From Farm
to Canal Street

From Farm to Canal Street

CHINATOWN'S ALTERNATIVE FOOD NETWORK IN THE GLOBAL MARKETPLACE

VALERIE IMBRUCE

Cornell University Press

Ithaca and London

First published 2015 by Cornell University Press
First printing, Cornell Paperbacks, 2015

Printed in the United States of America

Library of Congress Cataloging-in-Publication Data
Imbruce, Valerie, 1977– author.
   From farm to Canal Street : Chinatown's alternative food network in the global marketplace / Valerie Imbruce.
      pages cm
   Includes bibliographical references and index.
   ISBN 978-0-8014-5404-2 (cloth : alk. paper) —
   ISBN 978-0-8014-5686-2 (paperback : alk. paper)
   1. Produce trade—New York (State)—New York. 2. Food supply—New York (State)—New York. 3. Food habits—New York (State)—New York. 4. Chinese Americans—Food—New York (State)—New York. 5. Chinatown (New York, N.Y.) I. Title.
   HD9008.N5I46   2015
   381′.4108995107471—dc23   2015010706

Cornell University Press strives to use environmentally responsible suppliers and materials to the fullest extent possible in the publishing of its books. Such materials include vegetable-based, low-VOC inks and acid-free papers that are recycled, totally chlorine-free, or partly composed of nonwood fibers. For further information, visit our website at www.cornellpress.cornell.edu.

Cloth printing   10 9 8 7 6 5 4 3 2 1

Paperback printing   10 9 8 7 6 5 4 3 2 1

To Kevin,
for your support

CONTENTS

PREFACE

New York City, like many American cities, is in the midst of an agricultural awakening. Farmers' markets, community gardens, farm-to-chef collaborations, and urban agriculture are popular and financially successful. New Yorkers are taking more of a personal stake in how their food is grown and city officials are considering how they can sustain their agricultural hinterlands. For a city that once ruthlessly devoured its market gardens in Brooklyn and Queens at the turn of the twentieth century to make way for a growing urban population, it seems that now, one hundred years later, New Yorkers are thinking more carefully about their food supply.

Since its early colonial days, New York has never been an isolated state. It was a colony built on trade. Meat, lard, and grains from the New York environs made their way from New York Harbor to the British plantations of the Caribbean in exchange for sugar. Throughout the nineteenth century, canals and rails connected the eastern port city to the interior and the south of the United States, and Manhattan imported much of its food supply. The steady stream of immigrants from the mid-1800s on contributed to a rapid urbanization of the greater New York region and to the decline of agriculture.

One of the smaller groups of immigrants of the late 1800s, the Chinese, began provisioning their own foods. The Chinese enclave in Manhattan grew in population throughout the 1900s to become the largest concentration of Chinese immigrants in the United States. Today Manhattan's Chinatown remains iconic of New York's immigration history. It is also an iconic food destination, where tourists and New Yorkers alike go to eat and shop. There is no other marketplace like it in New York City. What is less known about Chinatown is its food system. At a moment in time when more and more people are interested in how food is produced and distributed, there are many questions to ask about

Chinatown's food system. This marketplace is strikingly different from that of the average supermarket and the myriad fruits and vegetables sold here are not sold anywhere else in the city. Where does all the food come from and how does it get here? Is there something fundamentally different about the way that Chinatown's produce is grown and supplied? What are the livelihoods and rural transitions associated with agricultural bounty for sale in Chinatown's markets?

This book tells the untold stories of how the food system of New York's oldest and most famous ethnic enclave has developed. I consider how Chinatown's food network continues to operate amid the citywide push to centralize food distribution and the nationwide trend in the vertical integration of food production, processing, and retail that have transformed the way that food is grown and sold. I describe how the street-level produce markets of Chinatown have survived in the wake of the consolidation of the grocery retail sector and the city's removal of pushcart and wholesale produce vendors; how and why farmers from New York, Florida, and Honduras choose to grow niche Asian fruits and vegetables that carry no price premiums and have no mainstream market; and how risk-taking entrepreneurs orchestrate a dynamic and flexible global network of trade without the use of mergers and acquisitions to keep Chinatown's shelves bountiful.

Chinatown may be a unique ethnic enclave, but it is by no means isolated. Chinatown is part of the global economy. Produce markets in Chinatown have no doubt been shaped by free trade and liberalized American immigration policies that characterize global economic integration. Yet Chinatown's produce markets also display characteristics that are alternative, or contradictory, to globalization. The retail and wholesale sectors are small and fragmented. The wholesale, not retail, sector sets prices. Asian immigrants and their descendants continue to consume ethnic foods, resisting acculturation and the mainstreaming of Asian diets into American ones. Chinese food in New York's Chinese restaurants continues to change with shifting immigration trends from China and urban trends in eating, reflecting current tastes and ideas about dining.

Chinatown's agricultural reach is also global in scope. The purchasing power of the area's shoppers provides livelihoods to small and large farmers struggling to stay afloat in the United States as well as in less developed nations. But instead of fostering monocropping and one industry-wide style of farming, the farms that grow Chinatown's produce use crop diversity and other practices that reflect cultural and biophysical specificity. Chinese vegetable growers in the United States today, with few exceptions, are members of multigenerational and new immigrant families who choose to grow and sell the ethnic foods of their people. The styles of agriculture that immigrant farmers bring from their homelands are often overlooked in discussions of food and agriculture, again seen as operative in spite of global capitalism instead of a viable economic form in themselves. The Honduran farmers that are part of Chinatown's food system are very much in need of good market opportunities. They report that Asian vegetables are the most stable market they can participate in. They have made small steps in improving their relations with export firms without explicit labor organization or the formation of grower cooperatives.

The way that Chinatown procures food demonstrates another kind of globalization, one that does not threaten regional agricultural economies, is not homogenizing cultures, and is not controlled by mega corporations. Rather, Chinatown's food system embodies a global economic network that is constructed by people who may have been marginalized but instead are carving out their own global niche in an economic network based in the cultural and biological specificities of the people and places involved. Although this particular network may persist only as long as Asian immigrants keep coming to the United States and eating diets filled with tropical, subtropical, and temperate fruits and vegetables, it is an adaptable model that connects farmers to market, one that can persist within the highly dynamic global environment.

The story of Chinatown's food network is one of interdependence between the local and global, the rural and urban realms. If we take *local* and *urban* in this story to be synonymous as representative terms for New York City–based produce markets, then these particular Asian markets don't conform to theories about other local, urban markets. Chinatown markets are dependent on neither a social movement, such as the push for local food, nor the "quality turn" in local markets that enables the price premiums garnered in farmers' markets or for organically certified foods. Unlike other markets for local food, there are no political dictates about which farmers can participate in Chinatown's markets (dictates such as New York City's Greenmarket program's definition of the radius in which farmers must live). New York City–based produce wholesalers set prices and quality standards but display flexibility in their relations with farmers. Thus it becomes the will of the farmer (the rural dweller) as much as the will of the produce broker (the urban dweller) to define this spatial relationship.

There are lessons that can be drawn from Chinatown's food system that have significance for urban planning and politics. Ethnic neighborhoods should be analyzed for the means by which they provide culturally specific foods to their residents. It may seem novel that today New Yorkers are claiming more and more of a stake not just in purchasing and consuming food but in procuring and producing it as well. Chinatown residents have been doing this since they formed their Manhattan enclave in the 1800s. I would hypothesize that the development of culturally specific food networks are integral to the formation of immigrant neighborhoods. New York City celebrates its ethnic restaurants; why not learn how they are maintained? In Chinatown, the decentralization of produce distribution and the proximity of food-related businesses, from produce wholesalers to restaurant menu printers, are vital to the success of Chinatown's food industry cluster. Policies that support upscale real estate development and centralization of wholesale food distribution threaten Chinatown's vibrant food economy.

The business and culture of ushering food from farm to table has won the hearts and minds of many talented entrepreneurs and enthusiastic eaters across the nation. But the media about food and farm culture is so focused on building and defining the "local food movement" that it is missing an array of issues that are equally as important, both socially and ecologically. The role of ethnicity in shaping food systems and the intersections between alternative and conventional economies and dichotomous spatial realms (urban/rural and local/global) are critical issues that this book takes up.

Part of the allure of reading, writing, and caring about food is that eating is *a shared experience.* Eating is something that everyone participates in and something that connects each of us to other people, to other places. We need to be concerned about the United States' eroding agrarian base and need to promote the inclusion of more diverse whole foods in the nation's diet, but supporting one's regional food economy, contrary to what is often purported, is not the only way to address these concerns. The singular focus on local foods to achieve the goals of strengthened economies, environmental stewardship, and public health obscures other means of achieving those same goals. The true test for the future is whether we will be able to balance global and local food systems; account for the needs of culturally diverse groups; and maintain interdependence with other peoples, places, and climates. After all, the way each of us eats and thinks about food is fundamentally quite different.

Chinese immigrants in the United States have long prided themselves on creating their own jobs—and the business of supplying culturally specific foods is no exception. Chinese and Southeast Asian Americans have started farms all over the United States. They have used their personal connections abroad to source Asian fruits and vegetables from many other locales. Many people assume that since Chinatown's produce is so cheap and not certified organic, it must represent the worst ills of industrial agriculture—the food must be pesticide laden, leading to soil erosion, and grown by exploited laborers and underpaid farmers while brokers are rolling in dough—when really, price isn't always the best gauge for food quality and labeling doesn't account for all methods of production. Despite a flood of recent books about food in the United States, consumers simply do not know where or how ethnic produce sold in New York is grown.

THIS book recounts the personal trajectories, serendipitous events, and social networking that has enabled the global expansion of Chinatown's food system. It highlights farmers from three distinct agricultural landscapes, examining multimillion-dollar farms near the Everglades Agricultural Area in Florida; backyard and commercial "homegardens" around Homestead, at the southern tip of Florida; and small farmers in a central valley in Honduras. Each of these regions offers insights into how the particularities of a place shape the global marketplace. The livelihoods of farmers from these areas illuminate the desires and practices of agriculturalists in a global market. Their lives and practices reveal, in vivid detail, a kind of globalization from below that needs to be better understood and accounted for.

This book was designed to investigate socioeconomic and environmental aspects of Chinatown's food system. I conducted field research between 2001 and 2006. I used the Global Commodity Chain approach as an organizing concept to select field sites for this project because the original intent of the approach was to understand the integration of processes over geographical areas.[1] Chinatown's fruit and vegetable markets in New York City are supplied by many places, many more than could be covered in one book, so I conducted preliminary research to determine which sites could most meaningfully be combined into one book.

New York City, southern Florida, and central Honduras were selected as sites for empirical study because they function as an integrated commodity chain and because of their social, environmental, and logistical importance to the food system. New York City is home to the country's largest Chinese population. Since the founding of Chinatown in the late 1800s, Chinese Americans have been organizing their own food system. South Florida has been a winter source of Asian vegetables since the 1950s. Miami-Dade County has the only tropical climate in the continental United States; subtropical and tropical fruits common to Asian diets are grown there. Further, the Port of Miami is a critical distribution point for produce imported from Latin America. Honduras was selected because distributors in South Florida play a key role in facilitating production there. Working in a newly emergent site of production, small farmers are contracted to grow an assemblage of crops complimentary to those grown in Florida.

New York City, Florida, and Honduras are coherent field sites because they are bound together not only by commodities but also through a social network of brokers, importers, exporters, and farmers. Network actors at each site engage in complimentary as well as antagonistic business practices, display a range of styles of farming, and grow distinct arrays of crops. Furthermore, actors at each site are influenced by nationally as well as internationally significant trends. Variation in the political-economic climate, biophysical environment, and social structure within each site makes for meaningful comparisons and distinctions between producers. Although the producers operate in the same market, differences in regulatory environments, capital resources, crop genetic resources, household size, climate, growing season, and labor, to name a few variables, shape practices and perceptions of producers within each site. Analysis of their practices illuminates local responses to larger-scale processes.

The methodology of this project combines anthropological with ecological techniques of data collection and analysis; it generated qualitative and quantitative data. It follows methodologies used in leading international in situ conservation projects (Jarvis et al. 2000; Zarin et al. 1999). The primary data is supplemented with quantitative marketing and pricing data drawn from government and industry sources.

Semistructured interviews were used with market owners, packer/exporters, farmers, and government and nongovernment agricultural workers in all sites. Farmer interviewees were selected through the help of agricultural extension agents in Florida and exporting firms in Honduras. All packers and distributors were contacted for interviews. Farmers' fields in Florida were mapped and sampled for cultivated plant species content and percentage coverage (see appendix D for detailed research methods).

The field research presented in this book ended in 2006. Archival research about Chinese food and restaurants for chapter 6 was undertaken in 2013. Observations about particular events and New York City food policy initiatives up to 2013 form the basis for chapter 7. The book is a case study that is limited to one snapshot in time. Given the dynamism of the food system described here, some of its actors and production practices have surely changed. But many of the people described in the book have been growing and distributing Asian vegetables as their life's work, and I believe they are still doing so. In an age in which trade liberalization is the dominant political-economic ideology, small and large growers compete for near and far specialty markets, and immigrants continue to cross borders from rural to urban areas, the relevance of this book remains strong.

The book also bounds the market-side analysis to Manhattan's China-town. This is the first Chinese enclave in New York City, and it is still the largest and most active in terms of its food system. It is where the wholesale sector and other food industry–related businesses are located. It is where the grocery marketplace most resembles "old" New York with its street vendors, pushcarts, and greengrocers. Flushing, Queens, rapidly transitioned from a largely white middle-class neighborhood to a Mandarin-speaking Chinese neighborhood with a Taiwanese flavor in the 1980s. The Chinese Americans in Flushing are proportionally at higher income levels and more educated than those in Lower Manhattan. Groceries are sold in fundamentally differ-ent ways in Flushing. Supermarkets, rather than greengrocers and street ven-dors, dominate. This is most likely a result of the later development of this neighborhood when supermarkets were the norm for grocery retail. I have no doubt that there are ties between the food supply in Manhattan's Chinatown and Flushing; investigating the relationships that form Flushing's supply chains would make an excellent study in itself. Sunset Park in Brooklyn emerged as a popular destination for poorer Chinese immigrants who wanted to escape the cost of living and congestion in Lower Manhattan. By the mid-1980s many Chinatown businesses established branches there. Some produce wholesalers in this book are setting up warehouses in Brooklyn—again, there are ties between Brooklyn and Manhattan's Chinatowns that would make for interesting further investigation.

THE introduction to the book describes how the geographic expansion of trade networks and agricultural globalization are often associated with corporate control and standardized practices. This is not the case for Asian fruit and veg-etables destined for Chinatown markets. The absence of any value added to Asian produce as well as the ethnic character of the produce may keep multi-national corporations and other mainstream interests from appropriating Asian commodity chains. Asian American entrepreneurs control the commodity chains. Chapter 1 lays the foundation for this argument by looking at the con-testation over space in Chinatown itself. The produce markets in Chinatown dominate the street space, and space is a precious commodity in New York. I look at the structure of produce markets in Chinatown—the greengrocers, street vendors, and wholesalers who organize the marketplace—to understand how this marketplace survives in Chinatown itself and how it gives shape to a global network of trade. Chapter 2 looks at how transnational trade networks are established and maintained. Transnational communities are known to build businesses through connections to co-ethnics and kin across continents.

Entrepreneurial immigrants use their cultural knowledge and language skills to build businesses. I take the position that ethnic entrepreneurship cannot be analyzed as an isolated unit within the enclave; rather ethnic businesses are embedded in interfirm relations on multiple scales.

The book then shifts focus to production sites. Three Chinese vegetable farms in Hendry and Palm Beach Counties in South Florida are discussed in chapter 3. At these sites, one farmer is the son of a Cantonese immigrant who farmed in New Jersey and, following in his father's footsteps, has been growing Chinese vegetables in Florida for over thirty years. Another farmer is the son of a Chinatown produce broker. A third is a newcomer, given access to Chinatown markets by special invitation. The three farms continue to make South Florida an important winter source of Chinese vegetables.

Southeast Asian farmers in Miami-Dade County compliment the Chinese vegetable farmers in Hendry and Palm Beach Counties by producing Asian tropical and subtropical fruits, herbs, and vegetables. The Southeast Asian farmers are the subjects of chapter 4. While the volume of produce that they supply is not great and their farms are very small, the diversity of produce they supply and their production methods merit analysis: their farms are commercial homegardens that illustrate how intensely diverse microfarms can operate in an international market.

Honduran farmers have been involved in export production of Asian vegetables for over a decade. They are the subjects of chapter 5. Three exporters currently organize production in the Comayagua Valley of central Honduras with partner companies in South Florida who handle all US logistics and provide market access. Between the three Honduran distributors there are more than four hundred small growers, cultivating thirteen varieties of vegetables. Chinese vegetables are the most lucrative and stable export crops that farmers in Comayagua can grow.

Chapter 6 addresses the role of food in the lives of Chinese immigrants in the United States. By looking at how Chinese Americans developed means to supply their preferred foods and present them to the public at large in Chinese restaurants, we can see that Chinese food was actively adapted to suit diverse palates. Chinese food is considered one of the great ethnic cuisines that have been successfully integrated into American culture. The Chinese restaurants and the supply chains that support them are not solely for the benefit of immigrants but are for many types of Americans.

Chapter 7 returns to Chinatown to bring home this newfound understanding of its food system. New York City has several political initiatives directed at reforming its food procurement. There are lessons to be drawn from China-town that can contribute to the political discussion. Finally, the principle findings are reviewed in the concluding chapter. Chinese American entrepreneurs have been managing the production and distribution of Chinese fruits and vegetables sold in New York City for over one hundred years. With more immigrants coming from Asia to New York City, the population size as well as cultural diversity of Asian communities has been growing. Manhattan's China-town is the preeminent place in the Northeast to buy ethnic East and Southeast Asian food products. To meet the increasing demands of residents and shoppers of Manhattan's Chinatown, the production and distribution of ethnic foods has been expanding to new production locales. Although Chinatown's food system is becoming global in scope, the system does not display characteristics of other global food systems. Chinatown's food system embraces small, diverse, minority-owned and -operated firms and farms. Actors in the system use social networks to build new trade relationships both within and between countries. Farmers specialize in a variety of crops and use biological diversity to improve production. Far from leading to consolidation of ownership and homogenization of practice, Chinatown's food system has shown us that global food systems can be filled with diversity and dynamism.

MANUSCRIPT revisions of this book were punctuated by the births of my two sons, Oliver and Felix. Their due dates provided me with hard and fast deadlines for revisions. I hope that when my boys are older they will understand this project as something I devoted myself to alongside them. They gave me the strength and clarity of purpose I needed to complete it. My husband, Kevin Lahoda, was my most stalwart companion throughout this project. From conception of my initial ideas to pursue research in Chinatown to the design of the cover art, he gave me witty advice and encouragement. It is to him that I dedicate the book. I am also very fortunate to have parents and in-laws who provide a stable foundation for me to stand on. I cannot thank them enough for all they do for me.

There are many people who have been of great help in the undertaking of this project. It would not have taken shape without my graduate advisor, Christine Padoch. From the first day I showed up in her office telling her my ideas to study something about New York City's food markets, she has been my advocate and a source of inspiration. I wholeheartedly thank Richard Andrus, my undergraduate professor, for teaching me to care about how food is produced. My editor, Michael McGandy, deftly ushered the manuscript through the revision process and made recommendations that pushed my thinking about the book, helping me to visualize and complete the additions of two new chapters to the original manuscript. He has been a pleasure to work with, and I owe him much gratitude for bringing the project to contract. My reviewers, Melanie Du-Puis and Lynn McCormick, did two very close readings of the manuscript and provided me with insights, questions, and suggestions that greatly improved the book. I cannot thank them enough for their time and thought. Two other readers, Susan Rogers and Julie Kim, contributed their knowledge and informed my understanding of Chinese food culture, greatly improving that chapter of the book. I enjoyed being a member of their reading group and thank them for inviting me.

The manuscript for this book has been greatly amended and revised over the course of my time as a faculty member at Bennington College. My students listened to me talk about my work, read my articles, and asked questions that helped me think about the relevance of my research in new ways. Kathy Williams at Crossett Library found all of the archival materials that I needed to finish the manuscript. Her care of the interlibrary loan services is invaluable. Two dear friends and colleagues at Bennington helped me most in the completion of this book: Carol Pal and Barbara Alfano. From the minute we started at Bennington College together, the three of us set our sights on publishing our books, and we've done it! Their friendship has been a grounding force in my life; I will always be appreciative of them.

Fieldwork requires a lot of assistance. Andrew Roberts shared his ideas and curiosities about Southeast Asian herbs, leading us to the homegardens in Homestead, Florida. He helped with the identification of many herbs, as did Hieu Nguyen with the Vietnamese plants and Ant Ariya with the Thai names. Many staff members of the University of Florida Agricultural Extension Service freely shared their knowledge and gave me many contacts in the south Florida farming community. I am particularly glad to have met Ken Schuler. His knowledge of the Chinese vegetable growers in Palm Beach County enabled my research in that part of Florida. He collected production data from 1987 to 2001 that provided evidence of trends in Chinese vegetable production that would otherwise be unrecorded.

Dr. Hugh Popenoe, professor emeritus at the University of Florida, gave me the contact I needed with Zamorano, the Pan-American School for Agriculture, to undertake research in Honduras. Mario Contreras and Dr. Alfredo Rueda of Zamorano helped me with much of the logistical planning and introductions I needed in Honduras. Most importantly, Dr. Rueda introduced me to Karen Jiron, my wonderful research assistant who spent time away from her young daughter and worked through the start of a new pregnancy with thoughtfulness and integrity. She and her husband invited me to their home and the homes of their parents, welcoming me into their lives. Dr. Rueda also introduced me to the employees of FHIA, Fundacíon Hondureño de Investigaciones Agricola, who facilitated my work in Comayagua. The many conversations I had with Dr. Dennis Ramirez and Jaime Jimenez provided me with great insight into the situation in Comayagua. Jaime also provided me with a place to live and a family to rely on for friendship and help. He, his sister Darriella, and Aunt Margarita were my surrogate family in Lejamani.

I had help with several maps that appear in the book. I have to thank Brian Morgan for the beautiful job he did on the Chinatown, Honduras, and Comayagua maps. Shane Chase, who was my student at Bennington College, completed the map of Florida out of the goodness of his heart and his dedication to learning, two traits that I know will serve him well.

Financial support for the preliminary research came from New York Botanical Garden; subsequent support for my research came from the National Science Foundation. Bennington College provided a generous subvention for the publication of the book.

Finally, and most importantly, I would like to thank all of the farmers, distributors and agricultural professionals who were very generous with their time and knowledge, and patient with my questions. Their livelihoods are sources not only of information but inspiration and admiration as well. I am truly grateful for the opportunity to have met the many people throughout this work that I would otherwise not know. The interactions that I have had with people involved in my research are a great privilege.

From Farm
to Canal Street

Introduction

SITUATING MANHATTAN'S CHINATOWN

In Manhattan's Chinatown colorful tropical fruits dangle from storefront awnings, stir-fry greens form pyramids on sidewalk tables, live blue crabs slide over each other inside plastic buckets, and Peking duck glistens behind windowpanes. The food landscape of Chinatown is in plain sight, on the street, for all to see, smell, and taste. The food of Chinatown is a stunning cornucopia that entices tourists, passersby, and everyday shoppers.

In Manhattan's Chinatown you can also see the juxtaposition of the informal economic sector and small ethnic enterprises with transnational capital. The sight of sidewalk peddlers plying their wares in front of the glass facades of some of the world's largest banking corporations illustrates that Chinatown is undergoing a transformation. Other signs are evident: following a crackdown on the illegal trading of fake designer goods on Canal Street, Starbucks moved in; luxury condos have risen on Mott Street, the heart of food commerce; and SoHo clothing boutiques inch ever closer to Chinatown. A long-planned information kiosk finally went up at the triangle at Canal and Baxter Streets in 2004, and the first Chinatown Restaurant Week was launched in 2012, efforts that attempt to create order in an otherwise seemingly disordered place.

Disorder, however, still feels like the dominant paradigm in Chinatown. In the popular media, descriptors such as *third world, dirty, smelly, congested,* and *illegal* are still frequently seen in reports about Chinatown. And more often than not, these reports refer to Chinatown's food markets, the striking plethora of greengrocers, fishmongers, and pickled, dried, and freshly prepared foods that can be found on numerous sites along Chinatown's main arteries. The putrid smell of aging fish and rotting vegetables fallen in the gutter can be overwhelming and unappealing. Chinatown is messy.

Nonetheless, food markets are abundant and perpetually busy in Chinatown. Within seven blocks there are as many as forty vendors of fresh fruits and vegetables. Pungent durians hang from vendor's stalls, bright red litchis signify summer, and seemingly endless varieties of leafy bok choy are available no matter what season it is. Many fruits and vegetables, no matter how uncommon—enormous winter melons, sharp Vietnamese coriander, and extremely bitter melon—can be purchased at rock-bottom prices, all year round. The neighborhood exclusively supplies over two hundred distinct varieties of fruits and vegetables that underlie Chinese, Korean, Thai, Vietnamese, Japanese, and other diets. It is a cultural jewel, a dietary lifeline to many first-, second-, and third-generation Asian Americans as well as the shopping destination of people of all ethnic backgrounds and culinary persuasions. Despite many rough edges, it is a food lover's and curious tourist's paradise.

The availability of fresh fruits and vegetables year round is a result of globally integrated, refrigerated distribution networks that link areas of consumption with areas of production. New Yorkers can enjoy tomatoes from Florida, lettuce from California, and grapes from Chile. The seemingly pedestrian activity of putting a bag of clementines in a supermarket basket is actually the result of major global shifts in the way that food is grown and sold. By and large, farms participating in the national and global marketplace specialize in one crop and companies that sell food at the retail level control distribution, processing, and production. There are varied impacts of specialization in agriculture and centralization of food distribution, but some of the most egregious include the abuse of agricultural workers, monocropping, overuse of pesticides, exhaustion of fresh water for irrigation, exclusion of small and medium-sized farmers from the market, the increase in political power in the hands of a few, giant agro-food corporations, and the overdependence on fossil fuels to maintain a globally integrated diet.

The migration of populations from their home countries to European and North American cities facilitates the trade of exotic produce to new points of consumption. The migration of Jamaicans to London, Mexicans to the United States, and South Asians to Toronto open up new markets for tropical and other fruits and vegetables not commonly eaten in those places. The size and cultural diversity of the Asian population in New York City has grown rapidly in the past fifty years, and a complex food system has developed to meet the diets of the new New Yorkers. What role does ethnicity play in shaping the way that immigrant communities supply their preferred foods? Can ethnicity define a food system that is an alternative to one dependent on monocrops and centralized supply chains?

Chinatown's food system displays characteristics that call into question modes of alterity in food systems. Alternative food networks can be seen as substitutes for dominant capitalist formations, not as relics that have not yet been penetrated by global capital. Alternative food networks present contradictions to the observations that the processes of global capitalism and neoliberalism are undemocratic, favor the rich at the expense of the poor, and create mounting social inequalities. Forms of social and economic organization used in alternative food networks, such as shortened supply chains and direct producer-consumer relations, can coexist and coevolve within capitalist society, rather than exist in spite of capitalism. Alternative food economies should be analyzed as responsive to space and place. Whether alternatives actively resist or transform existing social and economic structures, however, is up for debate, as is the polarization of conventional and alternative systems of food supply, and global (or neoliberal) and local economies (McCarthy 2006; Maye et al. 2007; Goodman et al. 2012). It is the relational and interactive processes that unite spaces of production and consumption, the local and the global, that form the basis of analysis of Chinatown's food network.

Actors in Chinatown's food network do not purport to be producers of alternative economic practices, nor do they articulate modes of resistance to an identified source of oppression. Through the observations and empirical data that I present in this book, I argue that actors in Chinatown's food network consciously work within the interstices of the global food economy, are producers of alternative practices, and do resist conventions in the global food supply by nature of their actions. These actors are mostly first- and second-generation immigrants, adding another analytical layer to this work. Transnational communities of immigrants have largely been left out of analyses of food and agricultural work, except as victims of oppression or abuse (Glick Schiller 1999; Basch et al. 1994; Appadurai 1996; Ray 2011). This work brings immigrants into the alternative food network and alternative food geographies literature as producers of processes that are spatially distended but also locally embedded and relational.

Manhattan's Chinatown is the oldest Chinese enclave on the East Coast, but it is not the only one in New York City. Flushing, in Queens, and Sunset Park, in Brooklyn, have also become Chinatowns in their own right. The study described in this book is bounded within Manhattan's Chinatown not because New York's Chinatowns are bounded but precisely because they are very interconnected, with each retaining unique characteristics. In fact, Chinese restaurants, markets, and population clusters across the entire East Coast are connected by private transportation, commerce, migration, labor, and supply chains. There are so many connections to be made and comparisons to be drawn between Chinatowns that new areas of research should be devoted to understanding these relations. It is my hope that this book inspires such work.

Chinatown in Manhattan is a central node connecting Chinatowns in the East Coast region. One of its unique characteristics as an urban neighborhood is that it uses the old, pre-supermarket, decentralized model of food distribution that was common sixty years ago, albeit with the extensive trade networks that are usual today. Produce is shipped from locations all over the world to the Port of Miami and Port of Newark and trucked to small wholesale warehouses in Lower Manhattan and Brooklyn. Wholesalers deliver produce from their warehouses to street vendors throughout the day, keeping the vendors' unrefrigerated displays fresh. Vendors use every inch of sidewalk space available to them, in both permanent and temporary displays. As I will show, the distribution system is dynamic and flexible and is innovative in its ability to supply diverse inventories and procure from producers of all sizes.

Another unique feature of food commerce in Manhattan's Chinatown, and one that is central to the food economy, is that in addition to street vendors and store owners, Chinatown houses several produce wholesale operations, which is not the norm in the city. Wholesale produce distribution in New York City is largely out of sight, taking place in the South Bronx at a restricted-access terminal market in Hunts Point, or in the private distribution centers of supermarket companies. But in Chinatown, Chinese American entrepreneurs have been managing the distribution of Chinese fruits and vegetables sold in New York City for over one hundred years, making the city the preeminent place in the Northeast to buy ethnic East and Southeast Asian foods.

Decentralized distribution and proximity between the wholesale and retail produce sector are two structural aspects of Chinatown's food network that need to be recognized and can be replicated in other neighborhoods and other cities. In current New York City food policies, government officials want to support more neighborhood-based retail options for fresh foods but are still focused on Hunts Point as the preeminent distribution site, possibly to the detriment of a food system like Chinatown's. Urban politics are a particularly important locus of study in food systems. Theorists of globalization have observed that the lessening importance of the nation-state in the formation of social identity and regulation of capitalism will open up new opportunities for regional and local levels of governance to more actively assert control over adjustment problems to new global regimes (Bonnano et al. 1994; Harvey 2012). Cities are at the forefront of social movements in American food politics. Urban consumers want to define what foods are available to them and how and where they are grown. The current local food movement seeks to create alternatives to centralized, corporately controlled networks of food production and distribution in order to lessen environmental and social burdens associated with their practices. New York City officials are responding to advocates of the local food movement with plans and policy proposals to reduce hunger and obesity, support regional farm economies and local food manufacturing, and decrease waste and energy usage. Immigrant food systems in New York need to be included in the debate about how New Yorkers can supply themselves with "good" food, particularly to avoid reforms based on only the views of privileged classes and racial groups.

Chinatown maintains the reputation that it is a place where one can find anything imaginable to eat. On any given day of the year, there are at least 135 different fresh fruits and vegetables to choose from! Restaurants in Chinatown reflect the tastes of immigrants from many regions of Asia and also consciously adapt Asian ingredients and cooking styles to American palates to attract a wider clientele. Chinatown's restaurants are a celebrated part of New York's cultural heterogeneity and its dining landscape. Why, then, has the structure and dynamics of Chinatown's food network that supplies restaurants and consumers of all kinds been virtually ignored by New York City officials, except when the area's street activities and microenterprises are deemed unacceptable to New York City's standards? Trade-savvy entrepreneurs work at international scales to supply Chinatown's produce markets. These entrepreneurs have transformed the area delimited as Chinatown as well as numerous production sites around the world. They have formed a flexible network that supplies Chinatown's street vendors, stores, and restaurants with copious and varied fresh ingredients. Some of Chinatown's produce comes from local and regional farms; much of it is imported from around the world. Bitter melon grows in Honduras, rambutan in Guatemala, and bok choy in Florida. In a globalized world, traditional food products come from nontraditional places. Chinatown's food network presents a decentralized model that supplies culturally specific foods from local, regional, and off-source producers. The means by which this network is organized should be of interest to food policy makers and practitioners in New York and elsewhere.

The spatial relations of Chinatown's food network show that Chinatown may be a unique ethnic enclave, but it is by no means isolated. Its economic and environmental reach are global in scope, and the purchasing power of its shoppers provides livelihoods to small and large farmers struggling to stay afloat in the United States and Latin America, as well as many other locales. Chinatown's food system includes peoples and styles of agriculture that are often overlooked in discussions of food and agriculture. It includes immigrant farmers in the United States who bring styles of farming from their homelands or who create entirely new ones, entrepreneurs who use connections made along uncanny personal trajectories to develop trading alliances across borders, and farmers in a developing nation who have found this ethnic-based export market to be its most stable market.

The story of Chinatown's food system ultimately portrays another kind of globalization, one that does not threaten regional agricultural economies, does not homogenize cultures, and is not controlled by transnational corporations. Rather, this story portrays a global economic network that is constructed by people who may have been marginalized, but instead are carving out their own global niche in an economic network based in the cultural and geographical specificities of the people and places involved.

While the supply chains of Chinatown's food system may be alternative to the supermarket firms that dominate global food trade, it is dependent on the same structural features of globalization: open borders, the continuous cool chain technology that is necessary for shipping perishable goods, and integrated transportation networks. Chinatown's food system is facilitated by national policies that support immigration, cheap and abundant fossil fuels, and multilateral free trade agreements. This particular network will persist only as long as immigration policy is open to great numbers of people of Asian origin, the reduction of trade barriers are maintained, and the cost of oil is low enough to allow the shipment of food from afar. But as the story will show, Chinatown's food system has altered with political and technological changes. It is an adaptable model that connects farmers to market, and one that has persisted within a highly dynamic, globalizing environment.

Chinatown in New York City's Food Landscape

New York City has seen a substantial increase in the variety of fresh fruits and vegetables for sale, shifts in the regions of origin of fruits and vegetables, and the consolidation of food retailing. As national and international trends have shown, sale of "exotic" produce has been a lucrative and fast-growing segment of the fruit and vegetable trade since the 1980s (Thrupp 1995; Cook 1994). This is in part the result of changes in consumption patterns. Immigration, travel, and culinary tourism affect consumption patterns. A rejection of mass consumption and corporate power, and interest in food safety and environmental sustainability—referred to by researchers as the turn to food "quality"—all foster interest in niche and value-added commodities (Marsden et al. 2000; Goodman 2003). The increase in sale of exotic produce, in particular, is also a result of political economic restructuring in less developed countries through free trade agreements, the participation of governments in the World Trade Organization, and the rise of new private standards set by international super-market firms meant to increase variety and year-round supply (Busch and Bain 2004, 329–30). In order to promote economic growth, the export of "nontradi-tional" agricultural products has been supported by government and non-governmental organizations, giving power to private firms to organize production and export.[1] Export-led growth strategies in Latin America have focused on high-value agricultural products like fresh fruits and vegetables (Thrupp 1995).

These consumption- and production-side trends are reflected in New York City's produce sales data. Over the almost two decades from 1981 to 1998, the number of tropical fruits and vegetables sold at Hunts Point increased by 70 percent, and the number of Asian vegetables increased by 200 percent (US Department of Agriculture [USDA] 1998). The number of fresh herbs as well as the USDA category "other fruits," which includes many tropical, specialty, or otherwise "exotic" fruits, has also increased by over 100 percent.[2]

Table 1 Diversity of products that reach New York City markets through Hunts Point Terminal Market

Tropical fruits and vegetables		Asian vegetables	Herbs		Other fruits	
apio	yucca	bean sprout	anise	caraway	fig	feijoa
arum	blanca	bok choy	basil	celeriac	fresh	guava
batata	coconut	daikon	chives	cilantro	olive	kiwano
breadfruit	date	gobo (burdock)	chipolinos	coriander	prickly	loquat
calabaza	jicama	bitter melon	dill	lemongrass	pear	litchi
chayote	pangana	don gua (winter	shallot	oregano	quince	manzano
cilantro	sapote	melon)	horse-radish	rosemary	Asian	passion
dasheen	sugarcane	gai choy (mustard)	mint	sage	pear	fruit
gandule	tamarindo	kobocha (Japanese	thyme	salsify	atemoya	pepino
ginger	yautia	squash)	watercress	savory	star fruit	
root	tomatillo	lo bok (radish)	arugula	sorrel	cherimoya	
honeyberry	yam	long beans	borage	tarragon		
malanga		mo gua (fuzzy				
quenepa		squash)				
taro		opo (long squash)				
		sing gua (Chinese				
		okra)				
		taro				

Note: Categories are according to US Department of Agriculture, Agricultural Marketing Service, Fruit and Vegetable Programs 1998.

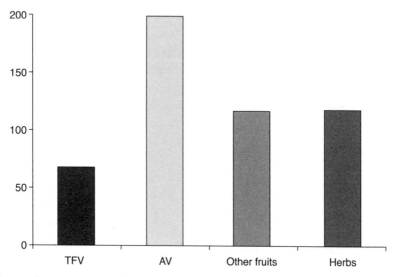

Figure 1 Percent increase in diversity of commodities in exotic categories, 1981–98, at Hunts Point Terminal Market. *TFV* stands for "tropical fruits and vegetables." *AV* stands for "Asian vegetables."

Source: US Department of Agriculture, Agricultural Marketing Service 1998.

The diversification of produce sold in New York City as documented by the USDA is substantial and yet does not account for all varieties of fresh fruits and vegetables sold in the city. There are a great number of items sold that are not recorded by the USDA because they do not flow through Hunts Point, or they do so in numbers too small to track. The city might officially state that terminal market use is up, or at least stable, but the volume of commodities flowing through the market has actually been decreasing (see figure 2).[3] The decline suggests an anomaly in the marketing data. Many products are simply unaccounted for. Undocumented specialty fruits and vegetables show up on the streets, in greengrocers and ethnic shops in Chinese, Southeast Asian, South Asian, and Mexican communities through distribution networks outside Hunts Point Terminal Market (see table 2).

Chinatown's food system accounts for, in part, the undocumented produce sold in New York City, as well as some of the loss of volume at Hunts Point. The majority of the volume loss, however, is caused by two other antagonistic national trends: the corporate consolidation of food supply and distribution and the response of local agriculture. The food retail sector has undergone a great concentration of ownership in the United States. By 2004, the top five food retailing chains controlled 48.3 percent of the market, compared with 28.9 percent in 1999 and 19.9 percent in 1995 (Konefal et al. 2007; Guptill and

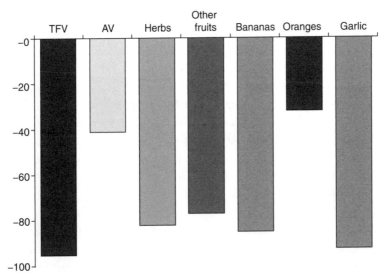

Figure 2 Percent decrease in volume of commodities imported, 1979–98, through Hunts Point Terminal Market. *TFV* stands for "tropical fruits and vegetables." *AV* stands for "Asian vegetables."

Source: US Department of Agriculture, Agricultural Marketing Service 1998.

Table 2 Some fruits and vegetables sold in ethnic markets in New York City not recorded by USDA Terminal Market Reports

Chinese and Southeast Asian		Asian Indian	Mexican
rambutan	water chestnut	paan leaf	epazote
Thai guava	celtuce	kerala	romero
jackfruit	lily bulb	chiku	rocoto
litchi	lotus root	tinda	guajes
longan	choy sum	amla	guazotle
jujube	snowpea tip	parvar	papalo
wax jambu	Taiwan choy	curry leaf	pepiza
pithaya	Shanghai choy	tumeric	
galangal	water spinach	olivar	
mah ohm	Chinese broccoli	malabar spinach	
rau ram	Thai eggplant	areca nut	
Kaffir lime leaf	Thai okra	lablab bean	
culantro	Chinese celery		
banana flower	bamboo shoot		

Wilkins 2002). Imports of fresh produce to supermarkets are critical to retailers' differentiation strategies. Consumers expect to find ordinary products like tomatoes or grapes as well as specialty products like tropical fruits on a daily basis throughout the year (Konefal et al. 2007).

Food retailers consolidate in one of two ways: by horizontal integration, whereby retail organizations acquire others to increase market share in the produce industry, or by vertical integration, whereby retailers make exclusive supply arrangements with manufacturers (Hendrickson et al. 2001). Consolidation renders the use of terminal markets obsolete because retailers manage the distribution portion of their operation or accept shipment directly from manufacturers. This sort of concentration is occurring in the supposedly "alternative" organic and natural foods industries as well. Yacaipa Companies took a 40 percent share in Pathmark and a 9.2 percent share in Wild Oats Market, Inc. (Rich 2005). Whole Foods subsequently tried to purchase Wild Oats in 2007 but was forced to divest itself by the Federal Trade commission based on antitrust concerns (Jones 2009). Walmart is attempting to gain more market share in organics and will carry Wild Oats products (Cheng 2014). An ongoing analysis of mergers and acquisitions in the organic processing industry since the USDA National Organic Standard was released in 1997 has revealed that food giants now own most organic brands.[4]

Walmart is the largest grocer in the United States and in the world. It has revolutionized the food retail industry by centralizing procurement and marketing through logistical and distribution innovations. For example, Walmart uses automated systems shared with suppliers to track store inventory and ensure deliveries of new produce to their wholesale distribution centers on a just-in-time basis. For efficiency, supermarkets have shifted to using one broker instead of multiple brokers for produce sales or to contracting directing with producers. In light of such buying power, supermarkets have been setting their own production and quality standards, even developing their own private labels to differentiate themselves from competitors. This has caused a shift in power along supply chains from producer driven to buyer driven (Konefal et al. 2007).

New York City, like almost all cities, has experienced the national food retail trends of horizontal and vertical integration. The warehouse club stores as well as national supermarket chains that have become big players in grocery retail are part of the city's food landscape. There are seven Costcos in the metro area—in Brooklyn, Yonkers, New Rochelle, on the Upper East Side of Manhattan, and three in Queens. Pathmark opened a new store on 125th Street in Harlem. Whole Foods has six stores in Manhattan, including the largest grocery stores in the borough (fifty-nine thousand to sixty-six thousand square feet) at the strategic transportation hubs of Columbus Circle and Union Square and in the newly gentrified Lower East Side. A seventh Whole Foods is to open on the Upper East Side in February 2015.

The backlash to the concentration of power in food supply and distribution has been a concerted effort in direct marketing to foster direct sales between farmers and consumers. The number of farmers' markets around the nation has exploded. Between 1994 and 2009 farmers' markets tripled from 1,755 to 5,274 (US Department of Agriculture, Agricultural Marketing Service 2011). New York City has been successful at direct marketing; there are fifty-four green-markets and thirty-six community-supported agriculture (CSA) arrangements around the five boroughs.[5] New Yorkers are embracing the perceived social, economic, and environmental good of direct sales. Parks are establishing farmers' markets to encourage safe use of parks, schools are organizing CSAs and the purchase of local produce in their cafeterias, and chefs are using locally grown foods in street food as well as haute cuisine.

Where does Chinatown's food system fit into the city's food landscape and into the nation's imagining of how food should be supplied? What is behind the chaotic, messy face of Chinatown's markets? Some people assume the worst. I was told by a New Yorker with a social conscience that the food sold in China-town "must be pesticide-laden food grown by nonunion, exploited agricultural laborers." The image of a dirty, disordered Chinatown in which illegal activity underlies the economic infrastructure has crept into the perception of its food system.

Global agricultural markets foster new relationships between consumers and producers. Although some agricultural commodities, such as sugar, have been in global circulation for hundreds of years, the compression of time and space with transportation and communication infrastructure has led scholars to examine globalization in a new context. The increasing expansion of global markets and transnational processes has provoked reconsideration of the meaning of culture and community as well as of the connections between urban cores and rural peripheries. Some global markets arise in response to the needs of transnational migrants to maintain social and cultural identities across political and geographical borders. Consumption of "ethnic" food products from home environments is an important part of building the identities and economies of transnational communities. Ethnic food is also one way for ethnic minorities to integrate into American culture by adapting their cuisine to American tastes or becoming part of the great diversity of cuisines savvy diners seek out and tastemakers write about.

In the agro-food literature, political economists have analyzed how the world is constituted and reconstituted around global processes, focusing on the transnational corporation and World Trade Organization as units of analysis in shaping governance, labor, production, and consumption in global agricultural markets (Bonnano et al. 1994; Goodman and Watts 1997; McMichael 1994; Magdoff et al. 2000; Burch and Lawrence 2007). The land-based nature of agriculture has called into question the industry's exploitation of biodiversity and other natural resources as a result of the need to drive down production costs and specialize in singular crops, needs exacerbated by global competition (Conway 1997; Pretty 1995; Altieri and Nicholls 2005; Gliessman 2007; Vandermeer 2011). In response to the critique of agribusiness and its effects on environments, there was pathbreaking work that defines the politics of "environmentalization" and "relocalization" of agriculture that has spurred much work on alternatives to conventional agriculture (Buttel 1992; Kloppenburg et al. 1996).

The growth of transnational communities that demand products that are impossible to grow in their new environments and must be imported from distant (often tropical) environments, has not, however, been included in analyses to this point. Nor have immigrants been included as producers of taste even though they have dominated food service occupations since the mid-1800s (Ray 2011). While metropolitan areas like New York encourage immigration and value cultural diversity, how the demand for ethnic fruits and vegetables fits into agricultural restructuring has not been studied systematically. The study of how the growth of transnational communities creates alternative pathways of fresh fruit and vegetable distribution will foster discussion about a growing population that has largely been overlooked in global and local arenas and will provide insight into how small-scale, ethnic entrepreneurs shape global trade and cultures of eating.

Asian immigrants in New York City support diverse and dynamic methods of production and distribution to satisfy their food preferences. Chinatown's food system counters the trend toward increasing consolidation of commodity chains by agro-food corporations. Although it is rapidly undergoing geographic expansion, three characteristics set it apart from the highly concentrated supply chains that rely on retailer-controlled coordination and crop specialization at the farm level: (1) enterprises from farm to retail level are decentralized, established by newcomers to the industry, and are often family owned and operated; (2) trade networks and businesses are established through ethnicity and kinship; and (3) cropping systems are diverse in cultivated plant species and management practices.

It is necessary to include ethnic entrepreneurs as a unit of analysis in addition to the dominant transnational corporation in the discourse on globalization of agricultural networks. These entrepreneurs are producers of alternative global processes. Enabled by the ease of global communication and transportation, as well as trade liberalization, ethnic entrepreneurs establish connections with co-ethnics across continents to create their own networks of trade. These initial findings have led to the main questions of this research: How is the distribution and production of Asian fruits and vegetables organized? Is this system fundamentally different from corporately controlled, globalized agriculture that uses crop specialization, monocropping, and consolidation of commodity chains to supply cheap fresh fruits and vegetables? What are its social and environmental impacts?

Global Alternatives

The analyses of global changes in fresh fruit and vegetable distribution and consumption has provided insights into the role of the consumer as well as the role of exogenous political and economic forces on the restructuring of global food systems (Bonnano et al. 1994; McMichael 1994, 1995; Burch and Lawrence 2007). This type of analysis, known as regulationalist, does not adequately deal with the diversity of practices in agricultural production and distribution.[6] By placing emphasis on macrostructural forces, regulation theory assumes a linear trend of economic development, following the logic of the Bretton-Woods institutions. Cases other than those predicted by this model are regarded as not yet infiltrated by these macro forces.

Global integration, although a reality, is hardly the only reality. The burgeoning literature on agricultural rurality and ecology parallels globalization and industrialization as objects of analysis and describes local examples of alternative scenarios (Nabhan 2002; Perfecto et al. 2009; Jackson 2011; Ackerman-Leist 2013). In the literature on alternative agriculture the social, economic, and geographic spaces that are not filled or passed over by industrial agriculture are analyzed in their own right. They are not considered spaces soon to be transformed into industrial efficiency (Lyson and Green 1999; DuPuis 2002; Goodman et al. 2012). There have been very good studies on alternative markets and pathways exploring a new or sustainable agriculture (Allen 1993; Hinrichs and Lyson 2007). Alternative trade has been considered an opportunity for progressive social change that takes advantage of political spaces above and below the nation-state and as opposition to the social and ecological injustices of industrialization and market liberalization (Tickell and Peck 1995; Friedmann 1993). Fair trade of agricultural commodities is one such alternative (Murray and Raynolds 2000) and organic agriculture another, although organics have not quite lived up to their promise and have been susceptible to similar trends of consolidation of conventional supply chains (Guthman 2004).

This turn inward to the endogenous pressures and needs of a locality has stirred much research as well as activism. The "local" has become the antidote to the "global" in the search for diversity and sustainability. But in thinking about how the formation of a transnational community is simultaneously a global (spatially expansive) as well as a local (spatially bounded) process, one can see that a transnational community fills different spatial fields simultaneously. Marginalized or minority peoples are creative in finding ways to meet their needs. Immigrants in the urban environments of New York City rely on diverse and dynamic processes of procurement and distribution to fulfill their unique requirements. The analysis of the single homogenous, modern capitalist system tends to ignore or trivialize the diversity of practice that the progress story cannot explain, or explains as inferior. The notion of the universal, the perfect, and the essential challenges us to readmit explanations of agricultural change based in social and political contexts and their spatial relations, linked to historical analyses (DuPuis 2002; Ploeg 1994). In this way, we can look at the exceptions to the rule as not only relics but also alternatives linked to institutionalized and organized activities. Seeing how these alternatives survive is interesting not only because of the value of diversity in itself but also because it shows how society really works behind the mask of the most efficient form. Alternative economies are contradictions to assumptions about advanced, capitalist societies (McCarthy 2006). Alternative economic practices not only are reacting to the forces of agricultural industrialization and globalization but are also results of dynamic, adaptive strategies that persist.

This book focuses on transnational entrepreneurs in a highly integrated political economy in order to understand how they are using opportunities and dealing with pressures of globalization. It explores a diversity of scenarios that exist in the global marketplace. Reliance on internationally grown products may be enabled by vertically and horizontally integrated commodity chains that link distant production areas with northern consumers, but not as a result of the forces of modernization and globalization guiding agriculture into one efficient form. Fresh fruit and vegetable commodity chains have shifted from producer-driven ones governed by firms, such as the Standard Fruit Company and the United Fruit Company, that controlled agricultural production as well as distribution and marketing, to buyer-driven processes, where supermarket retailers shape production and marketing without being directly involved in production (Dolan et al. 1999). But Chinatown's food network shows us that the supermarket-driven chains are not the only global models of agriculture. The influence of one "global model of agriculture" can be so pervasive that it drives policy to make its vision a self-fulfilling prophecy and masks the true diversity of processes that exist.

Food systems that openly contest, resist, and oppose global agro-food systems are working toward the goals of ecological sustainability, economic viability, and social justice. Alternatives are united in the practice of reconstructing a locally situated, decentralized food system, or in commodifying ecologically and socially responsible food production and trade. Tensions between local and global food supplies are constantly negotiated and it is clear that the local-global binary is problematic. Although it has been recognized that the ideology of alternative food systems has been better theorized than the practice itself (Allen et al. 2003), the tensions between the local and global are just starting to be reconsidered both in theory and in practice (DuPuis and Goodman 2005). The commitment to the relocalization of agriculture is indeed an important one, but it can obscure merits of other systems, particularly those that feed people across class boundaries. We cannot ignore that farmers' markets, artisan "slow foods," organic and fairly traded foods can often be prohibitively expensive and only appeal to certain demographics as well as class sensibilities. We continue to face the challenge of defining the many manifestations of "alternativeness" (Watts et al. 2005).

Comparing part of the mission of alternative agriculture—to conserve agricultural diversity and protect local and traditional foods—to Chinatown's food system for a moment reveals clear commonalities. Supplying a market with over two hundred types of fresh, culturally specific ingredients year round, as Chinatown's food system does, helps to conserve biodiversity as well as gastronomic traditions. Slow Food's Cittaslow (Slow Cities), according to their website, seeks to promote something "less frantic, yielding, and fast—no doubt more human, environmentally correct and sensible."[7] Chinatown at any given moment may appear frantic, but when one considers how the community has retained so many of its cultural traditions as the city has been constantly changing and hybrid cultures have been constantly forming, one realizes that Chinatown has not yielded but has adapted.

The pace of immigration and trade may deliver change, but it can also slow change. New immigrants sustain old habits, as does trade, but not exclusively so. Over the course of the twentieth century until today, Chinatown's food system, and the very category of Chinese food itself, has shifted to accommodate new modes of trade as well as new styles of cooking. Chinese restaurants have played a large role in defining the heterogeneous category that is "Chinese food," adapting cooking styles and ingredients to cosmopolitan tastes, mainstream American tastes, and regional tastes of new Chinese immigrants. In this way, restaurateurs and cooks have taken the products supplied by Chinatown's food system and produced public perceptions of Chinese ethnicities and food cultures.

This book brings global networks into the alternative food system discussion by examining Chinatown's food system. While the Chinatown food system in practice displays part of the vision of alternative food systems, it does not share in its political agenda. The global expansion of the food system follows processes outside the dominant industrial and corporately controlled food system but not by consciously resisting it. Chinatown's food system constitutes an alternative global food system in which individual entrepreneurs are making new spatial relations through their lived experiences. This system contributes biological diversity to the produce stands of the city, supports ethnic food cultures, and promotes crop diversity on farm fields. Through the supply of specific ethnic food items, Chinatown's food system helps sustain cultural practices of new and old urban inhabitants, as well as create new food traditions that are an important part of New York City's cultural landscape and should be supported by city government.

## CHAPTER 1

Greengrocers and Street Vendors

Over the past century, wholesale food distribution has been virtually removed from Manhattan, mirroring the consolidation of food distribution that has occurred across the nation. New York City built Hunts Point Terminal Market in 1967 in the South Bronx to rid Manhattan of the congestion and garbage associated with wholesale food distribution. The city's produce and meat distribution have taken place at Hunts Point since then, with fish entering the trade at Hunts Point more recently. In 2006, New York's last iconic wholesale market, the Fulton Fish Market, was closed and fishmongers moved to a new facility at Hunts Point. And a wholesale farmers' market followed. Over one hundred local and regional growers of fruits, vegetables, flowers, herbs, and plants also ply their wares at Hunts Point.

In Chinatown, however, wholesale produce vendors remain tucked into the nooks and crannies around Canal Street. In fact, an entire food industry cluster is at the heart of the culture and economy of the neighborhood. Restaurateurs; retail food vendors; wholesalers of produce, meat, and fish; restaurant supply businesses; food manufacturers; food industry labor exchange agencies; and printing companies support each other's needs and provide a soup-to-nuts food industry. In interviews, members of each of the food industry sectors chant the same refrain: "Location, location, location." The location of the historic Chinatown district in Manhattan is well known to city residents as well as Asian immigrants, tourists, and industry members from all over the United States (and abroad). The food industry keeps growing, as it has for the past 120 years. From 2000 to 2007 employment in the restaurant sector grew by 59 percent, durable goods wholesale grew by 18 percent, and retail grocery grew by 36 percent. Even nondurable goods wholesale, the category into which fresh food items fall, grew by a modest 2.5 percent.[1]

Chinatown-based wholesalers and retailers depend on their location and proximity to other businesses that support their enterprises. Many greengrocers in Chinatown don't have much storage space or refrigeration. They depend on frequent deliveries from their wholesalers. A study by faculty and students at the Department of Urban Affairs and Planning at Hunter College confirms that clustering is important for restaurateurs, restaurant supply companies, and manufacturers. One owner of a Cantonese-serving restaurant whom they interviewed assumed that 80 percent of the supplies of Chinese restaurants in the Tri-state area comes from Chinatown, regardless of the type of supplies. She said, "Everyone [who] wants to open Chinese restaurants knows to come to Chinatown to get their supplies because of the variety and competitive price." Another restaurant supplier affirmed that "the location is especially important to us since Chinatown serves as a gateway for those immigrants [non-English-speaking Fujianese restaurant owners] and is the first stop when they come to city. We will lose profit and our customer base if we move out to Brooklyn or Queens because those immigrants [who are our customer base] would not go to Queens or Brooklyn for business services. We rely on geographical proximity to other services that attract new immigrants who keep coming to Chinatown to take advantage of these services" (McCormick et al. 2010, 25).

The space that Chinatown's food industry occupies in Lower Manhattan is highly contested, however, creating tensions for produce wholesalers and retailers. The politics of space in Chinatown include formal litigation and illegal tactics like extortion. Embedded in these politics are histories of racism and exclusion and contemporary class warfare between gentrifiers and Chinatown's old guard. Neighborhood residents, city officials, street vendors, and store owners are frequently at odds over the structure and location of produce sales. The disagreements among Chinatown's stakeholders feed reports that perpetuate the "foreignness" of Chinatown. Comments about disputes printed in New York City media indict the wholesale sector for wrongdoing with statements claiming that "these wholesalers have turned my block into the black hole of Calcutta" and that Chinatown's former Dragon Gate Market of stall vendors "looks like a shantytown" (Kirby 1998).

The rhetoric of foreignness is a tactic commonly used when there are contesting visions about a particular geographic space. Gentrification as a geographic process has explicitly used the ideas of frontier and foreignness to inject private capital into poor neighborhoods, remodel housing to entice the middle class, and foster zones of commerce and consumption (N. Smith 1996). Chinatown is currently surrounded by recently gentrifying zones: the Lower East Side to the east, NoLIta (short for "north of Little Italy") to the north, and SoHo to the west. The encroachment of upscale and trendy boutiques, cafés, and bars, as well as so-called luxury housing, has created sites of conflict in Chinatown. Wholesalers are feeling more and more pressure operating within Chinatown. In the late 1990s Chinatown's council member proposed a wholesale market for Chinatown, but nothing has come of it to date. Space is not plentiful in Chinatown, and areas that were once exclusively zoned as industrial are no longer so. Wholesalers have to be much more wary of previously common practices like idling trucks, double parking, and working on the sidewalks in front of their store. The police department has been issuing more and more parking tickets for trucks that are parked incorrectly or exceed standing limits. This has made loading and unloading very difficult and costly: parking tickets are $115 each. Many wholesalers have moved to Brooklyn or purchased additional warehouses in Brooklyn to load and unload fewer orders in Chinatown. But they continue to deliver to clients in Chinatown all day long; distribution is still a ubiquitous activity. Delivery trucks, stacked boxes on the sidewalk, and men pushing hand trucks are constant features of the business day.

In addition to New York City's crackdown on disruptive activity by wholesalers, neighborhood groups have become vocal opponents of Chinatown's produce wholesalers. An extreme case is exemplified by a conflict between World Farm and the SoHo Alliance. Several wholesale companies moved to the fringes of Chinatown, along Chrystie Street to the east and around Broome and Lafayette Streets to the west. The western fringe proved to be a contentious battleground over two very different ideas of how to use the abandoned manufacturing loft space. The chic restaurants, shops, galleries, and apartments of SoHo abut the fruit and vegetable warehouses of Chinatown.

In September 1996 the SoHo Alliance, which represents over one thousand SoHo residents, filed a ten-million-dollar lawsuit against World Farm and commenced to seek a permanent injunction as well as monetary damages on grounds of nuisance and trespass. The allegations included complaints about the use of the sidewalk to operate forklifts and unload produce, trucks parked in front of fire hydrants and on crosswalks, and garbage left on the sidewalk. On November 27, 1996, the Supreme Court of New York State set up provisions stating World Farm would not (1) operate its vehicle in a manner threatening the safety or health of plaintiffs, (2) drive forklifts on the sidewalk, (3) use sidewalks to display and sell produce, (4) use sidewalks to store shipments for more than one hour, or (5) leave machinery on the sidewalk when not being used. The stipulation also set up an advisory committee to deal with problems that would arise (Saxe 1997).

Problems persisted for the next five years. Upon the allegations of 1996 the wholesalers united to form an association, the Chinese Wholesalers and Retailers Association of Greater New York, and attended community board meetings to defend their right to operate their businesses. They continued to violate agreements, arguing that some restrictions were trivial, unreasonable, or unavoidable. The SoHo Alliance continued to fight over the noncompliance of World Farm. Disputes over World Farm's compliance went to court again in 2001 when the company was told to pay an estimated two hundred thousand dollars in legal fees and a one-thousand-dollar fine and other costs (M. Williams 2001). World Farm's lawyer stated that they would appeal. World Farm continues to operate from this location; they have not left as many had hoped.

The Development of Chinatown and Its Food System

Chinese immigrants have been negotiating the space in Lower Manhattan that is now commonly referred to as Chinatown since they began arriving in New York City in the second half of the nineteenth century. The development of Chinatown's food system is intertwined with the history of Chinese immigration, the development of the Chinese enclave in Lower Manhattan, and the formal and informal use of urban space.

The first major wave of Chinese immigration to the United States was from Canton (now Guangdong) Province over one hundred years ago. In the mid-1800s, prior to the migration from Canton, only small groups of Chinese sailors, cooks, and others involved in the US-China trade lived in Lower Manhattan in the multiethnic Five Points area. After the British forced open the ports of southeastern China in the first Opium War (1839–42), Chinese laborers from the port city of Canton (now Guanzhou) were transported to California to work as laborers in the Gold Rush and then to build the western spur of the Transcontinental Railroad. By this time the Chinese diaspora was well under way. Chinese "coolies" were sent to the Caribbean and South America, and many Chinese emigrated to locations throughout Southeast Asia. During these labor migrations, the Chinese population of New York expanded steadily in the late 1870s.

Economic recessions late in the nineteenth century heightened antipathy toward the Chinese. Many Chinese left California to return to China or to travel to the East Coast to escape California's racially charged environment. Anti-Chinese sentiments were codified by the United States with the passage of the Exclusion Act in 1882. Chinatowns along the East Coast grew both involuntarily and voluntarily. Because they were denied structural assimilation, the Chinese developed enclaves for self-protection as well as social and economic improvement (Zhou 1992).

The food system of Chinatown arose out of the desire to feed the enclave. Like much of Chinatown's social and economic activity, the food system operated outside the mainstream of New York. Restaurants were one of the first business sectors to develop in Chinatown and they generated a steady demand for Chinese ingredients. In 1937 over forty types of plant foods were available in Chinatown, including dried items like fungus, fruits, and lily flowers in addition to fresh roots, tubers, fruits, and leafy vegetables (Porterfield 1937). Restaurants catered to Chinatown's bachelor society. Teahouses and "chop suey houses" were places where men could get hot, homemade meals and socialize with others. Typical Cantonese dishes that would come to be known as Chinese American food—chop suey, lo mein, chow mein, and fried rice—were served because they were quick and inexpensive yet contained a mixture of meats and vegetables. It has been said that this new style of Chinese cuisine was so different from cuisines in China that the chefs were not sure if the joke was on them or their customers.

Chinese cuisine prepared in Chinatown restaurants catered to the American palate beginning in the late 1800s, and by the 1920s chop suey houses were opening outside urban enclaves. Chinese food further developed general appeal in the 1970s when President Richard Nixon's trip to China in 1972 stirred American interest in Chinese food (Wong 1988).[2] This widely publicized trip coincided with a time when Chinese immigration was increasing following the immigration reforms of 1965. The new demographic flows increased both the number and ethnic variation among Chinese immigrants in the United States. Between 1963 and 1973 the Chinese restaurant industry expanded from 560 to 1,700 restaurants in New York City. Likewise, the number of grocery stores in Chinatown increased from fifty in 1965 to seventy in 1988 (Wong 1988). The increase in American interest in Chinese food, combined with the increase in Chinese immigration, propelled the expansion of the variety and quality of food preparation in Chinese restaurants. Diners no longer looked for simply functional meals; they wanted a culinary experience.

The First Chinese American Farmers

Records of Chinese crops in the United States date back to the nineteenth century. The prominent American horticulturalist Liberty Hyde Bailey wrote about Chinese crops in the United States in 1894 and their great potential for assimilation into the American diet. Mainstreaming "ethnic" crops is still a preoccupation of agriculturalists, but few Chinese vegetables have been successfully mainstreamed. The demand for basic Chinese vegetables like bok choy, lo bak (Chinese radish), ong choy (water spinach), and dau mui (snow pea shoots) encouraged Chinese immigrants to establish farms in agricultural areas outside New York City. Produce for winter trade and some subtropical items were supplied from gardens in Florida and even Cuba in the 1950s. Chinese Americans cultivated Chinese vegetables for Chinese restaurants and groceries because these vegetables were unfamiliar, and perhaps unpalatable, to Americans (Porterfield 1951).

I was fortunate to interview Karen Lee of Sang Lee Farms, the first Chinese American farm on Long Island.[3] The story of Sang Lee Farms provides insight into the means and motivations of the first Chinese American farmers in the New York area. The Lee family founded Sang Lee Farms in 1948. The Lees were part of the Cantonese migration to New York City in the early 1900s. They ran a laundry business in which their sons would help after school. After returning from military service in World War II, George Lee, father of the current owner of Sang Lee Farms, went to the State University of New York at Farmingdale to study agronomy. His Cantonese parents approved of his career choice. In an interview with the *New York Times*, George Lee's wife said, "In those days, being a farmer was different than in China, where it was considered low. Here, they knew you had to have an education and know what you're doing" (Toy 2003). George Lee and his cousin established Sang Lee Farms. At that time Chinese farms were already well established in southern New Jersey, but the Lees preferred Long Island because of its extensive underground aquifer. Southern New Jersey has a longer growing season, but the aquifer promised a competitive advantage during dry periods.

The Lees' intuition proved right. Sang Lee Farms quickly became the main supplier of Chinese vegetables for the eastern metropolises of New York, Philadelphia, and Boston to as far north as Montreal, west to Detroit, and south to Miami. They established a strong reputation in Chinatown among wholesalers as well as market shoppers. The farm expanded to Hobe Sound, Florida, in the late 1950s to grow vegetables during winter months. At the peak of production the farm was double cropping six hundred acres in East Moriches, Long Island, and several hundred in Florida during the winter. Half their acreage was in bok choy, and the other half was planted to a mix of about two dozen types of vegetables.

Sang Lee Farms grew in tandem with the immigration rates of the Chinese to the United States. In 1965 there was a turning point in US immigration from Asia and subsequent boom in immigration rates. Although sixty years of Chinese exclusion ended in 1943 when China became allied with the United States in World War II, it was not until 1965 that the US government abolished nation-of-origin quotas that had favored immigration from northwestern Europe for eighty years. Whereas the first half of the twentieth century saw 85 percent of its immigrants from Europe, the second half saw the reverse: 85 percent from Asia, Latin America, and the Caribbean. Between 1961 and 1970, the number of Chinese immigrants to the United States was just over 100,000, over

Table 3 New York City residents of Asian origin

Origin	1990	2000	2010
Asian Indian	94,590	170,899	196,704
Bangladeshi	4,955	19,148	35,961
Cambodian	2,565	1,771	3,918
Chinese	238,919	361,531	493,154
Filipino	43,229	54,993	74,882
Indonesian	1,443	2,263	3,522
Japanese	16,828	22,636	24,817
Korean	69,718	86,473	97,522
Malaysian	845	1,368	2,076
Pakistani	13,501	24,099	46,091
Sri Lankan	811	2,033	2,787
Thai	3,944	4,169	6,802
Vietnamese	8,400	11,334	13,937
Other Asian	10,207	24,330	34,063
Asian total	509,955	787,047	1,045,806

Source: Data are from the New York City Department of City Planning.

four times that of the previous decade, and from 1971 to 1980 the number jumped to roughly 240,000 (Immigration and Naturalization Service 1988). The majority influx of people from Asia came from mainland China, Hong Kong, Taiwan, Korea, and India. Refugees and others from Southeast Asian countries such as the Philippines, Cambodia, Laos, and Vietnam made up a small percentage. New York City residents born in China (including Taiwan and Hong Kong; each locality has a separate immigration quota) make up almost half the Asian immigrants in New York City today.

Currently New York City has 502,724 Chinese inhabitants, the largest Chinese population in the country (New York City Department of City Planning 2000, 2012). The population has doubled since 1990. The rapid growth quickly saturated Lower Manhattan's Chinatown, spurring the growth of satellite Chinese neighborhoods in Flushing, Queens, and in Sunset Park, Brooklyn. Whereas the first Chinese immigrants to New York City were largely from Canton (now Guandong) Province, the recent waves of Chinese immigrants are from Fujian Province, changing the demographic makeup of Chinese immigrants in New York City.

Agricultural production to meet the demands of the new Asian Americans continues to develop today. Many Chinese farmers followed the Lees to Florida, making the southern region of the state an important source of Asian vegetables from November to May and fruit from May to September. New Jersey continues to be an important summer supplier of Asian vegetables for the East Coast, with new

Chinese immigrants still going into agriculture there.[4] But as agricultural trade has been globalizing, so has Asian fruit and vegetable production. This has caused farms in the New York area that once grew for Chinatown, like that of the Lees, to shift their focus to higher-priced agricultural commodities, such as heirloom tomatoes, herbs, and wine, that are more competitive in the metropolitan area.[5] Now Chinese produce comes from the large expanse of sandy and muck soils of southern Florida, the horticultural heartlands of California and Western Mexico, the backyard gardens of Miami-Dade County, the two-hectare farms of central Honduras, and many other uncounted locations. Produce from each of these locales ends up on Chinatown sidewalks under the day-to-day, sometimes emergent, sometimes well-rehearsed choreography of Chinatown's produce brokers.

The Structure and Politics of Chinatown's Produce Sector

New York City is known as the produce capital of the United States. Boxes of fruits and vegetables pour through the city to feed its 8.3 million residents as well as the residents of the eastern region. Just as Hunts Point Terminal Market acts as a site of distribution for nearby eastern cities, so does Chinatown. Distributors from Philadelphia and Boston drive to Chinese wholesalers in Lower Manhattan and Brooklyn to make purchases. This gives New York wholesalers an upper hand in the regional market. They use buyers in other cities to spread rumors about price fluctuations, create artificial demand, or dump extra produce to preserve prices in New York. Produce trade is run by day-to-day negotiations. There are no provisions for price, quality, or volume guarantees. One wholesaler in New York explained that wholesale produce sales depend on volume: "If the quality is good we can take 15 percent profit, if it is bad, then 10 percent, and sometimes we lose money." Wholesalers try to squeeze as much profit as they can out of every sale.

But unlike the national concentration of produce distribution, the wholesale and retail structure of produce sales in Chinatown has been subject neither to vertical or horizontal integration nor to corporate appropriation. As one of my informants told me, "Chinatown works on a micro basis." The retail and wholesale produce sector of Chinatown is composed of small, highly competitive businesses: all wholesale and retail produce businesses have under twenty employees and about 80 percent have only four employees (McCormick et al. 2010). Nine wholesale firms are located in Manhattan's Chinatown, and another ten are located in the growing satellite Chinatown in Sunset Park, Brooklyn. Eighty-eight produce vendors are located in Manhattan's Chinatown, clustered along Grand, Mott, and Canal Streets, with other vendors scattered along

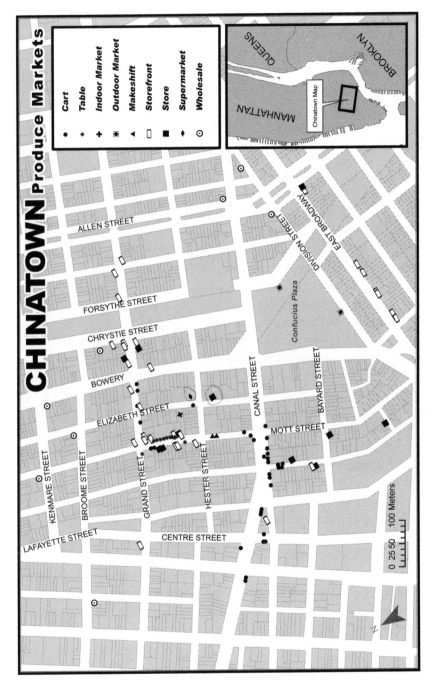

Figure 3 The produce markets of Chinatown. Map created by Brian Morgan.

Mulberry Street, East Broadway, and other locations (see appendix A for a list of produce retail and wholesale markets in Chinatown).

The structure of produce retail in Chinatown precludes its wholesale sector from moving very far. If Chinatown wholesalers were forced to move to the South Bronx, it could be the end of the retail sector in its current form. Wholesalers have constant face-to-face interaction with their retail clients. They deliver orders to their clients and deliver and pick up order forms. Most retailers work on the street and do not have typical business infrastructure, such as telephones and fax machines, to allow them to be in contact with their suppliers. Nor do they have refrigeration. They rely on personal service and proximity to their wholesalers.

Chinatown produce wholesalers are very powerful businessmen and -women. They not only control access to Chinatown in New York; they control the eastern metropolises. They distribute to Washington, DC; Baltimore; Philadelphia; and Boston. New York is considered the produce capital of the country because of the volume that passes through it, and its Chinese produce is no different. Some Chinatown wholesalers own warehouses in other cities; some own or are invested in farms in New Jersey, in Florida, and outside Toronto. They do not always follow rules of fair business; it is no wonder that they do not like to comply with the demands of their SoHo neighbors.

Much of the produce brokers' control of the market stems from the structure of the production and retail side of the industry. Wholesalers work with many individual clients, farmers as well as merchants, who are competitors in their sectors. There is no unification among farmers or merchants, so neither group has the power to demand set prices. It is the wholesalers, as the brokers between the farmers and the retail merchants, who are in the position to set prices. Nevertheless, price setting is the most tenuous aspect of this industry. Prices fluctuate widely on claims of quality, overproduction, and underproduction. Rumors, as well as real events, have equal effects on price setting. Furthermore, wholesalers accept produce only on consignment. Farmers are paid after delivery. Because of the perishability of produce, farmers have to ship on good faith. Working on consignment increases the power of the wholesalers in their role as brokers: they determine prices *after* farmers have shipped their products. Farmers have to take what they are offered. Both merchants and farmers are dependent on the wholesalers, who control the industry.

The Micromarkets of Chinatown

Produce sales in Chinatown happen on the street. Every market makes use of sidewalk space to create an outstanding visual bounty to entice passersby.

Figure 4 A vegetable display in front of a dry goods grocery advertises to many different Asian nationals.

Figure 5 A storefront fruit stand on East Broadway illuminated for evening shoppers.

Each morning produce vendors meticulously stock their shelves with brightly colored fruits and vegetables in a very specific way. Delicate herbs like watercress are packed in ice, and leafy greens like bok choy and Chinese broccoli are stacked with the cut end outward to display their cleanliness and freshness. Durians, pomelos, litchis, and longans are hung above the shelves, making use of vertical space and further increasing the illusion of plenty. Large squashes like winter melon are cut and sold in pieces by weight. In the winter months when shopping continues into the darkness, vendors set up spotlights to aid evening rush hour shoppers.

Many of the fruits and vegetables sold in Chinatown cannot be found elsewhere in the city. Produce markets are part of the character of Chinatown, contributing to its "exoticness." The markets are part of tourists' experiences—one is never alone in taking pictures of produce in Chinatown. Chinatown holds the reputation that if you know where to go, you can find any edible product imaginable. There have even been a number of field guides written about Asian produce that seek to translate Asia's bounty of freshness to those unfamiliar with it.[6] A colleague of mine commented that when she moved to the Lower East Side and started frequently shopping in Chinatown, she had to purchase one such guide in order to be able to shop there and has subsequently increased the variety of foods she consumes in her vegetarian diet. Chinatown would simply not be the same if the quality, quantity, and variety of produce disappeared from its streets.

The produce vendors are mostly first-generation Chinese immigrants, many of whom speak limited or no English. Their life unfolds on the streets of Chinatown through the heat and humidity of summer and the frigid air of winter. They seem to be complaisant toward their surroundings, perhaps as a means of self-protection against their unforgiving place of business. I often stand in front of a vendor for several minutes, recording the business's inventory, and am usually left alone. I rarely experience inquisition into what I am doing. Because of this social dynamic, the vendors have been the hardest set of people to get to know in my study. I was never able to get more than simple answers to my questions, if that. This is in part because of the vendors' guarded attitude and that I do not speak any Chinese dialects or have any personal contacts of influence in Chinatown.[7] The few times that I went to Chinatown with an interpreter to talk to produce vendors they were just as distrustful, and always busy. They need to be attentive to customers and cannot entertain many questions. I resolved to make my market survey mostly quantitative, colored with some observations and comments from wholesalers and farmers I have interviewed and supplemented with secondary sources.

Chinatown works on a micro basis; its vendors are very small scale—some sell as few as two or three types of vegetables on a sidewalk table—others have a store packed with produce-filled tables. There are two supermarkets in Chinatown, Hong Kong Supermarket on East Broadway and Dynasty Supermarket on Elizabeth Street. Their produce is terrible, the quality is very poor, and people do not shop there for produce but rather for other groceries that they carry.

The produce vendors other than the two supermarkets vary in infrastructure and permanence. There are stores and street vendors that anchor produce sales in the community and others that are subject to change. Since I began taking market inventories in 2003, there have been a total of eighty-eight produce markets that were present for at least one inventory. There are forty markets, or 47 percent of the total, that have been present for every inventory and that I determined to be permanent. But over the three years (2003–2005) that I inventoried produce markets, there was a gradual decline of the number of markets by 25 percent. This results from the varying types of markets that come in and out of life in Chinatown. I categorized four different types of markets according to infrastructure and location: store, storefront, street vendor, and makeshift store.

The first type of market, stores, use both the sidewalk space in front of the store and the inside of the store for produce, and the inside and outside are operated by the same owner. There are thirteen stores that sell produce, some exclusively. Others are general grocery stores or supermarkets that sell other grocery items as well. One store is a pharmacy run by a Vietnamese couple that carries Vietnamese herbs in a small, refrigerated display in the back. The stores are the most permanent market type; they anchor produce sales by having a wide selection as well as being open every day. The only day I ever saw a store closed was during Lunar New Year.

The second type, storefront produce markets, make use of only the sidewalk space of a store for produce sales. The store inside may be a grocery, fish shop, or other type of store. The store owner sometimes manages the storefront space, or

Table 4 Typology of produce markets in Chinatown

Market type	Number	Percent
Makeshift store	2	2
Store	13	15
Storefront	30	34
Street vendor	43	49

Source: Data collected by the author in 2003–5.

it is rented to outside parties. Sometimes one storefront is split between multiple tenants. Tenants can pay a premium for storefront space. Since the 1980s speculative capital has caused immense inflation in the value of Chinatown's real estate, and in some cases renters are taken advantage of by store owners. Indeed, those who are established in Chinatown hold much influence over those who are not. Peter Kwong describes the tenure of one merchant: "Retail space has become so scarce that unusual situations have developed. . . . One vegetable seller on Canal Street rents a 150-square-foot storefront, which he uses only as storage, and displays his produce on stands set up on the street. He pays $1,500 a month for the storefront, having also paid $20,000 as "key money" to the landlord" (1996, 51).

Public space is very valuable in Chinatown; in one instance, in 2010, a business owner on East Broadway reported the illegal demand for a fee to renew her lease. Real estate values affect the street vendors and ground floor merchants. Another merchant reported that his rent rose from three thousand dollars a month in 2000 to six thousand dollars in 2008 because the landlord was passing on increased property taxes to him (McCormick et al. 2010). The demand for key money and inflation of rents no doubt has put some merchants out of business.

The third type of market, street vendors, are the most common type of market and can be divided roughly into two categories—those that are licensed by New York City and those that are not. Street vendors are located where there is the most foot traffic, such as along Canal Street, at the subway entrance on Centre Street just south of Canal, and at the corner of Grand Street and Bowery. Street vendors are very territorial; each has his or her own location. I have never seen a street vendor change location, although there are some vendors who are present every day and others that are part time and seasonal. There are itinerant vendors, those who buy two or three boxes of vegetables and set up a scale and a chair on the sidewalk, such as women who are often seen sitting, shelling and selling ginkgo nuts. And there are those vendors who make use of space that is in limbo.

A unique example of markets in limbo is two makeshift stores (the fourth category of market) that were set up on the edge of a parking lot. These were shacks built of plywood and painted bright colors. They had an enclosed area in which the vendor could stand behind the counter space where the produce was displayed. One vendor specialized in seasonal fruit and the other in leafy vegetables. The space they were in was a parking lot destined to become the site of a high-rise building; for two years it served as an informal market space. Likewise, the triangle at Canal and Baxter Streets, which was long slated for an information kiosk, became home to vendors until the city forced them to leave.

Confucius Plaza continues to occasionally serve as an informal market space. Pushcart vendors will congregate there to sell extraordinarily cheap, low-quality leftover produce. The lines there can wrap around the plaza, particularly when longans are in season and being sold for two dollars less a pound than at other vendors.

The street vendors are an integral part of Chinatown's commerce. In a survey of street traders conducted in October 1995, Lin (1998) counted 122 vendors. The largest category was produce vendors, with forty-four vendors, or 36 percent of the total. One farmer who supplies a Chinatown wholesaler told me that he had a 25 percent decline in his sales one week that it was bitter cold in New York and the street vendors could not withstand working outside. Chinatown truly does work on a micro basis.

Street vending, although a very common form of commerce, is politically problematic. Street vending licenses for food are no longer available from the city: it offers three thousand permits, all of which have been granted, and an additional one thousand seasonal summer permits. The waiting list for city-issued permits is rumored to be over twenty-five years long. Permits, like yellow cab medallions, can be bought, sold, or rented only from existing owners, leading to inflated values. In 2003 Mayor Michael Bloomberg signed an executive order barring nonprofit and government agencies from asking the immigration status of permit applicants, to allow for a legal way of making a living for the city's undocumented immigrants. But many street vendors continue to work illegally and are vulnerable to fines. Others pay inflated prices for vending licenses from the few that possess them.

There are a number of street vendors in Chinatown who have permits; you can see these permits strung around their necks. But legal or not, street vendors are constantly under the influence of policing, construction, lease arrangements, and weather. They are seen as a problem and have had to fight to stay in business. Merchants and street vendors are often at odds; merchants simply do not want vendors on the streets. The former pay property taxes and have much higher overhead costs than do street vendors, who can undercut prices. Each group has its own association—numbering among the hundreds of associations in Chinatown—the Grand Street Merchant Association and the Chinatown Vendors Association, each of which advocates for different uses of the precious space of Chinatown. The Vendors Association supports unregulated public access to Chinatown's streets for its vendors and has defended this idea by demonstrating at City Hall and at community board meetings; by contrast, the Merchants Association believes that the vendors make the streets congested, dirty, and unsanitary.

Many city administrations have taken the same view as the merchants and have sought to clean the city streets of street vendors. New York City lives with the legacy of moving vendors inside. Starting in 1938, Mayor Fiorello La Guardia attempted to clear the streets of Jewish, Italian, and other ethnic vendors by requiring proof of citizenship. Mayors Ed Koch, David Dinkins, and Rudy Giuliani cleared the streets to improve the "quality of life" for its residents. These campaigns have affected multiple ethnic groups in many neighborhoods, from vendors outside elite property on Fifth Avenue and in Times Square, to African vendors in Harlem on 125th Street and Chinese vendors in Chinatown.

In the early 1990s Chinatown street vendors were ordered off the streets and moved into Sara D. Roosevelt Park. The park was an unused and unsafe space, with vagrants and drug users as its primary population. Hoping to simultaneously clean up the streets and the park, the Parks Department contracted the University Settlement House of the Lower East Side to oversee a market of one hundred stalls, named the Dragon Gate Market, which opened in September 1994. The market did not last long—the vendors perceived the allowable hours of operation from 7:00 am to 7:00 pm as restrictive. Perhaps a more important deterrent to the market's immediate success was the closure of the adjacent Grand Street subway station for renovation. The closure severely limited the flow of people through the area. In October 1995, a year after Dragon Gate's opening, only twelve active traders were at the site.

The battle over Dragon Gate Market went on and on, and the city, which initially encouraged its formation, called for its demise (Kirby 1998). In 1999 the market was vacated by city order. A number of complications had arisen. The city claimed that the vendors did not comply with the regulations of the market. They were building permanent market stalls in the park when only temporary structures were allowed, and there were reports of unsightliness and illegal tapping into electric and water lines. Since the opening of the market, a Chinatown real estate agency, Century 21 New Golden Age Realty, had assumed oversight. It was the agency's responsibility to inform the vendors of the city's restrictions and advise them on their behavior. Instead, the agency invested in the permanent structures and encouraged vendors to put their savings into their market stalls. Unfortunately the vendors bore the brunt of the fiasco, and they took to protesting and civil disobedience to defend their rights to vend. The vendors who held permits for street vending were eventually reassigned to the streets. Today, street vendors are still a very important part of produce sales and many take the risk of doing this highly visible work to make an illegal or legal living on the streets of Chinatown.

The Fruits and Vegetables of Chinatown

I found 209 distinct types of fresh fruits, vegetables, and herbs for sale in Chinatown.[8] Each represents different sets of culinary, cultural, agronomic, and economic practices associated with Chinatown's markets. Months in advance of the moment you see a head of bok choy sitting on the shelf for sale, a grower was ordering seed and preparing the fields for planting. Tractors (or oxen) tilled the soil, irrigation (or rain) watered tender green shoots of emerging seedlings, growers kept an eye on pest populations, and when the crop reached maturity, farm laborers crouched over in the blazing sun to slice the newly formed head of bok choy from its rootstock. Then, that head of bok choy was neatly place in a box, transported to a cooler for a few hours, and loaded onto a refrigerated tractor-trailer to make its way to Chinatown.

The agronomic practices associated with each of the 209 fresh produce items are surely a black box to most consumers. Consumers can let their imaginations associate possible scenarios of how food is grown according to what the media says, or what one might know about agriculture from experience. So, at most marketplaces, consumers can only truly know what is available and when, what the quality of the produce is by sight, and how prices fluctuate without an obvious reason why.

As a consumer, the number 209 can be misleading. It does not mean that during any given visit to Chinatown one can find 209 different fresh produce items. This number was compiled over a two-year period, with certain items making only a brief appearance. Fresh jackfruit and Cambodian eggplant were only in the marketplace once. Nor does it mean that there are 209 botanically different living edible plants for sale in Chinatown. Sometimes different parts of the same species, subspecies, or variety are sold under different names, like pea shoots and peas, or sweet potato leaves and sweet potatoes. Or sometimes the same fruit is sold at different stages of ripeness under a separate name and price. Green papaya is unripe and papaya is ripe. Whole, fresh, immature coconut is sold with a straw to slurp up its coconut water and fresh mature coconut is sold without the outer husk for eating raw and cooking. Finally, these 209 fresh fruits, vegetables, and herbs are not all confined to ethnic Asian diets, or to sale in Chinatown. About 40 percent of the 209 are conventional produce items like lettuce and grapes that many people eat and that are commonly sold throughout the city.

July and August are the best time of year to find a bonanza of fresh produce in Chinatown. This is the time when the market is supplied by the greatest variety of production locales. Temperate climates in the northeastern United States and Canada are at the height of production, tropical fruits from Florida are being harvested, and year-round climates in California, Mexico, and Honduras are keeping up production. Several fruits are available only in the summer and early fall. Fruits like litchis and longans explode onto the market in July. Other fruits such as jujube, rambutan, sugar apple, and Thai guava appear in smaller volumes. Vegetables like amaranth, boxthorn, hyacinth bean, lablab bean, and birdhouse gourd are available only in summer.

In September and October one of the strangest vegetables in Chinatown is for sale: *Trapa bicornis*, the seed pod of the aquatic species, also known as water caltrops, the devil pod, bat nut, goat head, bull nut, and buffalo nut. It bears these names for good reason. As described on the University of Connecticut's Ecology and Evolutionary Biology's website, "This naturally sculpted botanical oddity looks like nothing so much as a leering goat-horned devil, an enraged bull demon, a flying bat, or an alien chupacabra! The illusion of an evil face appears on both sides of the pod, and the two faces are usually quite different in visage."[9] There are certainly many vegetables to know and eat in Chinatown.

The diversity of fruits and vegetables declines in November and reaches a low in January. But in the winter months of December and January there are seasonal items. Pomelo, pomegranate, and two varieties of persimmon come into season in the winter. Likewise snow peas, snow pea tips, watercress, baby Shanghai choy, and bitter melon, which are available all year, are more abundant in the winter because of Mexican and Honduran production. Also, around Lunar New Year in January, certain products are popular and become more abundant in the market. Chinese celery and daikon radish are popular because they are considered lucky vegetables, and clementines sold with leaves and branches are popular for offerings of good fortune. These products are sourced specifically for the holiday.

Although the markets appear more bountiful in the summer, produce sales actually decline in summer months. Restaurants, as well as individual consumers, buy more produce in the winter. Wholesalers pare back their hours in the summer and work from 5:30 am until 2:00 pm, whereas in the winter the workday lasts from dawn until 7:00 pm. One wholesaler's explanation for this trend is that people don't want to cook in the summer. People also take vacations in the summer. But while money is lost on vegetables in the summer, fruits offset the loss. The value differential between seasonal fruits and vegetables is astonishing: longan is eleven times more valuable than Shanghai choy. In the example one wholesaler gave, she may lose 13¢ to 16¢ per pound of Shanghai choy, but she may make 25¢ to $1.25 per pound of longan.

Table 5 Example of pricing structure of longan and Shanghai choy given by wholesaler for summer prices

Point of purchase	Price/lb longan	Price/lb Shanghai choy
FOB (Farm, w/o freight)	$2.25–2.50	$0.20
Freight (paid by wholesaler)	$0.11–0.15	$0.11–0.15
Wholesale	$2.75–3.50	$0.23–0.26
Retail	$4.00–4.50	$0.60–1.00

Note: Longan is a high-value product. People try to use it to make up for the lower prices of vegetables in the summer. Wholesalers often take a loss on vegetables in the summer because supply is high and demand is low.

The longan, a botanical relative of the litchi, rambutan, and ackee, is a gold mine for Florida growers and distributors. The longan tree is a subtropical tree well adapted to tropical climates, and its fruit is a common one throughout southern and eastern Asia. In the 1990s Florida growers began producing it commercially, with limited competition from other production locales. Southern Florida is the best climatic zone in the continental United States for growing longan because longan twigs and leaves suffer damage when the temperature falls just one or two degrees below freezing. Its range extends only as far north as Tampa on the west coast of the Florida peninsula and Merrit Island on the east coast. Longan's fruiting season is short, from late July through September, with very little off-season fruit produced, keeping it highly valued and in demand during the summer.[10]

Because fruits are more lucrative than vegetables, when seasonal fruits are available, everyone tends to sell them. Eighty-five percent of markets were selling litchis and longans during the summer. Longan can be priced around four to five dollars a pound when it is abundant, but when few markets have longan—at the beginning or end of the season—prices will be seven to eight dollars a pound. The prices of products that are supplied year round are relatively stable. There are small margins of difference depending on quality and volume of the supply, affecting the consumer little. It does, however, affect wholesalers and farmers. A few cents difference on a pound matters when there are tens of thousands of pounds sold at one time.

Apart from these seasonal items, many fruits and vegetables are evenly distributed across markets and are found with the same frequency over the year. After all, that is the goal of the global marketplace—to keep our shelves full.

Bitter melon, taro, Chinese eggplant, Japanese pumpkin, long beans, daikon, Thai chilies, Korean cabbage, Chinese broccoli, bok choy, and Chinese mustard are mainstays of the marketplace.

Chinatown markets offer an outstanding variety of products for low prices and, most of the time, good quality. Chinatown's food system has developed over the past 120 years to become one that is firmly embedded both within the enclave and within global networks of trade. The location of Chinatown is of paramount importance to the myriad businesses that compose the food industry cluster there, and competition for the physical space of Chinatown is acutely negotiated on a daily basis. But in addition, in order for a marketplace that comprises many small vendors and a great diversity of products to be steadily supplied throughout the year, a dynamic, flexible network of production and distribution that extends beyond the confines of Chinatown exists. The ethnic enclave of Chinatown may primarily service and be served by first- and subsequent-generation Chinese Americans, but the enclave is not bounded in space. It is not isolated; it is very much embedded in global networks of trade. The next chapter will introduce the people who have shaped the distribution networks, describe how they "globalized" Chinatown's food system, and discuss how they maintain networks of trade.

## CHAPTER 2

The Social Network of Trade

The distribution networks that deliver the great diversity of produce to the numerous small retail vendors in Chinatown are flexible and dynamic; they are constantly changing. Entrepreneurs enter and leave the system and continually look for new suppliers and new products to sell—Thai guava is the hot new fruit among Florida growers; longans are now being imported from Taiwan and litchis from Mexico. The shift in product availability is as much a result of international as it is of intraregional competition. When a product grows well in an area, everyone wants to grow it; in addition, overproduction and market saturation push producers to look for new crops. Because of this dynamism and competition, successful farmers as well as brokers are constantly experimenting with new items and new production sites. Brokers do not shy away from global trade. Rather, Chinatown produce brokers use their social networks to develop new trade relations. The globalization of Chinatown's food system has occurred because individuals have been making contacts with friends, family, and associates abroad. Globalization, once thought to inevitably result in the homogenization of practices and the erasure of local identities, can include multiscale, network-oriented processes in which the particularities of place and culture are important determinants.

Chinese American wholesalers in Chinatown control access to the area's produce markets. They have shaped how the industry is structured, its business practices, and its networks of exchange. These brokers choose the farmers they want to work with and the terms of sale. They have maintained this control because they have *created* an ethnic industry. Their ethnic identity as Chinese in the United States and the ethnic character of the foods that they sell have both served to define their businesses, as well as provide a foundation on which to build them.[1] The Chinese American brokers use their ethnicity to keep control over their markets.

Chinese wholesalers are thought to be insular and unwilling to work with non-Chinese outsiders. Early in my research I interviewed two agricultural extension agents, one from Cornell University and the other from the University of Massachusetts, who had worked on two separate projects that attempted to connect local farmers with Chinatown markets. Both agents were highly discouraged by their experiences with Chinese wholesalers who were uninterested in collaborating with them. The disinterest led the agents to believe that the brokers would not work with people outside their ethnic groups. This assumption is untrue; brokers work with many non-Chinese growers, on local and international scales. I found that ethnicity is conveniently used as a way to justify refusing contact or protecting information. Once I was refused an interview with a Chinese American wholesaler in Florida on the grounds that she did not speak English well. After I interviewed a trusted friend and grower who worked with this wholesaler, one call from him was all she needed to provide me with one of the longest and most vibrant interviews I conducted. Industry outsiders speak of wholesalers with suspicion and distrust because they don't have personal experience with them, and insiders call into question their associates' trustworthiness because they do have personal experiences with them. When I asked a Chinese American grower who is the son of a Chinatown wholesaler if I could talk to his father he said, "You could talk to him, but he will probably lie to you anyway."[2]

Allegations of cultural difference, ethnic solidarity, trust, and distrust are both real and feigned in the Chinese produce industry. If they are feigned it is because there is a perceived advantage to doing so. Chinese brokers organize an industry that provides ethnic products to ethnic populations in the United States. Their markets are based in spatially and ethnically defined enclaves in urban areas, often in enclaves that have their own political structure. Brokers work to keep out competitors to protect their markets. The intentional "isolation" of these businesspeople may be what shields them from takeover by American food giants and has allowed them to organize the industry as they see fit.

Chinatown's food system is operating within the political economy of American agriculture, and it too is composed of complex, constantly evolving transnational networks of trade. Chinatown brokers work with many types of growers and distributors, from small Chinese-owned and -operated farms in New Jersey and immigrant Asian homegardeners in Florida, to agribusiness in California, large Chinese vegetable farms in Florida, and contract farmers in Honduras. Chinatown brokers are anything but isolated in an ethnic enclave. They are generators of transnational networks of distribution.

Ethnic Entrepreneurship in Chinatown

The role of ethnicity in New York's Chinatown is central to the discussion about Chinatown's political economy and its relationship to New York City society at large.[3] Chinese ethnicity in the United States can be expressed as shared values, kinship, language, and membership in associations. Shared ethnicity has been the grounds for positive business relations, friendship, and protection but also for exploitation. Prior to 1965, the year of US immigration reform, cooperation between Chinese and non-Chinese Americans was not common. Family, kinship, clanship, and membership in associations and "Tongs" were the common basis for business partnerships. The ethnicity of Chinese provided a solid basis for the economic activities of Chinese in the early period of Chinatown's development leading up to the liberalization of immigration (Wong 1988). Ethnicity was a resource for political, economic, and other goal-seeking activities, and ethnicity was used as an adaptive strategy within the opportunity structure of the larger society, even in post-1965 Chinatown when links outside Chinatown and use of city, state, and federal social services within Chinatown were more common.

The positive economic effects of ethnic solidarity are characteristic of what is known as an ethnic enclave. The ethnic enclave model was developed to describe the behavior of other successful immigrant groups in the United States, such as Cubans in Miami (Portes and Bach 1985). The ethnic enclave model shows how economic activity within an enclave leads to social mobility and status attainment of ethnic groups. An ethnic enclave is organized so that exchange can occur primarily within the ethnic group, thus protecting immigrants from undervaluation of their skills in their new society.[4]

The ethnic enclave can also foster injustice and exploitation. In Chinatown, the ethnic enclave can be a trap, manufactured by Chinese elites to keep the newest Chinese immigrants isolated and vulnerable to labor exploitation. Ethnic solidarity can be a manufactured concept to entice low-wage workers to give their loyalty to Chinatown's elite. Chinatown has a deeply divided class structure; there are those that live outside the area who bring in the capital to employ those that have no choice but to live in Chinatown's cramped conditions. It is inaccurate to conceive of Chinatown as an enclave whose inhabitants always cooperate and work to mutual benefit (Kwong 1996, 1997; Guest 2003).

Chinese use their ethnicity to take advantage of opportunities presented by the political-economic structure of the broader society. As technological innovations like refrigerated transport and such political innovations as free trade have encouraged produce to be transported at longer distances, Chinese Americans have moved to production sites farther afield from their urban enclaves. In the New York metro area, this move was from Long Island and New Jersey to Florida, Mexico, Central America, and the Caribbean.

In the case of Chinatown's food system, ethnic entrepreneurship cannot be analyzed as a process bounded within an enclave. The focus on labor earnings and opportunities in the ethnic enclave alone obscures the organizational pathways that ethnic businesses create with manufacturers, wholesalers, and retailers outside the enclave. Indeed, it is inaccurate to conceive of Chinatown as a bounded, isolated space, as the idea of an ethnic enclave suggests. Chinatown is a site of transnational activity, rendering the boundaries of the enclave fluid, if not limitless. Ethnic entrepreneurship constitutes interfirm relations on multiple scales (Werbner 2001).

The flow of commodities naturally connects multiple sites of production and consumption. Whether in raw or manufactured goods, the trade of niche goods for particular ethnic groups requires immigrants to work in a networked space, relying on complex local, national, and international relations to conduct their business. Trade of this sort has been documented not just for the Chinese in New York City but also for West African street vendors in Harlem (Stoller 2002).

Entrepreneurs in Chinatown's food system have used their ethnicity, specifically their language, kin, place of origin, and membership in social associations, to build business relations through social networking. Shared ethnicity, however, is not a strong enough value to sustain unprofitable relationships or to guarantee fair business practices. Relationships fluctuate over time with changing social, economic, and political pressures, subsequently affecting networks of trade and places and practices of production.

How and why are relationships formed within Chinatown's food system? How do relationships affect the stability and fragility of this system? The exploration of these questions is meant to shift the focus on globalizing trade from the anonymity of macroeconomic analysis to the personal world of individual actors within the system. Their life histories have shaped the food system.

Social Networking

Trade networks in Chinatown's food system are predominately established through social relations. Seventy-one percent of the actors in Chinatown's food system came into the system through a social relation and 62 percent maintain trade with a social relation. Every farmer who grows Chinese vegetables has entered the system through a relationship with a brokerage firm in Chinatown, because brokers control market access. In many cases, brokerage firms were established in partnership with farms through joint ownership or a verbal agreement to work together. In other cases, brokers have sought out farmers in new production locales to improve their supply.

The establishment and expansion of brokerage firms and farms has depended on social relations. As the ethnic enclave model suggests, kin ties and membership in associations are important foundations for business relations, but entrepreneurship is not limited by shared ethnicity. I found four kinds of relationships to be important: (1) kin ties, through which brothers or cousins have partnered and children of brokers and farmers have opened their own firms or farms; (2) social associations, which have enabled people to meet through membership in churches; (3) friendship, whereby friends or friends of friends have become partners; and (4) employment, in that prior experience as an employee in a brokerage firm or on a farm has propelled some people into ownership.

The significance of social relationships to the formation of trade networks within Chinatown's food system challenges the notion of nameless, faceless corporations making decisions about food sourcing based solely on competitive advantage and lowering production costs. The economic rationality of actors in Chinatown's food system is important, but where they establish their business and how they develop their business practices is based on their highly personalized life experiences. The following discussion provides examples of cornerstone actors in Chinatown's food system to illustrate how they have used their personal life trajectories to become actors in the trade network and how they maintain trade relations under changing circumstances. This discussion is not meant to be an assessment or critique of all their business practices. Questions about labor relations, venture capital, price setting, and politics are pertinent and unexplored aspects of the trade networks.

Kin Ties Linking New York to Florida

Firms run by patrilineal kinsmen, such as cousins, uncles, and nephews, were very common in pre-1965 Chinatown. This trend was largely a result of Chinatown being virtually a "bachelor society" (or more accurately, a society of married men whose wives lived in China). Families were relatively uncommon until the War Brides Act was passed in 1945, and they changed substantially with the immigration reforms of 1965. Many brokerage firms and farms have been established following the tradition of working with patrilineal kinsmen, although there are female entrepreneurs who have built their own businesses or who work in partnership with their husbands.

Sang Lee Farms, the first Chinese vegetable farm on Long Island, is a case in point. Two male cousins established Sang Lee Farms and they hired Chinese relatives and friends of relatives to work there. When the original owners retired, their sons, Fred and Richard Lee, took over the farm. The second-generation cousins worked together until 1992, when competition made farming on Long Island harder. Fred Lee still operates Sang Lee Farms; Richard Lee left to open his own greenhouses to grow perennials for landscaping. Fred Lee and his wife work full time on the farm and they have a core group of Chinese workers who have remained with them for years.

Another example of a father-son farm is Li Farm. Johnny Li, the son of a Chinese vegetable farmer in New Jersey, established a farm in Loxahatchee, Florida, in 1974.[5] Johnny and his wife, Judy, are still farming in Palm Beach County, Florida. Judy, who was born in Guandong Province and speaks Cantonese and Mandarin Chinese, handles sales. Johnny oversees the farm. They have been working with the same two wholesalers in New York since 1978, wholesalers who also worked with Johnny's father. In 2005, Johnny and Judy's son joined the farm; he plans to take over when his parents retire.

When Johnny and the Lees began farming in Florida in the 1970s there were two other Chinese farms located in the area. One of these, W.C. Farms, survived alongside Li Farm, but has recently changed ownership. A longtime Chinatown broker bought out W.C. in 1998. He sold his wholesale businesses in New York and Philadelphia and shifted his focus to farming. The broker encouraged his son to take over the farm; the son accepted the managerial role in 2000.

There are other examples of patrilineal kinsmen forming business relationships. Another Chinatown wholesaler sent his brother down to Florida to open a one-hundred-acre longan and Thai guava grove in 2000. A father-son farm and distribution firm in Florida City gained ties to a Cambodian supermarket owner in St. Paul, Minnesota, through marriage. Another farmer bequeathed his daughter-in-law a forty-acre Thai guava grove upon her marriage to his son. The sons of three other farmers in Miami-Dade County have joined the family businesses and expanded the farms.

Farms in the New York metropolitan area expanded to a winter-growing climate through kin ties. Florida became, and continues to be, connected to New York through kin ties, with subsequent generations taking over farms. As the average age of farmers in the United States is reaching that of retirement, the importance of younger people going into farming is extremely important for the viability of agriculture in the country. The number of farms producing vegetables for Chinatown on Long Island and in Florida has decreased, and those that have remained have become larger. The increased acreage is attractive to the subsequent generation. Leo took his father's place as manager of W.C. Farms because it was his chance to manage a multimillion-dollar business right out of business school. He does not see himself as a farmer. He is a grower, a manager who oversees production of vegetables. As mentioned above, Johnny Li's son, an engineer, joined his father's business in a managerial capacity. As the torch is passed down through generations, it would seem that carrying on a family enterprise is a positive thing. But questions of family social dynamics, work relations, and how expectations and desires are met or not would make for interesting research in multigenerational family businesses.

Taking Chances with Associates and Friends

The story of the Double Green brokerage firm and farm illustrates how people use shared membership in an association in the enclave to identify common interests and goals and develop new business opportunities. The founders of Double Green Farm Inc. and Double Green Produce Inc. in Florida City, and Double Green Wholesales Inc. in New York City, met through a church in Flushing, Queens. They recounted their story to me with pride, surely leaving out a critical perspective. But their telling of their business history is instructive, showing how they want to be seen. Laura Huang, a Taiwanese immigrant and resident of Flushing, took it upon herself to help the Wus, a Taiwanese family who wanted to move from Haiti to New York. She assisted the Wu children in getting into a preferred school and helped the family find an apartment in Flushing. Laura Huang and Yun-Feng Wu quickly discovered they were both interested in going into business. Wu suggested importing fish from Haiti because it was plentiful. Huang saw the need for vegetables for the growing Taiwanese population in Flushing. Since Wu had expertise in agriculture (he is an agronomist), he and Huang decided that they could open a production and distribution business. Wu would run the farm and Huang would run the wholesale warehouse in Manhattan's Chinatown.

Wu and Huang opened Double Green in 1985 but faced many challenges in their first years. It was more difficult than Wu expected to farm Chinese vegetables under Florida's ecological and economic conditions. In China, agriculture is very labor intensive. In Florida, however, it is too expensive to use the labor-dependent methods Wu knew from China. He was forced to develop new techniques and needed time to learn how to farm in Florida City. Laura, however, was not willing to wait and went on to find new farmers. Although the partnership dissolved, Wu and Laura helped one another realize their goals of opening a business and they both went on to build successful enterprises.

Wu used his professional experience and his contacts in Haiti and Honduras to develop export agriculture there. In Haiti he had been the chief agronomist of the Taiwanese Mission for agricultural development. There is also a Taiwanese Mission in Honduras, where Wu had many friends. In Honduras, the mission is a key part of the Chinese vegetable industry. The Honduran Mission put Wu in contact with a new exporter of Chinese vegetables from Honduras. In 2005 Wu was importing three to four container loads of produce a week from Honduras. Haiti has more infrastructural challenges for exporting goods than does Honduras, and Wu's production there has waned. Production in Honduras, on the other hand, is growing. Since he has established himself as a successful businessperson and farmer in Florida, he consults the Honduran Mission on the production and marketing of Chinese vegetables. Wu was invited to Honduras to speak at a workshop for agronomists in Central America interested in the export of Asian vegetables to the United States. Wu now considers himself the "father of Chinese vegetables" in South Florida because he has brought so many people into the business.

After Laura Huang left the partnership with Wu, she looked for potential business partners through her social networks. Some friends went into partnership with her; others introduced her to their own friends as potential partners. She "took care" of growers who turned out to be good. By "taking care," Laura means giving her farmers a good price and keeping them aware of exactly what the market wants. Farmers and wholesalers both talked to me about the need for special relationships and treatment of each other to maintain trust and, ultimately, positive business relations.

One of the growers with whom Laura took an extraordinary risk is Jack. At the time, Jack was growing chili peppers for Pace Foods. His friend and neighbor, Tommy Yee, grew Chinese vegetables for Laura. Jack spent a lot of time in Yee's packinghouse because he borrowed the vacuum cooler to pack his chili peppers and herbs. Inadvertently, Jack learned about farming Chinese vegetables from Tommy.

At that time Laura was looking for a new grower, and she requested to meet Jack. Jack felt he could not afford to take the risk of trying new crops; nor did he have the capital to expand. During their first meeting Laura offered Jack twenty-five thousand dollars to start growing vegetables for her. Jack left that meeting with a check and a verbal agreement to grow Chinese vegetables for Laura. Now he owns seventeen hundred acres south of Lake Okeechobee and ships about one thousand boxes of Chinese vegetables a day to New York.

From Employee to Owner

Yi Jen recounted to me what she sees as an extraordinary success story as a female entrepreneur in Chinatown's food system. She got her start by working for Yun-Feng Wu at Double Green's packinghouse in Florida. She aspired to own a business and wanted to educate herself about the produce industry by working for someone else. When she was ready to go out on her own, she raised seventy thousand dollars in cash from friends and family and set up a farm and packinghouse in Homestead, Florida. While Yi Jen was working at Double Green she had opportunities to be in contact with many suppliers. Yi Jen had lived in the Dominican Republic after emigrating from China and before coming to the United States. She spoke some Spanish. Yi Jen made a connection with a Honduran export company that was started by two Japanese Dominican men whom Yi Jen knew from her time living in the Dominican Republic. When Yi Jen was ready to open her own business she called her acquaintances from the Dominican Republic. They were unhappy with their importer and were interested in building new relationships. In 1994, Yi Jen went into business importing Chinese vegetables from Honduras. The business between Yi Jen and her Honduran supplier has been the one of the most stable and most well regarded in the Chinese vegetable trade today.

One Hand Washes the Other

Chinatown's food system is built upon social networks. Kinship, friendship, former employment, and community associations are the means by which entrepreneurs form partnerships and trade relations. While social networking is undoubtedly a feature of many industries, it is significant to note the importance of social networking in the expansion of agricultural trade because vertical integration and corporate mergers have been the dominant means of expansion in the industry. The cases presented here represent a rather small industry but are illuminating because they show that flexible, risk-taking individuals can prosper in the global agricultural economy. Analyzing the social relations embedded in global trade also presents an opportunity to understand trade based on social, rather than only economic, terms. In Chinatown's food system, profit is the underlying motive, but it is not the only motivation behind decision making and practices. People accept monetary losses to preserve relationships.

Yi Jen, for example, does not work with many people. Rather, she builds strong relationships with the few with whom she does work. She says that she treats her business relationships as long-term investments. She will take a loss so that her farmers can turn a profit. Yi Jen has explicitly stated in an interview, "After all, what was one season's loss on one crop with one farmer, when you have had that farmer working with you for many seasons and you will have them for many more?"[6]

Tommy Yee has worked with the same two brokers in New York City for almost thirty years. Of course there were others who came and went. Tommy has averred that in business, "one hand washes the other." In interviews he has stated that he knows that if he compromises with his brokers to their benefit, they will return the favor.[7] Long-term stability appears to be more important to Tommy than garnering the highest price he can in the short term.

Both Yi Jen's emphasis on cooperation and Tommy's attitude of reciprocity are philosophies I heard espoused numerous times by successful farmers and brokers in Chinatown's food system; such outlooks are why people build trade relations based on social relations. Trust and mutual respect, in addition to a quality product (from the farmer) and a good price (from the broker) are continually pointed out as necessary ingredients for long-term success. Timely payment is also crucial. Each of these necessary ingredients does not always exist. Farmers are very vulnerable to market conditions because they sell highly perishable goods. Chinatown brokers in New York City work on consignment, which means they do not pay farmers until after shipment is received. Farmers have to ship their product in good faith, making trust more important in this trade network than in other subcontracting systems, where prices are predetermined. Brokers refuse to pay for a product that they haven't yet seen. If the produce is of poor quality or if there is overproduction and the market is flooded, the broker will lower the price. All farmers have experienced not getting paid for shipped produce or getting paid what they believe is under market price. The only way to survive in a consignment system like this market is to find buyers and sellers who can be trusted. Trusted partners are found through social networks.

Changing Relations, Changing Practices

Entrepreneurs in Chinatown's food system have established and expanded their businesses through relationships of trust. They meet potential partners through social networks and they strengthen and expand relations that prove to be mutually beneficial. The examples of these entrepreneurs highlight the social aspects of trade relations and show how individuals function in global markets. But relationships change. Trusted partnerships go awry. Actors in the system use the resources they have to overcome competition, sometimes to the detriment of others. Just as there are the examples of cooperation and respect built through social networks, there are instances of deceit and distrust that have ruined relationships. Shared ethnicity, language, kinship, and friendship are not enough to maintain business relationships if these are not profitable, and sometimes social relations are used for exploitive purposes.

The mantra of Chinatown's wholesalers is "Quality is no good!" It is true that the market demands very high-quality produce, and wholesalers cannot sell produce of low quality—items that are bruised, wilted, or discolored. Because wholesalers have the final say in price setting, farmers often feel that they are purposely told their produce is of low quality so that they can be paid less. Unless farmers fly to New York to confront their wholesaler, there is no way to prove their suspicions correct. Also, wholesalers in New York sell produce to other wholesalers in Philadelphia; Boston; and Washington, DC, so they try to keep prices down to allow for one more exchange before the produce goes to retail. Because of this dynamic, New York, the largest market for Asian produce, is considered a "dumping ground," a place to sell produce that cannot be sold elsewhere for whatever price a farmer can get. Some farmers can't stand to deal with such a lack of control over their selling prices.

Sang Lee Goes Chichi

Sang Lee Farm has a new shingle outside the farm gate. It announces Sang Lee's positioning in the farm-chic rurality of the North Fork of Long Island. The farm boasts of "over 250 varieties of naturally grown produce"; *naturally grown* means "utilizing sustainable agricultural practices and integrated pest management."[8] Sang Lee's competitive advantage is the farm's ethnic twist. Online or at the farm stand you can buy premium baby greens like mini bok choy and yu choy for premium prices ($5.50 for eight ounces of snow pea shoots). The farm, along with its image, has drastically changed since its inception as the first Chinese farm on Long Island in 1948. But of course, agriculture on Long Island has also changed. Now it is an industry that fosters agritourism at high-end wineries and caters to the elite summer lifestyles of the island's East End.

Fred Lee, son of the founder of Sang Lee Farms and its current proprietor, just gave up his last account in Chinatown. It was a hard decision for him, but he couldn't emotionally or financially accept having truckloads of his harvest returned, unpaid. This practice became more and more frequent when Fred's wholesaler could not sell his produce. It was simply too expensive compared with Mexican-grown products. Not only did Fred lose the sale of his harvest; he would also have to pay to dump it. His longtime associate offered him the chance to go to Mexico and set up a farm, but Fred refused. He wanted to stay on Long Island; he didn't want to radically change his lifestyle. So he did what the other farms around him were doing: he diversified his product line and began marketing directly to restaurants, consumers, and catering companies. He produces baby vegetables, cut flowers, and heirloom tomatoes. He kept many of his Chinese vegetables, and he now assembles bags of ready-to-cook stir-fry greens and sauce. He set up a farm stand and began to advertise his own organic philosophy. In this case, internationally grown produce was undercutting Fred's business, and loyalty to Chinatown was not enough for him to market his produce profitably.

Jack's Divorce

Jack, a Florida grower, maintained a relationship with Laura, a Chinatown wholesaler, for ten years. In 2005 that relationship ended. In Jack's opinion, Laura lost her aggressiveness in the market. Without Laura fighting for a good price for him, working closely with him to understand his needs, and keeping him informed about market demands as she had done in the past, Jack felt that he could no longer continue to work with her. Jack clearly emphasizes that the Chinese vegetable market is not a niche market. There is no added value in growing Chinese vegetables, and competition is growing every day, particularly from Mexico, where high-quality vegetables can be grown at a fraction of the cost. If he does not have a broker working for him, pushing his product and demanding the prices that he needs to make a profit, then he will not continue growing Chinese vegetables. In fact, in the 2003–4 growing season Jack lost money on his Chinese vegetables. The other vegetables he grew carried his farm. Jack left Laura when another broker in Chinatown offered to buy his produce at higher prices.

Entrepreneurship has been a traditional path to success by overseas Chinese. Many aspire to own their own businesses or form partnerships with friends or relatives. When businesses prospered, owners would help others start businesses. That's why one often finds Chinese businesspeople dominating a particular trade in a country—with many owners related (Kwong 1996). Personal relationships, or *guanxi*, have been described as the cornerstone of Chinese businesses, important for the establishment of trust and for facilitating smooth business transactions (Kiong and Kee 1998). Indeed, ethnic Chinese have established themselves strongly in commercial and financial sectors, particularly in Southeast Asia. The World Bank has estimated that the combined economic output of the ethnic Chinese outside China was about four hundred billion dollars in 1991 and up to six hundred billion dollars in 1996 (Yeung 2000). But it can be easy to essentialize the role that shared ethnicity plays in Chinese business outside China. The motivation to build personal business relations based on ethnic, linguistic, and kin ties may reflect not loyalty or nationalism but simply profit seeking. In her critique of narratives of Chinese nationalism and capitalism, Aiwa Ong states, "Despite the tantalizing appeal of 'our kind of people,' and the racialist construct of overseas Chinese, the official view [given by the director of overseas Chinese affairs in China] is that in practice, one cannot count on the loyalty of overseas Chinese, only on their desire to make a profit off China" (1997, 338).

Ethnicity is used in networking; kinship, community associations, friendship, and shared nationality and language do unite entrepreneurs in Chinatown's food system. The ethnic character of the food products, as well as the community in which they are sold (Chinatown), further characterizes the system as separate from society at large and shields Chinatown businesses from takeover by American agribusiness and grocery corporations. Because Chinese language skills and a Chinese identity are needed for individuals to work within Chinatown to supply the retail end of this system, Chinese brokers control market access. Non-Chinese are involved at other points along the commodity chain—in farming and exporting from Latin America—but trustworthy relationships with Chinatown brokers are necessary for long-term success. Trust can be very elusive; it is not guaranteed by shared ethnicity or other types of social relations. Yet social relations are the first place to look for trusted business partners. Successful farmers and firms are constantly negotiating their business relationships, extending and intertwining the social network that unites those involved in Chinatown's food system.

CHAPTER 3

Okeechobee Bok Choy

Chinese vegetable farming in Florida developed to supplement the summer growing season of the Northeast. Sang Lee Farms was one of the first farms from the New York metro area to move to Florida in the 1950s. Chinese growers from New York, New Jersey, and the Toronto area followed the Lees to Florida, making the southern state an important source of winter Chinese vegetables. Chinese farms are now scattered around Central and South Florida. Their contribution to Chinatown's food system is substantial, particularly in Palm Beach and Hendry Counties, where there are over thirty-six hundred acres of Chinese vegetables in production.

A defining characteristic of a food system as an analytical unit is that it connects consumption with the natural environment. The building blocks of our bodies, the proteins, sugars, vitamins, and minerals we need to function, come from the foods we eat. It is easy to recognize the fundamentals of nutrition, but it is harder to appreciate how the fundamentals of plant nutrition are connected to human nutrition—how the elements that make up the nutrients in our food enter that food. Nutrients either come from the biological and physical properties of soil or they come from fertilizers that amend the soil. This is how human biology is intimately connected to the natural environment, to agriculture, and to the industrial processes that produce fertilizers. Ensuring that the necessary nutrients are in the soil, so they can flow through plants and animals into human bodies, is a highly complex process dependent on biological, political, and economic variables. We, as consumers who require food to live, have to work very hard to understand the variables that underlie the sources of our nutrition.

The move backward to the production sites that give life to the fruits and vegetables displayed by Chinatown's vendors is meant to uncover some of the processes and variables that shape our food system and that connect us to distant environments. Whether we acknowledge it or not, the act of eating has many ripple effects in the distant places that feed us. The growers that produce Chinese vegetables in South Florida have to work within its geographic constraints as well as the economic constraints of land, labor, and produce sales. The geographic particularities of production sites are important determinants in the shape of a food system, whether the production site is in the backyard of the marketplace or across a continent.

Social ties between Florida farmers and their brokers in Chinatown may facilitate the trade of Chinese vegetables, but it is the attempt by human beings to control nature that enables vegetable production in South Florida in the first place. Such an attempt is seen in the extensive drainage of wetlands, which opened up hundreds of thousands of acres to the production of vegetables and sugarcane. Further, chemical fertilizers provide crops with nutrients in sandy soils devoid of nutrition. The consequences of agricultural runoff and water pollution have become impossible to ignore in South Florida, and development pressures are encroaching inland from the highly desirable coastal areas. Agriculture in South Florida is now the enemy of both the environment and developers. The stories of the Chinese vegetable growers tell a personal story within a seemingly faceless and nameless industry, but they also exemplify the challenges that many farmers today face.

South Florida's Land Squeeze

The agricultural importance of South Florida is undisputed: it is the United States predominate source of late fall, winter, and early spring vegetables and about half of its cane sugar (Baucum and Rice 2009, 3, and Vallad et al. 2014–15, 1). But South Florida is naturally best at producing saw grass marshes, hardwood hammocks, and alligators, not sugarcane and tomatoes. Food production could not take place in South Florida without extreme alteration to the natural environment. South Florida was *intentionally* engineered to be exactly what it is: central to the nation's food supply. Its natural environment, wetland, was not agriculturally friendly until the 1950s, when the Army Corps of Engineers began draining the wetlands south of Lake Okeechobee to create the Everglades Agricultural Area.

The Everglades Agricultural Area is an area of seven hundred thousand acres that occupies the heart of South Florida. It is the result of channelizing the Kissimmee River, which flows into Lake Okeechobee, and impounding Lake

Okeechobee. Instead of water flowing naturally off the lake in sheets to create wetlands to the south, it is diverted into three Everglades water conservation areas totaling 869,800 acres through an intricate system of over fourteen hundred miles of canals and levees with pumping stations and floodgates. All this is maintained through the Central and South Florida Flood Control Project, which manages flood control, drainage, and irrigation in South Florida. Runoff from rainfall is removed by pumping stations and forced into the conservation areas or siphoned off into the Atlantic Ocean and Gulf of Mexico.

All the water now intricately managed once flowed naturally from Lake Okeechobee over the Everglades into Florida and Biscayne Bay. Moving sheets of water fifty miles wide and one hundred miles long would flood the entire southern shore. The Everglades Agricultural Area (EAA) now occupies one-third of the historic 2.3-million-acre Everglades wetland system and disrupts the natural flow of water from the lake over to the bay. There is also an agricultural extension to the EAA. The C-139 Basin is located southwest of Lake Okeechobee entirely within eastern Hendry County, west of the EAA. It covers approximately 170,000 acres. Both the EAA and the C-139 Basin are highly productive agricultural areas with rich organic peat or muck soils known as histosols.

The alteration of the water regime of South Florida, initially to support agriculture and increasingly to support residential development, has been a major cause of wetland decline and degradation and has pitted agriculture against the environment. Agricultural fertilizers and tillage practices have exacerbated the water quality problem: oxidation of the peaty muck soils as they are drained, dried, and tilled causes the release of nitrates into the water cycle and the formation of excess nitrogen leads to eutrophication of Lake Okeechobee and contamination of drinking water from leakage into the Biscayne Aquifer. Further, phosphorus runoff from chemical-intensive sugarcane and vegetable farms has changed the native plant communities of the Everglades and there has also been a negative effect on the fauna supported by native plants.

The environmental impacts of the fundamental alteration of the complex hydrologic patterns have led to many political challenges for South Florida. In 1988 the U.S. attorney's office in Miami filed suit on behalf of the Fish and Wildlife Service and the National Park Service against the Florida Department of Environmental Regulation and the South Florida Water Management District for pumping water that exceeded pollution standards into the Everglades without a permit. A settlement to clean up the pumped effluent from the EAA was reached in 1991, but counter legal challenges to water regulation by agricultural interests delayed action.

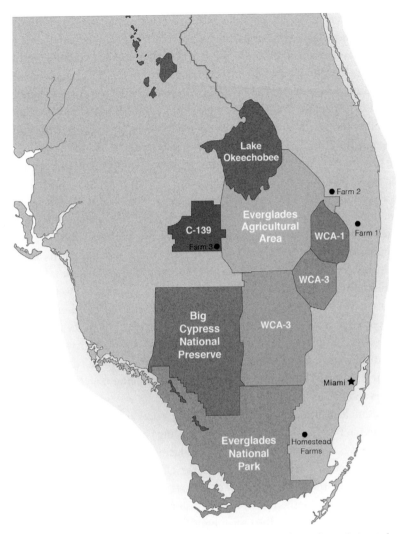

Figure 6 Map of South Florida showing the locations of the farms in this study in relation to the alterations made to the watershed to accommodate agriculture. *WCA* stands for "water conservation areas," and *C-139* designates another agricultural area. Map designed by Shane Chase.

Finally, in 1994 the Everglades Forever Act mandated that the implementation of stormwater treatment areas and best management practices (BMPs) for the EAA and the C-139 Basin. The practices use the best available technologies for achieving the interim phosphorus water quality goals of the Environmental Protection Agency. EAA farmers are required by the Everglades Forever Act to reduce the total phosphorus in the runoff from their land by 25 percent each year by implementing BMPs to clean the water. The annual phosphorus load reduction is calculated by comparing the current year's amount with that of the ten-year base period of 1978–88, before BMPs were in place, and adjusted for differences in rainfall between the two periods. Unlike the EAA's goal of achieving a 25 percent reduction of total phosphorous loads from historic baseline levels, the goal of the C-139 Basin is to maintain total phosphorous loads at or below historic baseline levels. The Everglades Forever Act mandated that landowners within the C-139 Basin should not collectively exceed the annual average phosphorus loading observed during the base period extending from October 1, 1978, to September 30, 1988.

To reduce the levels of phosphorus coming off their farms EAA farmers have implemented various BMPs, of which the main ones include efficient fertilizer application, control of erosion and sediment, and effective storm water pumping operations.[1] Instead of water being directly pumped off farms into water conservation areas, the Everglades Forever Act mandated the creation of stormwater treatment areas. These areas are large, constructed wetlands that remove pollutants from storm water runoff. Runoff from the EAA is routed through an inflow canal to stormwater treatment areas, where the phosphorus removal occurs naturally by deposition or by plant growth. After water has passed through the stormwater treatment areas, it is then discharged to the Arthur R. Marshall Loxahatchee National Wildlife Refuge and two other water conservation areas located to the east.[2]

The implementation of Best Management Practices and Stormwater Treatment Areas in the EAA has been successful in reducing pollution. 3,500 metric tons of phosphorus have been removed as of 2010, reducing phosphorus concentrations in Everglades bound water from 170 parts per billion before the construction of Stormwater Treatment Areas to a low of 12 parts per billion today.

As of April 2010, the EAA BMPs and stormwater treatment areas together have removed more than thirty-five hundred metric tons of total phosphorus from water entering the Everglades Protection Area. In 2010, more than 1,400,000 acre-feet of water were treated in stormwater treatment areas, reducing phosphorus by 76 percent. A decade ago, before treatment areas were constructed, phosphorus concentrations in Everglades-bound waters averaged 170 parts per billion (ppb). Today, the concentrations in discharges to the Everglades have been as low as 12 ppb, but biological recovery of the marsh system after continual exposure to high nutrient loads will be a long and unpredictable process.

As if the alteration of the natural environment in South Florida was not extreme enough, development pressure is squeezing the land even more. In 1998 the Sierra Club designated Palm Beach County as the most sprawl-threatened medium-sized metropolitan area in the nation. Between 1992 and 2002 Palm Beach County lost 16 percent of its farmland, a decline from 637,934 to 535,965 acres. To counteract this trend, in 1999 the county adopted the Managed Growth Tier Systems and designated use-specific development areas: urban and suburban, exurban, rural, agricultural reserve, and the Everglades.[3] Inflation of land values is a big problem, and farmers struggle with the cost of land, as well as with the threat that land they rent may be sold off to developers. Farms on the edge of residential zones are finding it harder and harder to keep going.

It would seem that the remoteness of the EAA would protect it from development, but there are signs that this may not be so. A Tampa-based developer approached a farm in the EAA and expressed interest in converting fifteen hundred acres of that property into an aero-club development with a runway for private planes, one- to two-acre home sites, a golf course, and stores. Current residents and farmers in western Palm Beach and Hendry Counties have seen inflation of land values as a result of this speculation. A Hendry County agricultural extension agent told me that three years ago he bought forty acres that include natural wetlands for four thousand dollars an acre. Before the real estate bubble burst that land was worth fifteen thousand dollars an acre. At those values it is unclear whether it will be profitable to farm such expensive land. Since cattle pasture, a common form of land use in the area, has a very low return per acre (about $0.03 in Southwest Florida), rangeland has already turned into vegetable production areas or preserved wetlands. Conversion to more intensive, lucrative types of agricultural land use may be a solution, but it must be understood that intensive land use will have more nutrient runoff that can easily throw the delicate water system out of balance. In the face of sprawling residential developments with sod lawns and artificial lakes, developers are still considered to be far worse than farmers by those interested in conservation. As the vice president of the Audubon Society of Florida commented, "It's obvious the continuation of agriculture in the EAA would be more benign environmentally than having the area turn into South Florida's version of Los Angeles Valley" (Santaniello 2004).

Growing Baby Bok Choy in Florida

Small and medium-sized Chinese vegetable farms are scattered around southern and central Florida, but the three farms that grow the majority of vegetables that make their way to Chinatown do so against the backdrop of extreme environmental alteration in southeastern Florida. Whether it is complying with

BMPs for water conservation or being squeezed by development pressure, Chinese vegetable growers are dealt many curveballs. Yet the acreage, volume, and value of Chinese vegetables grown in southeastern Florida have risen sharply since the 1990s (see table 7 for a listing of the major crops that make up the category "Chinese vegetables"). Between 1998 and 2004 the harvestable acres of Chinese vegetables increased by 38 percent, the volume of sales increased by 114 percent, and the value increased by 160 percent (see figures 7, 8, and 9). This growth is attributable to the increase in the extent of production as well as an

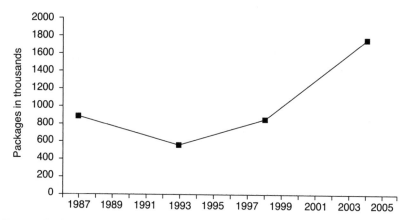

Figure 7 Total volume of Chinese vegetable sales. Between 1998 and 2004, the volume of sales increased by 114 percent. Data presented for Palm Beach County, farms 1 and 2. Data collected by Ken Schuler, former extension agent of Palm Beach County, for 1987–2001 and by author for 2004.

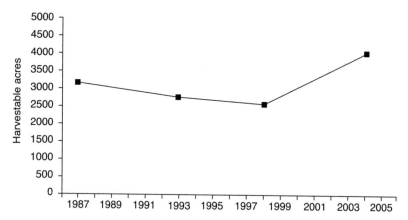

Figure 8 Harvestable acres of Chinese vegetables. Between 1998 and 2004, harvestable acres increased by 38 percent. Data presented for Palm Beach County, farms 1 and 2. Data collected by Ken Schuler, former extension agent of Palm Beach County, for 1987–2001 and by author for 2004.

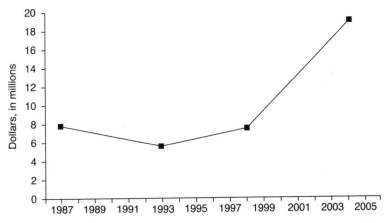

Figure 9 Total value of Chinese vegetables. Between 1998 and 2004, the value of vegetable sales increased by 160 percent. Data presented for Palm Beach County, farms 1 and 2. Data collected by Ken Schuler, former extension agent of Palm Beach County, for 1987–2001 and by author for 2004.

increase in production per acre. In the 2004–5 growing season there were 3,877 harvestable acres of Chinese vegetables, 1.77 million packages sold, and a farm value of $19 million.

Florida is not just for retirees, socialites, and vacationers; it is home to the United States' leading agricultural counties. Sprawl aside, Palm Beach County is the most valuable agricultural county east of the Mississippi River and is within the top ten of the United States. When you sweeten your coffee or eat an ear of supermarket sweet corn in January, chances are you are ingesting nutrients that came by way of Palm Beach County. And when you pick up a head of bok choy from Chinatown in December, you should think of Palm Beach County's balmy winter climate, sandy soils, and extensive drainage system. More specifically, you can think of Johnny Li, Leo Cheng, and Jack Varney— the farmers growing your vegetables.

These three farmers supply the majority of Chinese vegetables from southeastern Florida. The farms differ in their history and philosophy, but what they have in common is that they are all large farms harvesting vegetables on over one thousand acres and grossing millions of dollars (see table 6). They are conventional farms: they practice integrated pest management to control insect populations, use herbicides to reduce competition from weeds, and rely on fossil fuels to run their tractors and to cool freshly harvested vegetables before they are packed on trucks and shipped up to New York. They are also diversified vegetable farms rotating between fourteen and thirty-four different vegetables over the course of a year. Like most farmers, they rely on immigrant labor.

Table 6 Characteristics of Chinese vegetable farms, Palm Beach and Hendry Counties

Farmer characteristics	1	2	3
Ethnicity	Chinese American	Chinese American	American
From a farming family	Yes	No	No
Full-time farmer	Yes	Yes	Yes
Age of farmer	57	30	50
Years farming	30	5	20
Relative in Chinese vegetable business	Yes	Yes	No
Household size	4	4	4
Family members work on farm	Wife, son	None; children are babies	Wife, son
Other household income	No	No	No

Farm Characteristics	1	2	3
Acres	900	1,000	1,700
Harvestable acres*	1,205	2,517	1,147
Acres owned	450	0	1,700
Number of Chinese vegetables	14	16	14
Number of non-Chinese vegetables‡	0	4	20
Maximum labor force	80	60	100
Annual output-volume in cartons, 2004–5	380,000	1,350,000	1,201,929
Annual gross income, 2004–5	$4 million	$15 million	$11 million

* Harvestable acres takes into account crop rotations and number of harvest cycles per year.

‡ Farm 1 grows strictly Chinese vegetables; Farm 2 is experimenting with green beans, calabaza, and lettuces in a joint venture; and Farm 3 has maintained 66 percent of its acreage in eggplants, peppers, basil, and other specialty crops.

They have crews of Latino farmworkers that can reach up to one hundred members.

Each of these three farms has a particular relationship with its Chinatown produce broker. If the farmers didn't have such connections, they would not be in the game, since brokers keep their growers abreast of market dynamics in the short and long term. Prices fluctuate on a daily basis and consumer preferences shift over time. The brokers are the eyes and ears of the growers in the marketplace. When selling wholesale, and especially when growing at a great distance from the marketplace, growers need their brokers to tell them what the market wants.

Consumer preferences have shifted in Chinatown over the past few decades. In part the shift reflects demographic changes in Asian immigration to the

Table 7 Shift in composition of Chinese vegetables grown in Palm Beach County

Crop	1987–88 % volume	1992–93 % volume	1996–97 % volume	2001–2 % volume	2004–5 % volume
Napa cabbage	32	31	21	13	24
Bok choy	21	16	9	12	3
Chinese radish	13	8	11	18	10
Yu choy	12	20	14	9	13
Chinese broccoli	10	11	7	9	12
Chinese mustard	8	8	10	6	12
Choy sum	3	5	2	2	1
Kohlrabi	1	1	1	2	1
Baby bok choy			10	10	15
Cilantro			2	3	1
Shanghai bok choy			10	12	2
Winter melon			3	4	2
Chinese celery				0.3	0.1
Chives				0.5	0.2
Baby Shanghai choy					4

Source: Data for 1987–2001 collected by Ken Schuler, former extension agent of Palm Beach County. Data for 2004–5 collected by the author.

Note: In 1996 baby bok choy, cilantro, Shanghai bok choy, and winter melon were added to the suite of vegetables grown; in 2001 Chinese celery and chives and in 2004 baby Shanghai choy were added. The percentage of napa, bok choy, and yu choy decreased to accommodate the new vegetables.

United States, but it also reflects trends within the produce industry at large. Bok choy, napa cabbage, and daikon radish made up about two-thirds of Florida's harvest until the 1990s, when yu choy, cilantro, winter melon, Shanghai bok choy, and Chinese celery became part of growers' inventories (see table 7). Baby vegetables became all the rage in the late 1990s, and it was no different in Chinatown. Baby bok choy and baby Shanghai choy have surpassed their "adult" counterparts in popularity.

Chinese vegetables might seem to be a niche crop because they are for a specialty market. In fact it is quite the opposite. They do not have the added value typically associated with niche crops. This means that there is no price premium for Chinese vegetables, and they are sold for dirt cheap in Chinatown. It costs one dollar for a pound of bok choy and seventy cents for a pound of Chinese eggplant. As one would expect, given the retail value of Chinese vegetables, the value of Chinese vegetables at the farm level compared with that of other vegetables is quite low. Chili peppers are by far the most valuable crop in southeastern Florida, bringing in about $39,977 per acre. At the other extreme is kohlrabi, a popular vegetable in Chinatown, which brings in about $1,700 per acre. Even the most valuable Chinese vegetable, Chinese celery, is worth only about $4,400 per acre. That value is on par with that of the common string bean, cucumber, sweet corn, and cabbage. As one grower emphasized the point, "Chinese vegetables are not niche crops!" I would add that Chinese vegetable crops are not mainstream either; they can occupy only a limited share of the market.

The economics of growing Chinese vegetables is very tenuous. In addition to the relatively low value of the crops, the average farm value of Chinese vegetables per package has not changed since the 1980s. There is much fluctuation around the average values with much to gain or lose per season, but the net result is very little change in value. Thus playing the market, so to speak, is a gamble. Growers report big differences in the prices they receive from their wholesaler for the same growing season (see table 8). A grower needs to have a secure relationship with his or her broker to be assured of receiving a fair price.

The only direct control growers have over their profit is to reduce production costs, experiment with new crops, increase output per acre, or increase acreage. The alternative is to try new markets, which is considerably more difficult. Each one of these three Chinese vegetable farms constantly experiments with each of these variables. As a whole, the farms have succeeded in increasing harvestable acres, a measure that accounts for multiple harvests on the same land, as well as the volume of vegetables produced per acre. From 1987 to 2005, the harvestable acres increased from thirty-two hundred to just around four thousand acres (see figure 8). The average volume of packages produced per acre also increased, from 280 to 430 packages.

Table 8 Reported average package price of select crops, 2004–5 growing season

Crop	Farm 1	Farm 2	Farm 3
Napa	6.70	12.00	11.73
Bok choy	7.50	8.00	11.93
Baby bok choy	7.50	6.00	15.00
Yu choy	9.00	15.00	22.00
Chinese mustard	7.12	8.00	8.25
Chinese radish	6.50	8.00	7.20
Chinese celery	17.00	—	29.62
Kohlrabi	10.30	—	10.00

Note: Prices differ considerably per farm although farms are part of the same markets.

These trends are not restricted to Chinese vegetable production and distribution but rather are part and parcel of American agriculture—farms are getting larger and producing more per acre because profit margins keep getting thinner. Farms in very different biophysical as well as economic environments compete for the same markets, putting farms with very different production costs in competition—Mexico has cheap land and cheap labor; California has plenty of sun and flat, fertile land. In the international climate of agriculture, how do farmers stay in business? How has Johnny Li been growing Chinese vegetables for thirty years? Why did Leo Cheng, a young business school graduate, decide to grow Chinese vegetables? And why did Jack Varney, a grower who had the most profitable crop, chili peppers, bother to grow Chinese vegetables? The stories of each of these Chinese vegetable growers illustrate the ways and means of American farmers. These three farmers operate in a natural environment that would not be hospitable to the crops that they grow if it were not for major works of engineering as well as industries that synthesize and mine the nutrients needed to grow plants and kill pests. The biological and physical constraints of agriculture are real—but the economics of labor, land, and produce sales is what preoccupies these farmers and drives their decision making.

The Story of Johnny Li

Johnny Li and his wife, Nancy, operate the oldest Chinese vegetable farm in Florida.[4] Much to Johnny's delight, his son finally decided to leave his career in engineering and come on board. Johnny grew up on a Chinese vegetable farm in Warren County, New Jersey. His father was a Cantonese immigrant who kept Chinatown supplied with vegetables. When harvest season ended in the Northeast, Johnny's father would buy and ship vegetables from Florida to his brokers in New York and Boston. This was a way to stay in business in the winter months, but it was also a way to keep up year-round business relations with his brokers so they wouldn't wander toward other suppliers.

When Johnny was in his twenties, he worked as a truck driver for his dad. He hauled produce from Florida to New York. As a go-between traveling this route, Johnny identified a "broken link" in the commodity chain. Brokers in New York couldn't supply a steady product to the marketplace, and farmers in Florida didn't have consistent buyers. Johnny saw this problem as an opportunity to become a supplier of winter produce. In 1974 he began his own farm in Florida, growing vegetables to seasonally complement the crops grown on his father's farm in New Jersey.

From an initial 110 acres, Li Farm has grown to its current size of 900 acres. The farm is divided into nine fields across Palm Beach County and, recently, St. Lucie County to the north. Johnny's son joined the farm in 2005; the plans of father and son are to continue farming as the family has for the past two generations. Li Farm is the only farm in the group of three that grows exclusively Chinese vegetables. Johnny and his family want to keep doing what they know how to do best. They don't experiment much with new crops. They focus on ways to keep costs low while maintaining high quality in their produce.

Li Farm has an established reputation in Chinatown. It has been working with the same two wholesalers in New York since the 1960s. Johnny attributes his success to the loyalty of his brokers, and his wife, Nancy, who handles all the marketing. She sits at her desk, sometimes seventeen hours a day, dancing between Cantonese, Mandarin Chinese, and English to deal with the business of farming. She says that she enjoys her work, when everything in sales is going smoothly and they have steady orders. They take the feedback from their brokers seriously and use their suggestions to produce a marketable product. Johnny knows what and how much to plant because he trusts the opinions of his brokers. He also understands that not all his products will be profitable. Of ten crops, only eight may turn a profit. He can accept the loss on two crops because he knows that prices fluctuate and that if he accepts a low buying price when prices are low, his broker will make it up when the price is high. He feels that volume and consistency of supply are most important in maintaining business relations for the long term.

Li Farm began as a growing, packing, and shipping operation. This is the norm for the Chinese vegetable farms in Florida. They retain more control over the marketing of their produce by packing and shipping their own produce instead of selling their vegetables to a local packinghouse to pack and market them. This business model has certain advantages. For one thing, packing and shipping produce enables growers to sell directly to Chinatown wholesalers rather than through a third-party broker. For another, growers control the quality of their pack. They can decide what produce is "good" verses "bad" quality. A third advantage is that they can market their produce under the farm name. Produce boxes proudly display the farm name, address, and phone number, serving as advertisements and making the farms well known in Chinatown. By building their reputation, they attract the interest of new customers and build brand loyalty.

Li Farm is a strong brand in Chinatown, but Johnny does not let himself get too comfortable with his situation. He knows the farm could collapse at any moment. He said to me, "Good thing you came today, we might not be here tomorrow!" Roland, Johnny's son, keeps his expectations low so he won't be that disappointed should something untoward occur. Like many farmers, Johnny likes to complain—and has much to complain about. He is an inquisitive skeptic who thinks about agriculture on many levels: labor, migration, state and federal government, free trade, international competition, land conservation and development. Not to mention the day-to-day pests, weeds, and weather. It is a dizzying number of concerns, but Johnny tries to stay in control.

Since the ratification of the North American Free Trade Agreement, Chinese vegetable production has continued to move to Mexico. Johnny has had to cut back his production by 25 percent as a result of competition from Mexico. The only advantage of growing in Florida is a lower transportation cost; they are slightly closer to the market. Mexican produce is just as fresh though, and the quality of their pack is better because labor costs are low. Leafy vegetables from Mexico are ready to sell out of the box; outer leaves and stems are trimmed to market standards on the farm. Johnny's boxes might have to be trimmed down by as much as one-third the weight by the wholesaler because he can't afford that kind of labor on the farm. Johnny and his son have thought about going to Mexico. They say everyone has—and many have gone. Much like Johnny's expansion of his father's business to Florida over three decades ago, Chinatown brokers have sent family members and business partners to Mexico. Mexico is the new frontier for Chinese vegetables. But Johnny and Roland don't want to live there, and they wouldn't trust someone else to run their farm. They are staying in Florida.

The pressure of development in Palm Beach County is starting to push Johnny northward. He owns only about half the land that he farms and his leases are on parcels on the edge of development. Boynton Beach, Loxahatchee, and Lake Worth, where Johnny has five fields, have been converted from sleepy towns with citrus groves to retirement and single-family home subdivisions and shopping malls. Agriculture now seems out of place in the area and certainly doesn't keep pace with the value of land, which peaked at eighty thousand dollars an acre before the housing crisis.

Conservation easements are not the solution to this problem. Palm Beach County, like many other counties in the nation, has a program to buy development rights from farmers in order to protect agricultural land from development. On the surface, conservation easements seem to be a good idea. Farmers get paid for the development rights and the land stays in agriculture, preserving its rural character and open space. Johnny regrets selling the development rights on one of his fields. He was offered fifteen hundred dollars an acre in a place where land is selling for forty thousand dollars an acre. If he wanted to sell his property, he could not get market value for land that cannot be developed. He feels that it is unjust to expect farmers to bear the financial burden of preserving open space. Farming pays the mortgage, but land valued at top development value is the capital gain.

Johnny's solution to the land squeeze is to move northward to St. Lucie County where development pressure is lighter. He bought small and medium-sized citrus farms and is in the process of converting them to Chinese vegetables. He has been growing vegetables on one of the groves for three years now and is planning to increase production there. The chance of frost in the winter is slightly higher there, but Johnny would rather swap the risk of frost for the risk of losing his leases to a developer. He tries his best to stay one step ahead of disaster. So far he has done so for thirty years.

The Story of Leo Cheng

Leo Cheng is the most optimistic farmer I've met. He's young, fresh out of business school, and ecstatic about having the chance to run his first business. Ironically, he never thought he would go into farming, although it was always a possibility for him, as his father ran a wholesale produce company in Manhattan's Chinatown and in Philadelphia; he knew many growers. After college Leo worked for a year for a well-respected grower of Chinese vegetables and mainstream herbs in the Tampa area. After this experience Leo thought, "I am never going to do this!" He went back to New York to start business school. During this time two things happened to change his mind about farming. The family wholesale business was under legal pressure to move out of Chinatown in Manhattan because the noise and garbage associated with running a produce warehouse did not mix well with the encroaching SoHo luxury lofts, galleries, and shops. And one of their Florida-based suppliers was looking to sell its farm. They decided to sell the wholesale company, and when Leo completed his master of business administration, he found himself back in Florida buying out W.C. Farms.

Leo worked with the previous owner of W.C. Farms for two years before he assumed primary responsibility for the farm in 2000. The first thing he did was change the name to W.C. International to show his aspiration to become an importer of produce as well as a grower. His year at Sanwa Growers outside Tampa shaped his business goals. They had experienced rapid growth by getting into mainstream markets in addition to Chinatown markets and by becoming an importer and packer of produce. This is exactly what Leo is trying to do. He doesn't think there is much potential for growth in the production of

Chinese vegetables alone and thinks there are too few brokers who control access to Chinatown markets. Even though he is working with his dad's old company and doesn't fear being taking advantage of, he doesn't want to rely too heavily on any one customer. Such a customer would have too much power over him. He wants to expand his customer base and product lines. And to do that, he is trying to court supermarket contracts.

Leo wants to grow lettuces. After all, lettuce is the number one consumed vegetable in the United States. He is renting land in the Everglades Agricultural Area in the heart of mainstream vegetable production and renting space at the packinghouse of a large corn grower. These growers sell to supermarkets, and by hanging around them and getting to know them, Leo is hoping that he too will win supermarket contracts.

While Chinese vegetables like napa cabbage and bok choy are regularly sold in mainstream supermarkets, most Chinese vegetables are not. Leo would have to convince supermarket buyers to try new products, or he would have to grow what they want. He is currently involved in a joint venture growing calabaza (a variety of squash preferred by Hispanic customers) and green beans. He also just acquired two small accounts with Piggly Wiggly and Acme for baby bok choy. At the time of our interview, he was waiting to hear about a new contract with a supermarket, an arrangement that may allow him to add two hundred more acres to his farm. Even if this deal doesn't come through, Leo feels that his business is progressing simply because he can now take the time to solicit buyers in whom he is interested, rather than just respond to buyers interested in him. He even hired a marketing firm in California to help him get new accounts. It seems ridiculous that someone in California could help him get accounts in Florida, but that is not important. Reputation and contacts are. Supermarket buyers have their favorite brokers. Leo wants to break out of his familiar world of Chinatown's food system and into the new world of American supermarkets.

While dreaming of lettuce, green beans, and squash, Leo plants and harvests yu choy and gai lan, the thin-stemmed, leafy, small-headed relatives of broccoli. He rotates the leafy vegetables through three-acre blocks that, minus windbreaks, canals, and ditches, gives him about two and one-half acres to plant on. He plants successively to harvest every day. The time to maturity for these leafy *Brassica* crops is thirty to forty-five days from seeding. The trick is timing. They have a very narrow harvest window—the flower buds must be fully formed but not opened when finally sitting on the retail shelf. But Leo likes to play another timing game: when there are droughts, floods, or hurricanes in Mexico and California, he seeds. Mexican growers can produce a box of gai lan for nine dollars. That is below his costs; he can't compete with that. But he feels that the weather protects him; if he has good weather and they have bad weather he can make big profits in small windows. One year he really hit it when Mexico had a hurricane and he was getting fifty-two dollars a box for gai lan. "It was so good it was scary," Leo recalled. He bought a new Ford F450 pickup that year.

Leo and Johnny Li know each other very well. Leo likes to share information with Johnny. He doesn't believe in secrets, such as hiding planting schedules. Leo feels that they are indirect competitors. They each have their own brokers, but their brokers are competitors. Leo has suggested that they work more closely together as a farming cooperative so they can control their supply and their prices better, but nothing has come of that idea. Instead they work on supporting agriculture in their own ways. They are both public advocates of agriculture in their areas: Johnny works closely with University of Florida Extension to improve production techniques and Leo is involved in the local Farm Bureau to protect agricultural land.

Leo's weakest point is that he leases all his land. He owns nothing. His landlord is an advocate of agricultural land, so Leo doesn't worry much about losing his leases to development, but the real mark of achievement for him is to become a landowner. Leo might have inherited his father's contacts in the Chinese vegetable business, but not land. He respects Johnny for staying small and steadily acquiring land. Leo, on the other hand, is focused on growth. Leo pushes his land, double cropping, and in some paces triple cropping, on the sand, muck, and "salt and pepper" soils—those that are a combination of sand and muck. This is chemically intensive. Herbicides, pesticides, and nutrient solutions are the primary means of farming in the big agricultural lands of the Everglades Agricultural Area and its neighboring lands. For Leo, his primary concern is not his reliance on chemical agriculture, which he should be more concerned about; it is what he is growing and whom he is selling it to. For him, Chinese vegetables are not enough.

The Story of Jack Varney

Unlike Johnny and Leo, Jack wasn't born into Chinese vegetables, or anything related to agriculture or produce sales for that matter. Jack is a self-taught farmer. His father was an academic and Jack lived abroad for much of his childhood. The academic path was not for him. He tried a semester of college but came home and got a job at a nursery. He worked all the time and found himself happy learning how to grow and sell plants. He decided to try out farming.

Jack moved to the Boynton Beach area and began growing peppers and herbs—high-priced vegetables. His farm was very close to Li Farm, one of the largest and most successful farms in the area. Jack made an arrangement with Johnny Li to use his vacuum cooler. A vacuum cooler is a talisman of success for a vegetable grower. It is an expensive piece of equipment that cools freshly harvest vegetables very quickly without the use of water. In just twenty to forty minutes the temperature of vegetables bathed in Florida sun can be cooled from 95°F to 45°F. Not using water means less chance of fungal rot and discoloration. For leafy vegetables like the Chinese bok choy relatives, the vacuum cooler ensures quality.

Jack spent a lot of time hanging around Johnny's operation. Jack knew nothing about Chinese people, let along Chinese vegetables, but while waiting for his herbs to cool at Li Farm Jack inadvertently learned a lot on these two subjects. It took a while for him to gain Johnny's trust and to engage in meaningful conversation, but when he did they talked a lot about farming.

Jack was doing well. He had a contract with Pace Foods to grow jalapeño peppers for jarred salsa. He also grew high-quality herbs—basil, cilantro, dill, and arugula (yes, arugula is considered an herb in the industry)—for a distributor at Hunts Point Terminal Market in New York. Yet he still had little capital to reinvest in his farm.

Johnny might have been Jack's first introduction to the world of Chinese vegetables, but it wasn't Johnny who got Jack into the business (although he might have helped open his mind to Chinese vegetables). Jack had a friend, Don, in New Jersey who grew Oriental vegetables, as they were called at the time, and was selling them to Laura Huang of Double Green in Chinatown. On a visit to Don's place, Laura requested a business meeting with Jack. Laura was looking for new growers and wanted Jack to grow for her. Jack's immediate reaction was "No way!" He didn't give it any thought because he was absolutely not interested. He had a good thing going and couldn't afford the risk because he had no capital. Or so he thought. He politely listened to Laura go on and on about the vegetables and what it is like to grow them. She grew up on a farm in Taiwan so she really understood how to grow things. Jack finally grew impatient and blurted out, "Laura, I am absolutely not interested. I don't know these vegetables and frankly, I don't trust Chinese people." Laura remained calm and replied, "What would it take for you to trust a Chinese person?" Jack said, sarcastically, "In America, there is an old saying. Shit walks and money talks." Laura reached into her pocketbook, pulled out her checkbook, and asked, "How much do you want?"

Jack was completely dumbfounded. Laura had called his bluff. He quickly went through some numbers in his head to come up with a reasonable amount. For twenty-five thousand dollars Jack got into Chinese vegetables. Laura had the utmost confidence in Don's opinion of Jack. She had never met him before yet made a risky investment in him. He learned fast and made good on Laura's investment. She even fronted him another fourteen thousand dollars to purchase a vacuum precision seeder, a tool that other Chinese vegetable growers were using to seed their cabbages.

Laura not only invested financially in Jack; she became his Chinese vegetable mentor. She told him, "If you don't understand the place of vegetables in the Chinese diet, then you can't understand how to grow and sell them." She flew down to Florida every two to three months to help Jack improve his understanding. Standing in the fields throwing Taiwan choy out of a freshly harvested box, she showed Jack how to trim the outer leaves and stems so it is ready for retail. The look of the leafy vegetables is a very important signifier of quality to the consumer. The stem ends need to be sliced clean and straight. Chinese cabbages are displayed with cut ends forward on the retail shelf so customers can be sure of it. Laura showed Jack how to trim vegetables correctly in order to increase their quality and value. She turned a nine-dollar box of poorly packed Taiwan choy into an eighteen-dollar box while reducing the volume by only one-third. This is the kind of communication needed between broker and grower. Without it, the grower would think he or she was sending a good product to market and would be offered a low price and ask, why is my broker trying to stiff me? Laura taught Jack about all the expectations of the market and how to deliver on them to both his and her profit. For example, bitter melon is eaten in the summer because it is excruciatingly bitter and considered to be a cooling vegetable; Chinese celery is used in dishes prepared for Lunar New Year—Jack would never know any of this without Laura.

Jack sent a semiload of Chinese mix—the group of vegetables that Laura specializes in—to her every day. Shanghai broccoli, bok choy, baby bok choy, baby gai choy, big gai choy, heading mustard, mustard greens, Taiwan choy, Sen Fin loose cabbage, and pickling cabbage made up 75 percent of Jack's production. He and Laura even tried new vegetables. Jack introduced green amaranth leaves to Chinatown, with Laura selling them.

The good times lasted about ten years, until Jack and Laura started to fight. Mexican produce was driving prices down for everyone, but Jack felt that Laura was slipping. She wasn't as aggressive, she worked less, and she was reaching her late fifties and realized her kids were not going to take over her business. In Jack's opinion, she had lost her drive. Laura and her husband were always complaining that Jack was sending them garbage. Jack got so tired of hearing the words "garbage, garbage, garbage." He jumped on a plane to New York to see why his perfectly good vegetables were being called garbage. He couldn't get a clear answer. Everyone was frustrated with the low prices of the market.

Jack started to feel out a new Chinatown broker and sold him a few boxes. Laura caught wind and called Jack right away. This treachery would not be tolerated. Jack had to stay loyal until he decided to "divorce" Laura. He made the trip to New York to do it in person. Jack still grows as many Chinese vegetables as he did before, but his attitude about it has changed. He has built his system of planting and harvesting around the Chinese vegetables and although they are not as profitable as they once were, it keeps his farm running and his three hundred employees working every day. That's one thing he likes about Chinatown: they work seven days a week compared to the regular five-day business week of other produce sectors.

Jack has had to do a lot more negotiating with his brokers than Johnny and Leo have. Perhaps its because they are insiders, but maybe it's Jack's way. He is affable, judgmental, humorous, and tough. He can also be seen as tyrannical. He works seven days a week and expects his crew to do the same. He built housing for his Hispanic workforce on the farm and is landlord as well as employer. After all, they live out in the heart of Florida agricultural land in the C-139 Basin without much housing nearby. The closest town is the sleepy Bell Glade, whose welcome sign just past the levees that bound Lake Okeechobee proclaims, "Her soil is her fortune." According to Jack, there is nothing else to do but work. Labor relations are not part of what is examined in this book, but there would be many issues to explore on Jack's farm, particularly in light of the struggles of resistance against labor abuse among the nearby Coalition of Immokalee Workers.

Jack forges ahead, multitasking all day long: answering his constantly ringing cell phone and citizens band radio, managing the harvest, assuaging his new broker's doubts about the quality of his produce, arranging trucking, and juggling a lawsuit of a hurt employee. He just paid off his mortgage on seventeen hundred acres of contiguous farmland and wetlands for water purification; he's been experimenting with a compost operation to stabilize his sandy soils (he's not on muck); and he's got some new crops in for Indian, Mexican, and Hmong markets. He was already offered a bid of ten thousand dollars an acre on his land by a developer looking to create a small airport. He realized he could cash in and run, but then he thought that would be irresponsible. It's not just his life that is supported by his farm; his employees are dependent on it as well.

THE three Chinese vegetable growers in this study have a range of experiences, but they all insist that they are still learning. Jack says that the unpredictability and problem solving involved in farming is what he loves about his work. Two

Figure 10 A typical field of Chinese leafy greens. Crops are planted three rows to the bed. Windbreaks are adjacent to canals.

University of Florida extension agents whom I interviewed consider these farmers to be "pros" who do not need much help from the cooperative extension.[5]

The Chinese vegetable growers have developed a style of farming that is akin to the norms of agribusiness at large. Most Chinese vegetables are continually sown from early to mid-September through late April. Planting fields are divided into two-acre blocks separated by irrigation canals or windbreaks. There are typically one hundred feet between irrigation canals, with cross ditches for surface drainage. Subirrigation (also called seepage irrigation systems) is used. Water is introduced into parallel open ditches from canals so that water can move with gravity under the root zone through the soil profile and into the root zone by capillary action. Beds are forty-four inches wide with six feet between centers and three to four rows per bed. Cage cultivators are used to prepare raised beds for planting, precision seeders sow seeds, and surface sprayers moisten newly seeded beds and apply herbicides. The farmers follow integrated pest management plans. Napa cabbage and bok choy face the most severe

Figure 11 Harvest time. Bok choy ends are cut, placed upright for cleanliness, and boxed in the field.

pest pressure and "soft" or "harsh" pesticides may be used, depending on the severity of the outbreaks. Preventative strategies are used to control pest and disease outbreaks, like using a pest scout to monitor pest populations, rotating crops, and attracting predatory insects by planting preferred species. Packing takes place in the field by full-time or contracted laborers. Boxes of harvested products are taken from the field directly to the packinghouse, where they are cooled with water or with a vacuum cooler in order to bring the field temperature of the crop down to refrigeration temperatures quickly. Packed and cooled boxes are stored in temperature-controlled coolers while they await shipment.

The stories presented here illustrate how the expansion of Chinatown's food system has influenced agriculture in South Florida, but even with sophisticated means of controlling natural biological and physical variables, agriculture will always be dependent on its local environmental conditions. Through social networks, farmers and produce brokers from the New York metropolitan area developed production in Florida. Since the 1970s production has been growing and new as well as second- and third-generation farmers continue to enter the industry. Farmers today have to cope with local as well as global changes. As

Chinatown's food system is expanding to more areas with starkly different agronomic and economic conditions, Florida farmers must continually adjust their practices to remain competitive. The Chinese vegetable farmers use irrigation, soil fertility, and pest control practices conventional in South Florida, but instead of specializing in one crop, they use crop diversity to their advantage. Because they grow between thirteen and thirty-four different crops, they can cope better with production problems and price fluctuations. Crop diversity and an overall increase in production volume per acre has been compensating for deflated prices in overproduced crops. But with increasing development pressures, rising production costs, and mounting environmental constraints, Florida farmers are unsure about the future of Chinese vegetables. They take it one day at a time.

## CHAPTER 4

Bringing Southeast Asia to the Southeastern United States

Chinatown markets in New York City have been diversifying to reflect the demands of new Asian immigrants coming to the United States. It is a mistake to think of Chinatown as a place that caters to only Chinese tastes; Southeast Asian products are an important part of Chinatown's offerings. In Manhattan's Chinatown there are markets that offer the flavors of Thai, Vietnamese, Filipino, Laotian, Malaysian, and Cambodian cuisines. There is a veritable Southeast Asian mélange in Chinatown, and tiny farms and homegardens in the tropical, southernmost part of the Floridian peninsula fill consumers' preferences for the fresh herbs, fruits, and vegetables of Southeast Asia.

The diversity of demand in Chinatown's markets has led to the development of new distribution networks for agricultural commodities as well as new types of agriculture. In Homestead, Florida, the manifestation of these two intersecting trends is visible across the agricultural landscape. Southeast Asian immigrants have been moving from their first homes in the United States to southern Florida in order to pursue agricultural livelihoods. They are producing specialty herbs, vegetables, and fruits traditional to Laotian, Thai, Vietnamese, Cambodian, Filipino, and other Southeast Asian diets. Farmers from Southeast Asia now living in Florida have been tapping into the distribution networks of South Florida that deliver produce to Chinatowns of the East Coast and Midwest. But the farmers have not only brought new crops to South Florida; they have also brought new styles of farming. Most interesting is a style of commercial "homegarden."

Homegarden farmers in Florida manage crop diversity as an economic strategy. The analysis of this type of agriculture is particularly salient for several reasons. First, it represents a striking contradiction to the generally held idea that small-scale, biodiverse farming systems such as homegardens are not commercially viable. Second, it exemplifies the functionality of small family farms in an era of the dominance of agribusiness in North America. Finally, it furthers the argument that crop diversification can be used to achieve economic stability. In a nation that is struggling to protect small farmers, to develop niche markets, and to aid minority farmers in purchasing and operating farms through state and federally mandated programs, the example of the South Florida homegardens should not be overlooked.

Agriculturally experienced immigrants from Southeast Asia have brought an alternative vision of agriculture to southern Florida. Southeast Asia has a rich tradition of homegardens, which are characterized by their complexity of structure and multiple functions. They can be defined as multistory combinations of various trees and crops around a home (Kumar and Nair 2004; Méndez et al. 2001). Homegardens are a popular subject of study because they can be interesting models of sustainable agroecosystems; they often foster efficient nutrient cycling, high biodiversity, low use of external inputs, conservation potential, and socioeconomic benefits (Torquebiau 1992; Padoch and de Jong 1991).

Most analyses of homegardens have been done in tropical Asia and Latin America. Homegardens are little understood in the political-economic context of developed nations, particularly in North America. Commercialization is assumed to lead to the dissolution of homegardens; however, a study of recently commercialized Vietnamese homegardens contradicts this claim: although anecdotal evidence suggested that commercialization was leading to decreased diversity in homegardens, quantitative analyses did not substantiate these claims (Trinh et al. 2003). In fact, there were higher numbers of total species in the more commercialized sites in southern Vietnam, where monocultures of single commodity crops like longan and rambutan are popular, as compared with other sites.

South Florida is similar to the Vietnamese case in that agriculture is highly commodified, yet total species diversity at the landscape level is high. There are at least twenty-three species of tropical fruits and twenty-five species of vegetables grown in monoculture, whereas there are hundreds of species of horticultural plants and approximately one hundred species of specialty crops grown in mixed cropping systems in South Florida's homegardens.

An important distinction to make about Florida's homegardens as compared with others is that they did not *survive* commercialization, they are not remnants of a past tradition of the area, and they were not formerly rooted in subsistence production. Instead, Florida homegardens emerged as an agricultural solution to the complexities of competing in an industry increasingly dominated by agribusiness firms and rendered borderless by international trade agreements. Homegarden farmers strategically choose to use crop diversity to exploit economic niches on the small plots of land they have available to them. They do not fear competition from farms with lower production costs because they realize that their choice of crops and their reliance on many different types of crops give them a competitive advantage in the face of high-yielding monocultures and the importation of fruits and vegetables. My interviews indicated that market flooding and international competition were major concerns of large-scale vegetable and tropical fruit growers, whereas these were not concerns for the homegarden farmer. Homegarden farmers rely on very specialized crops that are not grown on a large scale, and they plant a variety of crops for economic stability. The mean number of crops per homegarden is nineteen, with only Thai guava to be found across all homegardens, and many more crops are found in only one homegarden. Homegarden farmers also express that their multistrata style of farming helps to maximize area in the small plots of land to which they have access. One Homestead farmer, an immigrant from the Philippines, noted, "It's not how much space you have, it's how you use it. I would rather be small and diverse than big and specialized."[1]

Agricultural diversification has been a counter-trend to specialization, the form of production that has dominated post–World War II agriculture in developed nations. There are many empirical studies on agricultural diversification in North America and Europe, although the research questions that predominate in regions vary. Canadian researchers have been questioning the means of diversification, as well as the geographic scale of diversification, that is, whether it is on a regional or farm scale (Bradshaw 2004; Machum 2005). Ilbery and Bowler (1998) suggest that in Europe the agricultural trends of intensification and specialization have been reversed, and now diversification and dispersal are rising. Research in Europe has largely focused on quality of food production, reembedding food networks in regional relations, and implementing change in food supply chains as a means of rural development (Marsden et al. 2000; Murdoch et al. 2000; Ploeg and Dijk 1995). In the United States, research is focused on the importance of local food systems as more just and sustainable alternatives to industrial (and global) agribusiness, with agroecological principles of soil and water conservation, biodiversity, and biological pest controls as central to this alternative agriculture (Altieri and Nicholls 2005; Gliessman 1997).

The Florida homegarden case suggests that conventional and alternative agriculture may not be antagonistic styles or philosophies of farming but instead are interdependent. Florida homegarden farmers have found their advantage in the marketplace through their choice to produce a variety of crops, yet they do not exist outside single-commodity agribusiness. Rather, they survive *because* of it. Homegarden farmers produce for specific immigrant populations from South and East Asia that are concentrated in urban centers around the United States and Canada. The farmers need the tropical climate of South Florida to grow many of their crops, which locates them at a distance from their markets, and they depend on the marketing and distribution infrastructure established in southern Florida to pack, transport, and sell products to markets up and down the East Coast, as far north as Toronto and west as St. Paul, Minnesota. It is because of the volume produced by large growers in Florida, as well as the container loads of produce imported from the Caribbean and Central America, that homegarden farmers can easily and inexpensively reach their markets. Urban produce brokers and production point distributors organize farmers throughout the Americas who grow Asian fruits and vegetables in Chinatown's food system. Homegarden farmers benefit tremendously from this infrastructure and may not be able to survive without it.

The case of the Florida homegardens provides evidence that complicates the tendency among scholars to dichotomize conventional and alternative agriculture. The relationships that exist between use of space and agricultural practices are varied, rendering space a problematic indicator of alternativeness in agriculture (Hinrichs 2003). Sonnino and Marsden (2006) provide many examples of case studies that muddy the demarcation of conventional and alternative food networks. Although it has been recognized that the ideology of alternative food systems has been better theorized than the practice itself, we continue to face the challenge of defining the many manifestations of "alternativeness." The farmers described here do not espouse a politics of alternative agriculture as it is discussed in the United States, yet their practices clearly set them apart from most agriculturalists in their region and in the nation at large.

The commercial homegardens are part of a striking trend that began in the 1980s and continues today.[2] They have been in existence for almost two decades, yet there is little recognition of some of the new crops they have brought to the area, and no analyses of how they grow or market their produce (Lamberts 2005). Agronomists often overlook diverse systems, because they do not fit into the single-commodity approach of agricultural extension and USDA census surveys or the dominant paradigm of farming. Indeed, homegarden farmers have a different vision of agriculture, and they realize that they work apart from the growers around them. The son of a Laotian farmer who is planning to take over the family business told me, "There is a cultural divide in the local growers' organizations. Asians do not participate in the meetings; we should organize ourselves."[3]

The Crown Jewel of Agriculture

Miami-Dade County is home to what has been called the "crown jewel" of Florida agriculture. The subtropical climate, abundant water, and curious and innovative entrepreneurs from all over the world have created one of the most diverse agricultural communities on the planet.

R. L. Degner, S. D. Moss, and W. D. Mulkey, *Economic Impact of Agriculture and Agribusiness in Dade County, Florida*

Miami-Dade County is well recognized for its agricultural diversity at a landscape level, and there are a number of unique features that distinguish it from other agricultural regions around the state and the country, one of these being the size of its farms. Miami-Dade has the highest number of small farms in the state of Florida. Of the county's 2,498 farms, 71 percent are smaller than ten acres. The average farm size across the county is 27 acres, significantly smaller than the state average (195 acres) and that in the nation (418 acres). The number of small farms in Miami-Dade has been increasing over the past three decades, particularly in the size class of one through nine acres, which showed a 53 percent increase from 1997 to 2007 (US Census of Agriculture 1997, 2002, 2007).

Miami-Dade County produces a large variety of high-value agricultural products. The University of Florida's Institute of Food and Agricultural Sciences identified twenty-three species of tropical fruits, twenty-five species of vegetables and herbs, and hundreds of species of ornamental plants in commercial production across the county (Degner et al. 2002). Miami-Dade is an important source of conventional vegetables, including tomatoes, snap beans, and summer squash; tree fruits, such as mangoes, avocados, litchis, and longans; and ornamental plants, among them palms and orchids. With this abundance, the county ranks second in farm sales in the state. Fresh vegetable production represents the largest use of agricultural land in the county, 41.7 percent, and it is the highest grossing at $491 million. The nursery industry has the next-highest gross amount, at $439.8 million, although it uses only 11.8 percent of the land. Tropical fruits generate $137 million and use 16.1 percent of the land (Degner et al. 2002; sales figures based on 1997–98 crop years).

Another unique feature of Miami-Dade County is its tropical climate (Greller 1980). This distinction makes the county the sole producer of many subtropical and tropical crops in the continental United States. The Tropic of Cancer, 23.4° north latitude, is approximately 140 miles south of Homestead, the main farming region in the county. The region is wet and hot in the summer (May to November) and cool and dry through the winter (December to April). In Homestead, the average annual high temperature is 83.9°F and the average annual low is 64.2°F. Subfreezing temperatures may occur about once every two years with moderate to severe damage to agricultural commodities. Annual rainfall is on average about fifty-six inches and sometimes exceeds eighty. The greatest amounts of rain generally fall in June and September, with occasional flooding during the wet season, which lasts from May through October. The few feet in elevation difference across the county makes a great difference in flood risk; some fruit trees suffer from subterranean flooding and so "high" land (approximately seven feet) is considered more desirable for orchards.

In addition to these distinctions, Miami-Dade is the most populous county in the state, with 2,496,457 residents in 2010, according to the US census of that year. The population has increased by 23 percent since 1990 and is projected to continue to rise. Most inhabitants live on the Atlantic Coastal Ridge, or Miami Ridge, but are moving into the south Dade agricultural area. Since the agricultural land of southern Florida is squeezed between the protected land of the Everglades and Biscayne Bay National Parks and rapidly urbanizing land, agricultural land is the only "open" space that can be developed. Approximately 61 percent of Miami-Dade County is protected under the aegis of federal, state, and local parks, preserves, water conservation areas, and recreation areas. The severe development pressure has ignited policy debates and much community activism in favor of agricultural land preservation as well as government-sponsored studies aimed at retaining rural and agricultural land uses.[4] The demand for real estate has skyrocketed, inflating land values in some cases from ten thousand to sixty thousand dollars for a five-acre plot. In the two years I conducted my research I saw housing developments such as Farm Land Estates and Avocado Grove Estates succeed in subdividing five-acre units to build single-family homes starting at three hundred thousand dollars on half an acre of land. Land speculation assures farmers who own land of their equity, but many people do not want to see the rural character of south Dade disappear, so these changes have led to much debate. Many farmers have lost their contracts to rent land, lost the ability to purchase or rent new land at the high prices, and experienced extraordinary rent increases.

Tropical Fruits, Exotic Herbs, and Homegardens

The Homestead homegardens began to emerge over three decades ago. This was a very dynamic time for agriculture in South Florida. A tropical fruit "craze" began in the 1980s, and hobbyists, entrepreneurs, commercial fruit growers, and agricultural researchers were united in experiments in growing and selling new Florida fruits. Chris Rollins, the director of the Fruit and Spice Park in Homestead, expressed the attitude of those days well when he said, "In South Florida we used to plant lemons and grapefruit; now we're into carambolas and mamey. Some growers are cutting down limes and avocados and are putting in longans, litchis, atemoyas and sugar apples" (Vietmeyer 1985, 34).[5]

Several factors contributed to the shift in production. Experimentation in fruit crops was encouraged by instant market success. Many growers chose these new crops because they were culturally "exotic" and botanically interesting. They were also profitable. The market appeared to be insatiable. Prices that were unobtainable for the traditional fruits of South Florida (like citrus, avocados, and mangoes) were easily obtained with the new fruits. For example, a grower was guaranteed six dollars a pound for litchis and longans because supply was limited and competition from other production areas was virtually nonexistent. To fruit growers, tropical fruits were a gold mine. Growers didn't need to know or even understand the market; the demand was there. One of the commercial fruit growers I interviewed in 2004 commented about this time, "You could put anything in the ground and an ethnic group would come out of the woodwork to buy it."[6]

International trends in migration and trade liberalization fostered the new agricultural markets. The analysis of immigration trends at this time reveals that by the 1980s there were relatively recent, yet large and growing, Asian and Hispanic populations in the United States—between 1960 and 1980 the Asian and Hispanic foreign-born population increased fivefold, rising from 490,996 to 2,539,777 for individuals from Asia and from 908,309 to 4,372,487 for those from Latin America.[7] Also by the 1980s the diversification of fresh fruit and vegetable production and consumption was well under way both nationally and internationally. The sale of "exotic" produce was a lucrative and fast-growing segment of the fruit and vegetable trade.

Two natural disasters further propelled South Florida's crop diversification. Hurricane Andrew, a category-five hurricane, touched down in Homestead in 1992, causing major damage to fruit trees. Faced with the decision of what to replant, growers began replacing the staple tropical fruits of the area (mango, avocado, and Persian limes) with new fruits. An agricultural census taken in 1993 to capture the effects of Hurricane Andrew showed that avocado acreage declined from 8,987 to 5,965; Persian lime acreage from 6,071 to 1,668; and mango acreage from 2,424 to 1,398 (Degner et al. 1997).

At the time of Hurricane Andrew, there were close to sixty acres of litchi planted in the area. Hurricane Andrew caused severe damage to all the tropical and subtropical fruit groves (Crane et al. 1993); however, litchi trees were able to recover faster than other fruit trees. This motivated growers to plant more litchis in the Homestead area (Knight 2001, cited in Rafie and Balerdi 2002). By 2001, the estimated area planted to litchi in Florida was 330 acres, with an estimated annual production of fifteen hundred tons of fruit. By 2003 there were 650 acres. Longan production also increased. Before 1992 there were under one hundred acres; by 2003 there were eight hundred. Mamey sapote production increased from 150 to 500 acres, as did other tropical fruits like Thai guava, sapodilla, papaya, and jackfruit.[8]

The second natural disaster that contributed to the restructuring of the fruit industry in southern Florida was an infestation of citrus canker, discovered in urban Miami in 1995. Despite extensive eradication efforts, resulting in the removal or cutting back of over 1.56 million commercial trees and nearly six hundred thousand infected and exposed dooryard citrus trees statewide, the infected area continued to increase. The canker was further exacerbated by the presence of the citrus leafminer, which accelerated the canker's spread (Gottwald et al. 2002). As a result of much research and policy evaluation, a new regulation—the "nineteen-hundred-foot rule"—was established in January 2000 and put in practice in March 2000. The rule requires that all exposed and infected citrus trees be eradicated in a nineteen-hundred-foot radius (0.41 square miles or 1.06 km²). The rule was highly politically charged; it was challenged in court but upheld. It now serves as the operational basis of the citrus canker eradication program. Some residential areas that have been subjected to the nineteen-hundred-foot eradication method have remained free of canker for the prescribed two-year period and thus have been released from quarantine and farmers can now replant them if they wish. However, the lime industry is all but extinct in Miami-Dade County, with about 150 of 3,500 acres left in 2003 (John Crane, personal communication, August 1, 2003). Farmers continue to grow Kaffir lime, Persian lime, and pomelo on a limited basis, knowing full well that they risk disease and eradication. Agricultural extension agents regularly survey their trees.

As the profile of crops grown in southern Florida was diversifying, so was the profile of its inhabitants. Agriculturally experienced immigrants from Southeast Asia were attracted to Miami-Dade County because of the tropical climate. They brought knowledge of tropical and subtropical fruit and vegetable production from their home countries to Miami-Dade and developed not only new crops but also a new form of agriculture: the commercial homegarden. The commercial homegarden in this context is a type of small-scale production system that is biodiverse, mixing perennial and annual crops, trees, shrubs, and herbs for the purpose of commercial sales.

The oldest garden in my sample was planted by a Filipino American farmer in 1982. He is acknowledged by others to have developed one of the first farms of this type and to have introduced winged bean and lablab bean to the area.[9] Southeast Asian farmers continued to develop new farms throughout the 1980s, 1990s, and 2000s. The two youngest farms in this sample are each two years old. The growth of Asian-operated farms has been further documented by USDA agricultural census statistics. Between 1987 and 2002 the number of Asian-operated farms in Miami-Dade County increased by 322 percent, from 32 to 103 farms, and in land area by 410 percent, from 564 to 2311 acres (US Department of Agriculture 1987, 2002). In 2007, the number of Asian-operated farms showed another increase, to 169 farms (US Department of Agriculture 2007).

Land-zoning regulations in Homestead's agricultural areas support the maintenance of homegardens. Land is divided into five-acre units, so most homeowners have fruit trees on their property to supplement their incomes.[10] There are many part-time farmers in this area; 60 percent of tropical fruit growers in the county work in the groves part time. Homegarden farmers, however, intend their backyard garden to be their primary source of income. They began as, and most continue to be, full-time farmers (see table 9).

There are many socioeconomic commonalities within the surveyed sample of farmers. All are immigrants from Southeast Asia (specifically Thailand, Cambodia, Laos, and the Philippines). They grew up in farming families in their home countries, and most were the children of rice farmers. They had lived in other parts of the United States before moving to Florida and chose to move to the South Florida to begin farming as their primary source of income.

Table 9 Characteristics of surveyed households in Homestead, Florida

Characteristic	Households, n = 10
Farm founder born in Southeast Asia	10
Founder had other previous career(s)	8*
Farmer from farming family	10
Farmer full time	8†
Average age of farmer	43 years, range 25–65
Average age of farm	12.5 years, range 2–23
Children work on farm	4‡
Average number of permanent hired labor	5
Other household income	3

*The two operators who did not have a previous career are children who took over the farm from their parents.

†For the two main operators who were not full time, one was retired and the other worked with husband's orchid business.

‡Within the total sample this data point was not obtained for one household, three did not have children, and one had very young children.

Two farmers in the sample farmed in Central Florida and moved south for the warmer, mostly frost-free climate. Those who had not farmed had other previous work experience; of these, personal work histories vary. One farmer was a professional agronomist who had worked for the International Rice Research Institute in the Philippines and later for a large nursery in Miami-Dade, grafting mango cultivars. Another farmer had a bachelor's degree in electrical engineering and worked for many years in New England in engineering. He recounted to me why he decided to move to Florida and become a farmer: "After visiting my friend who lived in Homestead, I dreamed of living in a climate like my home in Cambodia and growing Cambodian fruits and vegetables. I told my wife I wanted to move to Homestead."[11] Another two farmers were grocery store owners, and the others did piecemeal work for hourly wages. A Thai farmer who grew up on a farm in Thailand said he decided to go into farming because "you can't build equity if you work for minimum wage."[12] A friend or family member introduced most people in this sample to the area.

For 70 percent of the farmers, the farm is their only source of income. All farmers work full time on the farm, but in three households children and wives work off the farm. For all but one of the households with children out of high school, the children work on farm. In three of the four households with adult children, at least one child is planning on taking over the farm when the parents retire. The other children are attending college or are working off the farm. Family members aid farms mostly in administrative tasks and marketing. In four households, children are relied on for English-language skills. Hired labor is sought for physical farm tasks. Each farm has a permanent core of, on average, five workers. Temporary crews are hired to harvest and pack. Most temporary laborers are Mexican and Guatemalan migrants and are hired through contractors or on the street.

Building Homegardens

When compared with what other researchers have described as homegardens, the Florida homegardens are similar to the general model in structure but differ from the norm in that their primary function is cash income. Farmers and their families consume some of the products they grow and plant a few items exclusively for home consumption. The underlying goal of this style of farming, however, is to achieve economic growth by maximizing production in a given area through crop diversification. It is a different approach from the more commonly practiced agriculture based on monoculture and economies of scale, the goal of which is to increase production of like goods and services in order to diminish costs.

The surveyed farms comprise multiple fields and cropping systems. Farm sizes range from 2.5 to 109 acres across one to nine fields. The homegarden

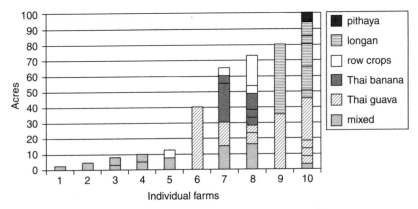

Figure 12 Size, type, and number of fields per farm in Homestead. Farms range from one to nine separate fields managed as mixed-cropping systems, annual row crops, or orchards. Each bar per farm is partitioned into the number and types of fields that make up the farm. The types of orchards are listed here by dominant crop, but some include a few individuals of other species or are interplanted. The forty-acre Thai guava orchard in farm 6 is interplanted with lemongrass and the thirty-acre longan orchard in farm 10 is interplanted with Thai guava. The row crop fields also include more than one species. The five-acre field in farm 5 is Thai basil intercropped with boniato leaves; the five-acre field in farm 7 rotates between Thai eggplant, long bean, and long squash; the five-acre field in farm 8 is half mint and half boniato leaves; and the twenty-acre field in farm 8 is half bitter melon and half Thai basil.

"core" is the original field that includes the farmer's house; this core takes a popular form of backyard homegarden described by other authors (Angel-Peréz and Mendoza 2004). Mixed-cropping systems are managed in the homegarden core. In subsequently acquired fields, mixed-cropping systems, orchards, or annual row crops (vegetables and herbs) are managed, increasing the overall size of the operation (see figure 12).

The number of managed fields per farmer changes over time; expansion and contraction occurs in times of opportunity and crisis. Only one farmer I spoke to had never expanded. She operates the smallest and one of the most intensely managed farms. On 2.5 acres she has approximately eighty raised beds for herb production. While she is alone in not having expanded beyond her backyard garden, others like her who manage only mixed-cropping systems (that is, they do not have orchards or row crops) have the smallest operations, with at most two fields.

The farms that practice only mixed farming are in the smallest operation category (2.5–12 acres) and are located on farmer-owned (rather than leased) land. The specialized treatment these fields receive, in terms of putting in perennial crops and structural features common to this style of farming, is too great an investment for leased land. Owning land is also preferable as a means of building equity; most farmers interviewed expressed a desire to secure their financial futures postretirement through land ownership.

Leases are most commonly held on orchards and open fields for row crops outside the core field. Leasing is very common in the Miami-Dade agricultural area, and contracts are constantly turning over. It is possible to lease mature orchards or to obtain long leases on young or new orchards. Whether land is leased or owned, managing multiple fields creates flexibility in the farming operation. Farmers can downsize if necessary; expand when opportunities arise; experiment with new crops; or rotate crops that are diseased, not producing, or not selling well. In contrast to those who manage only mixed-cropping systems, those who also manage orchards lease 63–100 percent of their land. One exception is a farmer who was given land as a wedding present and does not lease land.

The surge in real estate prices affecting many urban areas across the United States, including Miami, is also affecting outlying agricultural areas. The inflated land values are making it difficult for farmers to afford new land or find available land, and lease rates are rising. One farmer who recently turned over his lease experienced a doubling of his lease rate in one year—it had been at a fixed rate for the past ten years. Although he manages the highest number of fields per farm in the sample, he cannot afford to buy any land; the only land his family owns is the five acres where his mother lives and began farming. Another family, looking to acquire an additional five acres to increase its operation to fifteen acres, was unable to afford new property. They told me, "We had our eye on a piece of land, but we were too slow on acting on it and someone else bought it. Now we can't afford to buy something."[13] The newest farmer in the sample moved to Florida about seven years ago and waited five years to acquire a lease on land. He converted sixty acres of mango to Thai guava and longan orchards.

The Agrobiodiversity of the Homegarden

The core of the homegarden is a biologically diverse cropping system situated around the home of the farmer. It is a multistrata, multizone garden that uses vertical as well as horizontal space intensively and is from 2.5 to 16 acres in size. Habitats are created for moisture-loving and aquatic plants, as well as for shade-tolerant and sun-loving plants. The structural features discussed below that have come to characterize the homegarden core have spread, through farmers' social networks or via simply "peering over fences." A Cambodian farmer revealed that "although people think they have secret techniques, there are none here. You can drive around and see what other people are doing."[14] Farmers are constantly watching each other to learn from each other's successes.

Farmers choose their crops based on their knowledge of an unfulfilled demand for fruits, vegetables, and herbs common in their diets. Because the farmers in this survey are from a variety of countries and regions within Southeast Asia, each has tended to specialize in different crops. Most farms grow a wide variety of herbs, vegetables, and fruits as well as some medicinal and ornamental species (see figure 13). A few specialize in fewer than four fruits. Of the ninety-three crops that are grown across all of the homegardens, only one fruit, Thai guava, is grown on all on them. On the other hand, twenty-eight species are grown on only one farm (see table 10). In a report on the vegetable sector in Thailand completed by the Food and Agriculture Organization, one-third of the "underutilized" vegetables listed for Thailand are growing in Florida's homegardens.[15] They are special repositories of biological diversity.

A distinctive feature of the homegarden is the vertical stratification of plant life. Stratification is determined by a combination of the natural form of plants

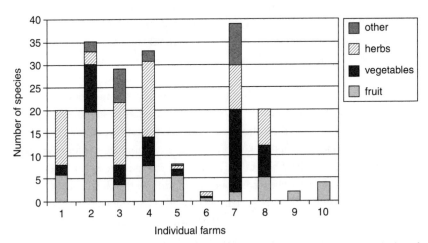

Figure 13 Species composition by farm. The categories in this figure are described in the list of species in appendix C. The herbs grown on these farms are exclusively grown by homegarden farmers. Some of the vegetables and fruits are grown by American, Chinese, and other farmers across southern Florida.

Table 10 Species distribution across farms

Variable	Species
Total # species	94
# spp/farm	mean 19, range 2–38
# spp grown in all farms	1*
# spp grown on only 1 farm	28

Source: Data collected by the author during August 2003 and February 2004.

*Thai guava is currently one of the most popular fruits, recently grown in monoculture because of its market value, easy vegetative propagation, and early yields and because it bears fruit year round.

and management practices of the farmer. The selection of shade tolerance in understory species, planting density, and pruning are practices that significantly affect the light gradient. Light levels influence and in turn are influenced by plant productivity. The composition of the strata will also affect aeration in the garden. High humidity may be preferred by some species but can also encourage fungal development and plant disease. The composition of successful vertical stratification in which each plant is yielding well reflects a sophisticated understanding of plant form and management.

The homegarden core can have several layers of vegetation. The canopy is made up of fruit and leguminous trees eight to fifteen feet high, such as mango, litchi, longan, tamarind, and acacia. There can be several layers in the understory, containing small trees, woody shrubs, large herbaceous plants, vines, and ground cover herbs (see figure 14). The small trees (three to six feet high) are generally light-loving species and are interplanted with canopy species to allow them sufficient light. Thai guava, the most commonly planted small tree, is easily vegetatively propagated and quick to bear fruit. It is frequently interplanted with larger, slower-growing species to maximize production per unit area. Other common small trees are Kaffir lime, sugar apple, and sapodilla. Sugar apple has sparse foliage and lets a lot of light through to herbaceous plants planted underneath. The Kaffir lime leaves are harvested year round. The Kaffir lime is grafted to lemon rootstock to produce trees without thorns for easier harvest. Grafted trees also fruit faster than growing from seed. The Kaffir lime, like all citrus, is under strict surveillance in southern Florida by the University of Florida Institute of Food and Agricultural Sciences (UF/IFAS) Extension because it is prone to citrus canker, a disease that destroyed the Persian lime industry in the area.[16]

There are two strata of shade-tolerant herbaceous plants in the understory. There are large herbs (one to three feet high) such as taro and pandan leaf. Taro is grown for its petiole, which is called *tun* in Laotian and Thai, instead of for its corm (known also as dasheen and eddoe, among other names). Because the taro corms are not harvested, the plant proliferates vegetatively and new petioles and leaf blades can be continually harvested. Pandan leaves are also continually harvested; an extract is made from pulverized leaves to impart a sweet flavor to rice and desserts. Pandan leaf spreads vegetatively, but is pruned back in winter to foster denser growth in the hotter summer months. There are ground cover herbs (0.5–1 foot high) such as Chinese lizard tail and pepper leaves. The two species spread vegetatively to form dense patches. The patches suppress undesirable species, but they do present a danger of invasion to other parts of the garden. Invasion is controlled through harvest and by ground cover cloth.

The shrub layer contains two species, neem and noni, that have well-known medicinal as well as culinary values. Farmers described the species to me as foods, so I believe that to be the main reason for their cultivation. In Thailand in particular, neem and noni are considered "underutilized species" by the Food and Agriculture Organization, so it would seem surprising to see them cultivated in Florida. However, species are usually considered underutilized because they could be cultivated on a wider scale but are not.[17] Underutilized species are typically grown on a very small scale or in backyard gardens, so it makes sense that homegarden farmers would chose to cultivate them in the United States as well in their countries of origin.

Noni has a long history of medicinal use in Southeast Asia and the South Pacific and now is the basis of a large industry, with over two hundred companies selling noni products in more than fifty countries (International Noni Communication Council 2005). However, noni is cultivated in homegardens, not for medicinal use, but so that its large, shiny leaves may be used as a wrapper for stuffed or rolled foods. Neem is used as an insecticide, as mosquito repellant, and as both topical and internal medicine. In these homegardens, it is a common food item. The extremely bitter leaves are considered a health food, and the sweet flowers are also eaten. New leaf growth is preferred to old leaves, and constant pruning encourages new growth, keeping the plant smaller and fuller than it would naturally be.

Aquatic and semiaquatic plants are grown in homegardens in innovative ways. The most complex aquatic habitat is a series of slightly terraced, plastic-lined pools that feed into a central drainage canal. At present there is only one aquatic plant grown in one garden in this way: the Laotian rice paddy herb pak van. Cultivation of this plant is noteworthy in the composition of these garden types because it requires an intricately developed and time-consuming management regime. Opening and closing a faucet at the upslope of each pool maintains the water level. Water overflows through the pools, spilling into the main canal or onto adjacent beds, particularly in the rainy season. Algae and duckweed quickly develop in these pools, and manual weeding is done frequently. No tools are used, because of the fear of ripping the plastic lining of the pools. One to two times a year the pools are emptied, the plants and soil taken out, and the linings cleaned. The old soil and plant matter is used to mulch and fertilize other beds. The pools are aesthetically pleasing. They attract fauna, including wading birds and frogs. Each time I have visited this garden there was a red ibis feeding in the pools (see figure 15).

Areas adjacent to the pools are used for semiaquatic plants. During the summer rains the pools tend to flood, reaching neighboring beds through a

Figure 14 Planting shade-loving herbs under trees is a common feature of homegardens. Here the ground-covering herb la lot, a kind of pepper leaf (*Piper lolot*), is planted under tamarind trees (*Tamarindus indicus*).

drainage canal. The drainage canal is used for moisture-loving species, such as the Laotian riverine tree called *ka don,* the only wild-collected species I found in these gardens. It has beautiful, cascading red inflorescences. Waterlogged soils are maintained in other ways as well, such as in raised beds, plastic-lined beds, or individually potted plants sitting in water. In these moist-bed arrangements, irrigation pipes are set up so that each wet bed has its own faucet and its water content can be carefully controlled.

Shade cloth is used to increase shaded surface area when the sun is most intense in the summer and is used in the winter to increase the tenderness of leafy herbs. Popular herbs such as Vietnamese coriander and ma ohm, another rice paddy herb, are grown under shade; these herbs are also grown in moist soils. Many herbs are eaten fresh in soups and are preferably harvested when they are young, delicate, and tender.

Figure 15 The pool system to grow the Laotian herb pak van (*Marsilea crenata*). Along the edge of the pool the vertical strata of the garden are apparent.

Herbs that reproduce by vegetative propagation are used to form ground covers to suppress weeds and trap organic matter, as mentioned above. Another ground cover feature is common to these gardens: black, permeable tarp on all uncultivated areas of the garden. One farmer claims to be the innovator of this method, and others followed suit. He alleges that he was tired of mowing the weeds each week, so he decided to keep them from growing. The tarp keeps the gardens neat and tidy and besides reducing the labor of weeding lowers the use of herbicide. Herbs and annual vegetables are often planted in a small hole in the tarp or in narrow row openings. The largest open areas of the tarp are where trees are planted. Here leaf litter is common, acting as mulch and suppressing weeds, retaining moisture and recycling nutrients. The tarp suppresses the spontaneous regeneration of plants; everything growing in the garden has been planted.

Most parcels of land in the agricultural area of Homestead are square or rectangular plots adjacent to other farms, orchards, or homes. Fences are commonly used to delimit property, as well as to keep thieves out. In the homegarden, vines are grown on perimeter fences, and shrubs and trees are planted along fences. Tindora, a self-seeding vine, is popular for outer- and inner-garden trellises. Curry leaf, which forms dense hedges, is used as a barrier, and on perimeters, small trees like dwarf coconut palm and sapodilla are planted. Every opportunity to grow a useful plant is taken.

Three farmers in the sample manage fields for annual row crops. Such crops include Thai basil, sweet potato leaf (boniato), mint, bitter melon, Ceylon spinach, long bean, Thai eggplant, and Chinese okra. Crop selection, methods of planting, and times of planting vary from year to year. Sometimes multiple crops are interplanted; other times five to fifteen acres may be planted to a single crop. Farmers typically try to exploit off-season production times for specific crops, to garner higher market prices. They watch the international and regional production patterns to know when it is a good time for them to plant; for example, Thai basil can be sold at $2.50 a pound in the winter, double its summer price. Farmers also plant crops that are not grown on a large scale either regionally or internationally. Chinese eggplant is imported in large volumes from Honduras and Chinese cabbages and leafy greens in the Brassicaceae, or mustard, family are produced on large farms in other parts of Florida. Instead of planting high-volume crops, homegarden farmers choose to grow crops like bitter melon, sweet potato shoots, and Malabar spinach.

Orchards are managed by half the farmers in this sample. The most common fruits grown in orchards are longan, litchi, Thai guava, and Thai banana. Thai banana plantings are renewed every three years, since production begins to decline at that point. Farmers who grow Thai banana usually have a few fields of different ages. Most orchards have a few trees of several other fruits mixed in, particularly along their perimeters. Jackfruit, coconut, sugar apple, and sapodilla are grown this way. More recently pithaya, or dragon fruit, is becoming popular. Pithaya is grown on fences or in sets of three individuals growing up a central stake. One farmer in the sample recently planted a five-acre orchard of pithaya and another farmer interplanted three acres of pithaya with Thai guava.

New orchards are often interplanted with herbs such as lemongrass or Thai basil while trees have not yet reached fruiting stage. New longan and litchi orchards are sometimes interplanted with Thai guava, since it is fast growing and reaches fruiting stage quickly. Thai guava has become a very popular fruit to plant in the past few years. Where litchi and longan have reached a point of oversaturation in the area, resulting in a decline in price, Thai guava is more limited in its production. Also, Thai guava is not currently imported on a large scale; by contrast, Florida litchi growers compete with Mexican imports and

Florida longan growers compete with Taiwanese imports (Rafie and Balerdi 2002). Although Florida has the advantages of lower transport costs and higher-quality fruit, Taiwanese and Mexican fruit undercut them in costs of production. Thai guava does not have this kind of competition and is fetching a good market price.

From Homestead Homegardens to Chinatown

Homegarden farmers are part of Chinatown's food system. The majority of their produce is shipped to cities along the Eastern Seaboard with large Asian populations as well as to Toronto, Chicago, Houston, and St. Paul. The farmers also sell locally, but the local market is not large enough to support them. They market their produce in a variety of ways. They sell retail and wholesale. They ship through local packinghouses and they ship directly from their own farms. Several farmers have become packers and shippers as well, buying and selling products from other farms. From using existing marketing channels to developing their own, homegarden farmers are constantly negotiating market fluctuations and looking for ways to maintain or increase their profits through marketing, rather than increasing production. Because the majority of the crops that they grow are specialty crops that are not grown on a large scale, these farmers are largely shielded from the problems of overproduction and international competition that plague other growers in the area.

Homegarden farmers do not exist outside or in spite of conventional agriculture. *They exist because of it.* In many ways, their marketing success hinges on the existence of large regional and international growers. Homegarden farmers benefit from the marketing infrastructure that exists because of the high-volume production of certain specialty crops. One farmer described this strategy well. He said, "I like to take advantage of existing packing, trucking, and cooling systems. Sometimes in the summer I will work with my neighbor to complete a pallet and I call a trucking company and they come here to pick up stuff. Other times I borrow the forklift and loading space at the local packers and I give them bananas in exchange."[18] The local packers referred to in this quote are two brokerage firms that were set up as offshoots of Chinatown produce brokerages, described in chapter 2. They run trucks to New York City all week long and accommodate these small growers' shipping needs.

The markets that homegarden farmers grow for are just as specialized as their crops. They grow almost exclusively for Southeast Asian, Indian, and Chinese populations across the United States. Local markets are not enough to sustain them. They have to ship to urban areas like New York; Atlanta; Boston;

Washington DC; Toronto; Chicago; Minneapolis; and Houston where large Asian populations are located. Normally it is difficult for small, specialty farmers to compete in distant markets, because they cannot produce the volume needed to make long-distance shipping economically feasible. This is not an issue, however, for homegarden farmers in Homestead. This area produces a large volume of Asian fruit and vegetables for the country's Asian populations. Furthermore, the Port of Miami is the main point of entry for produce from the Caribbean and Latin America. From Honduras alone there are over twenty container loads of Chinese vegetables imported on a weekly basis that are distributed by Homestead packinghouses and Miami shipping firms. Homegarden farmers piggyback on the transport of these products.

The firms that broker southern Florida's Asian produce developed alongside the diversification of Miami-Dade's agriculture. Farmers did not have to worry about market access. Some brokerage firms were outgrowths of Chinatown firms. The first distributor of South Asian fruits and vegetables in Miami began on his own, however, as a mango grower. He was attracted to the business because he saw that there were so many people from South Asia in the United States who wanted mango—green, unripe mangoes in particular—but had no commercial access to this fruit. In 1977 he began shipping boxes of mangoes direct to customers by Federal Express. His clients were asking him for Indian vegetables in addition to the fruits he was selling. No one was growing the vegetables. He felt that if he wanted to increase his profitability he had to import from abroad. The mango shipper recognized that he was on the cusp of major changes in agriculture around the world, not just in Miami-Dade County. He knew that the Dominican Republic was exporting produce. With little more than Indian seed, a "knowledge" packet of information on cultivation practices, and an interpreter, he went to the Dominican Republic to find farmers who would give Indian vegetables a chance. By 1987 he was importing crops like Indian bitter melon, tindora, and Indian eggplant. Now he has a warehouse in Miami where he imports and distributes eight hundred to two thousand boxes a week of up to seventy-two different fruits and vegetables.[19]

Over the next decade three more packinghouses would become established in Homestead, along with four more importing/shipping firms in Miami that specialize in Asian fruits and vegetables. Some firms developed as sister companies to brokers in New York City's Chinatown, others to exporters in Honduras. The brokers, along with their affiliate distribution firms at other points in the commodity chain, shape new areas of production, in Florida and offshore.

While homegarden farmers have these firms to rely on for marketing purposes, they do not sell their entire supply to them all the time. They are constantly looking for ways to increase their profitability through direct sales, although it is difficult. Brokers typically mark up the products they buy by 10 percent. If there are two brokers involved, there is a 20 percent increase in profit to be had by a farmer if he were to market directly to retailers. One farmer said that he could increase his profitability by 40 percent if he sold directly to retailers. In the Homestead area there is only one Asian grocery store and a handful of restaurants. There are more Asian grocery stores up the Eastern Seaboard from Miami to Ft. Lauderdale, to which Homestead farmers do deliver, but the market is quickly saturated. Also, it costs labor time and gas to deliver. One farmer commented that he didn't feel that delivering to Miami was worth his time. He said, "I'd rather sell to individuals in this community at cost."[20]

Local sales also occur on farms. Customers will go to the farm in order to buy direct. Farmers like this type of sale because there is no transport involved on their part. Preparation of small orders can be laborious, however; if the order is not already harvested, they will go into their fields on the spot to gather the order. Or they will accept orders from passersby and accommodate them immediately. Some farmers have developed strategies to accommodate small orders. One farmer now uses a box about one-third the size of the standard box. This aspect of the business is important economically, and culturally as well. It makes the farmers visible to residents and fosters social connections. One farmer said that a form of cultural tourism has developed around his farm. Laotian and Thai vacationers in Florida will stop by his farm, having heard from friends about items growing there that they have not been able to find outside their home country. This brings him a lot of pride, but he abashedly admitted, "I like to leave my driveway gate open, but sometimes there are too many people stopping by and I just don't have the time to spend with them."[21]

Although local sales are very important, they account for only 10–33 percent of homegarden farmers' businesses. In order to maintain the profitability that direct sales can offer, farmers sell at the retail level to distant cities, in addition to wholesaling through brokerage firms in Homestead. One farmer went to New York City to personally develop contacts with retailers. He gave out free samples and began relationships with new buyers by offering low prices. When his buyers determined that he was reliable, he increased his prices. To find customers, other farmers use the "Blue Book," the produce industry's listing of accredited firms. Shipping presents more of a challenge than does finding customers. Shipping is done by air or truck; shipping by air is expensive, but is necessary for delicate herbs with a short shelf life. The specialty herbs can be sold at high prices: $2.50–4.50 a pound from the farm, and up to $6.00 retail. If farmers ship by land, they sometimes use independent truckers who charge by the pallet.

Cooperation between homegarden farmers makes it possible for them to ship directly. A pallet contains forty-four to fifty-five boxes, so the farmers rely on one another to fill orders if they don't have enough to sell on their own. Also, since each farmer has varied crop inventories, farmers may offer customers products from other farmers and buy from them. By pooling their resources farmers can increase sales. One farmer noted that his customers like to think of him as "one-stop shopping." If they request certain items that he does not have, he will either try to grow them or buy them from someone else who may be growing the items in question. Some farmers buy and sell to simply increase their flexibility in taking and filling orders; others have developed this practice as a standard part of their operation.

Shipping on a regular basis requires some basic infrastructure, a shed or covered area to wash and pack, and a cooler to store product before shipping. Three of the farmers in this study have focused on developing the shipping aspects of their business. They purchased walk-in coolers and built packing sheds. Through becoming regular buyers of produce from area growers, they expanded the economic potential of the trade network. The largest distributor of Southeast Asian specialty products is the best example of this. He works with sixty to seventy growers, ranging from people who have a few fruit trees in their yards to Cuban producers who grow boniato leaves on a large scale. He provides market access to many who would otherwise not have it; about half his growers are part time and deliver produce from as far as Tampa on the weekends. He also buys from women who wild collect species such as *Solanum torvum* (called cherry, pea, or Cambodian eggplant) that rapidly spread around the land-scape.[22] He told me, "You wouldn't believe the old women that come to me with Cambodian eggplant they said they found growing, or with lime leaves from their backyard. People are not supposed to have them [Cambodian eggplant] growing, but these women do, and they are happy to earn enough money just to play bingo."[23]

THE Southeast Asian homegarden farmers are united in the strategy to stay small and specialize in a variety of products. They are opportunistic in using many ecological niches in their gardens as well as in taking advantage of multiple marketing niches. They like to be a source of "one-stop shopping" for their customers. The versatility and flexibility of these farmers give them strength in the face of competition with larger growers. While they do cultivate some crops that are grown on a large scale both regionally and internationally, they shield themselves from external competition by specializing in Southeast Asian herbs, vegetables, and fruits. The crop composition of each farm also contributes to the cultural landscape of the Homestead, reflecting the preferences of cultural groups to whom the farmers belong.

Although some scholars of Miami-Dade agriculture celebrate its diversity, they allege that the very diversity of agriculture in southern Florida works to fragment it as an industry, a factor that may lead to its demise (Degner et al. 2002). The diverse mix of farmers in Miami-Dade County has not fostered a shared industrial vision that defines agriculture in the county, to the dismay of some agricultural professionals. But the varied approaches that farmers bring to the pressures they face have been working for them. The differences between farmers are complementary, not conflicting. The small, highly diverse farmers do not survive in spite of large and international growers—they survive *because* of them. Small farmers benefit from the marketing infrastructure that exists because of the volume of produce imported and supplied by large area growers. They take advantage of Chinatown's trade network to reach large populations of Asian fruit and vegetable consumers. Long-distance trade is cost effective only in large volumes. A shipping container can hold approximately one thousand 35-pound boxes. One of the main reasons why small farms cannot survive as markets grow more distant is because they have to "get big or get out." But urban areas with large Asian populations across the United States and Canada—the main markets for these farmers—are home to a diverse mix of Asian immigrants from cultures that typically consume many fruits and vegetables. The market itself is so varied that there is room for many types of specialty growers. The large regional growers and numerous international growers enable sophisticated marketing infrastructure such as a "cold chain" (refrigerated loading docks and transport) that enables the shipment of fresh produce across continents and seas.

The Southeast Asian homegardens of southern Florida challenge many assumptions about the viability of high-diversity, biologically intensive agricultural systems on a commercial scale. While agricultural research today generally dismisses biodiverse agriculture and the general trend in agriculture around the world has been toward monocultures, crop specialization with increased commercialization, the group of farmers discussed in this chapter use diversity for economic gain. They also demonstrate a way for small-scale, family-run farms to survive in the competitive global marketplace. Ultimately, American small farmers have largely not survived the political-economic restructuring of global agriculture and thus have been relegated to the margins of agriculture. In response, proponents of alternative modes of agriculture have been united in a political agenda to resist the dominant agricultural structure and diversify small farms through initiatives such as community-supported agriculture, direct marketing, agritourism, and food microenterprises like wine and cheese making. But the commercial homegardens of South Florida offer a way of using, rather than avoiding, the global agricultural system to create an alternative.

The very nature of what constitutes alternative agriculture is so varied and complex that we cannot presume to know all its manifestations. Alternatives may be present within existing markets and distribution networks, particularly in immigrant food systems that have not been explored in this context. The Southeast Asian immigrant farmers in Homestead exemplify the innovation that people from other farming traditions bring to the countries to which they immigrate. They also show how small farmers who simultaneously take advantage of existing consumer demand and marketing infrastructure can occupy specialty niches.

## CHAPTER 5

Growing Asian Vegetables in Honduras

The influence of Asian immigration to the United States has been felt on agricultural landscapes outside of the US as well as inside. One such place is the Comayagua Valley of Honduras. Since the introduction of Asian vegetables to Comayagua in 1989, the number of farmers involved has grown from a handful to over four hundred. Half the area of export crops contracted to farmers in the Comayagua Valley is now dedicated to Asian vegetables.[1] For small farmers, Asian vegetables are the most lucrative and stable crops.[2]

Comayagua has been an important site of export production of fresh and processed fruits and vegetables since the 1970s, with government agencies and private industry collaborating to conduct field trials of nontraditional crops and implement plantation-style, spot-purchasing, and contracting arrangements to develop export agriculture. The historical approach to commodity agriculture in Honduras was vertical integration, whereby one firm would control the complete life cycle of a product, from production to consumption. On Honduras's northern coast, the economic and political power held by the vertically integrated firms United Fruit and Standard Fruit led to the characterization of Honduras as a "banana republic" (Jansen 1998). But in the 1970s the Honduran government sought to integrate smallholders into the agricultural economy and mandated that all agro-industries purchase some of their raw materials from contracted farmers (Glover 1987).

Contract farming is a common means of production of agro-exports in Latin America and Africa. It is a production scheme used since the 1960s, but it gained momentum through the 1980s with the development strategies of export-led growth and diversification of agriculture. It can be a solely private venture, but more often contract farming is a joint public and private endeavor. Small farm agriculture is central to economic development. Small farmers are competitive with large-scale agriculture in the production of high-value, labor-intensive commercial crops. Problems of access, however, can keep small farmers from being included in domestic and international markets. Lack of access to information, services, inputs, and markets often preclude small farmer participation in the production of high-value fruit and vegetable crops. Contract farming can be a way to unleash the potential of small farmers for rural development. If the crops selected for smallholder production are labor intensive, not easily harvested by machine, and of high value to ensure profit on a small piece of land, then smallholders are likely to benefit economically.

Proponents of contract farming see it as a win-win situation: the production risks and transaction costs for export firms are transferred to the farmer and marginalized farmers are provided with market access and input credit that are otherwise unobtainable. Optimistically, contracting is seen as a means toward technological growth, increased productivity, the formation of a peasant middle class, and the privatization of extension services. Outcomes of contract farming, however, have varied considerably. While most cases report economic benefits, the social and environmental consequences of contract farming have been more problematic.

One way to analyze if farmers' participation in Chinatown markets, as a model of a global market, is to their economic and social benefit or detriment is to focus on the power relations between export firms and contract farmers. Are Honduran farmers forced to be passive price-takers and to cede decision making over production of their crops if they want to participate in the global marketplace? Do the social ties between importers in Florida and exporters in Honduras convey market benefits to Honduran farmers?

Export firms prefer working with small farmers rather than with large landowners because small producers typically grow subsistence crops in addition to export crops to protect themselves against price fluctuations for home-consumed foods, enabling them to withstand periods of low prices on export crops. Small producers also have a propensity to exploit themselves by working as much as needed whenever the work is needed, not considering their income in the form of an hourly wage or their working hours during set times of day, week, or year. Small producers also tend to maintain production of export crops in the face of low commodity prices in order to keep their households going or because of lack of any other cash crop opportunities (Grossman 1997). Through contract farming many small farmers in the tropics have moved from purely subsistence farming or production for national markets to production for international markets and, in doing so, have become dependent on export firms to provide them with agricultural inputs as well as to buy crops for which there is no local market.

As a model of development, contract farming tends to emphasize individuals over households or communities (Carletto et al. 1999; Goldín 1996; Hamilton and Fischer 2005). An individual signs the contract and receives payment, even though he or she is not the sole laborer. Furthermore, contracting one's labor and land to a sole purchaser can leave the farmer with only illusory control over production when that farmer is essentially no more than a hired hand (Clapp 1994). The individualistic nature of contract farming leads many researchers and practitioners to believe that the only way for farmers to gain control over production relations is to form a cooperative to assert bargaining power (Glover 1984; Little and Watts 1994).

The argument that farmers are inherently dependent on export firms assumes that farmers are passive recipients of firms' policies and that the relationship between firms and farmers is static. It is more accurate to say, however, that relations of production are constantly evolving and that farmers actively engage in shaping production relations. The question remains whether contracting in itself is fundamentally exploitative of small farmers or whether contracting is a viable way for small farmers to raise their standards of living, levels of expectations, and skill sets in order to have more life choices. Morrison and colleagues (2006) recognize that it is important to differentiate contract farming itself from the larger political economic plan that it may be associated with. The question remains if it is contracting per se that leads to asymmetric power relations or if contract farming can be used to improve livelihoods.

The varied outcomes of contract farming illustrate the point that it is not the act of producing crops under contract that is the causal variable of a particular result but that political, economic, and cultural variables influence the outcomes of contracting as well. The heterogeneity of contract farming, as well as the context in which it is practiced, makes contract farming difficult to theorize. Rather, it must be situated in its particular local and global conditions to be fully understood. Local- and global-scale processes are mutually constitutive, and place-based characteristics influence global change.

In Comayagua, farmers have a choice to switch firms when their contracts expire, giving individual farmers the power to act on their perceptions and experiences of working with firms. In a contracting scheme where farmers have a choice of firms to work with, farmers' needs are more likely to be recognized by firm managers. Farmers' navigation of the contracting system and competition between export firms lead to change in the system. Through competition for a limited pool of farmers, firms adjust their policies in favor of farmers without explicit attempts of labor organization on the part of the farmers.

The Comayagua Valley of Honduras

The Comayagua Valley is in the Department of Comayagua and extends roughly from the city of La Paz in the south to that of Siguatepeque in the north, a distance of about thirty-seven kilometers. Comayagua, the capital city of the department, has been urbanizing; it houses 38 percent of the department's population (352,881) (Instituto Nacional Estadístico 2000). The ethnic makeup of Comayagua, both the department and the city, is homogenous; the population is largely mestizo. But there is a growing distinction between urban and agricultural workers, notably made by 68 percent of farmers in the survey sample when they were asked about their children; they hoped that their children would find work in the city. In part, this sentiment is reflective of the hardships of farming, but it also reflects the growing economic and educational opportunities in Honduran cities.

Despite the growth of the city of Comayagua, agriculture is still the most important economic activity in the Comayagua Valley. The valley is Honduras's primary source of fresh vegetables for export. Nevertheless, while vegetable farming is important, its extent is limited: only 10 percent of the valley, 5,309 hectares, is planted in vegetables. Well over half the farmland in the department is in basic grains, mainly produced for home consumption (Secretaría de Agricultura y Ganadería 1999). Although vegetable farming is limited to a small minority of farmers, the farmers in the valley have more opportunities to enter market-oriented agriculture than do mountain farmers because of the former's access to transportation and irrigation infrastructure. There are reliable irrigation canals and rivers, and the Pan-American Highway runs through the valley to Puerto Cortés on the Atlantic Coast.

Introducing Asian Vegetables to Comayagua

The development of nontraditional agricultural exports from Comayagua has been a collaborative endeavor between government and industry.[3] While there was export of nontraditional agricultural crops prior to 1985, export-led growth was embraced in Honduras with the ratification of the Caribbean Basin Initiative in 1984 (the forerunner of the Central America Free Trade Agreement, or CAFTA). From this point on growth occurred quickly. In 1983 the value of nontraditional exports in Honduras was $423 million and by 1993 it was up to $1.3 billion (Torres-Rivas 1993).

The years between 1985 and 1989 marked a turning point for the composition of crops exported from Comayagua. Market flooding in cucumbers led to

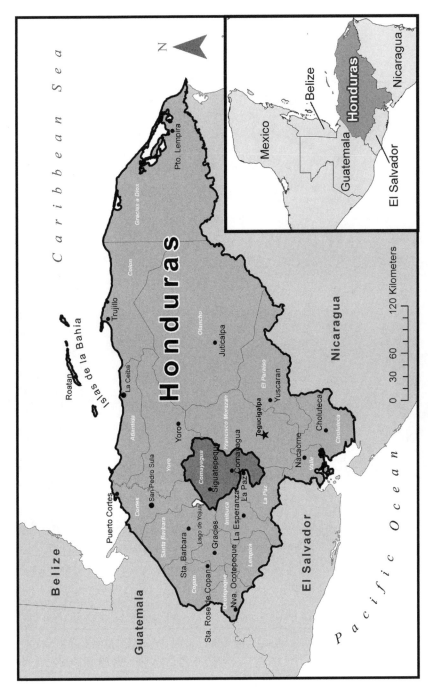

Figure 16 The Comayagua Valley extends from the city of Comayagua to Siguatepeque in the Department of Comayagua in Central Honduras. Map created by Brian Morgan.

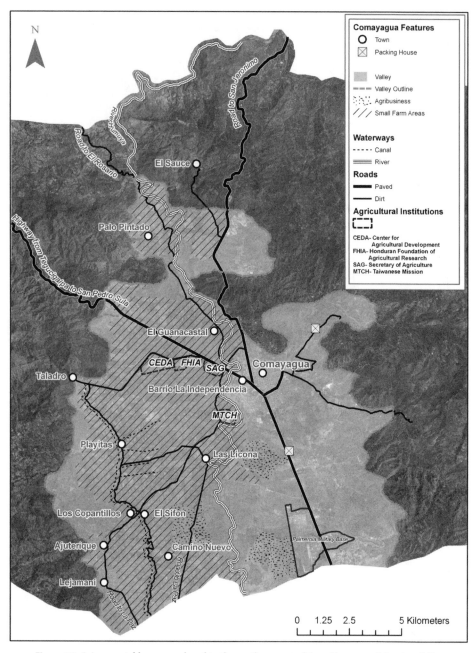

Figure 17 Asian vegetables are produced in the southern part of the valley around the city of Comayagua, but production is spreading north toward San Jeronimo. This map shows the proximity of towns of residence of Asian vegetable farmers, the areas where the farms are located, irrigation sources, roads, packinghouses, and agricultural institutions involved in Asian vegetable production. Map created by Brian Morgan.

the bankruptcy of several firms and the downsizing of cucumber acreage, although cucumbers remain in the valley today. More severely, fruit fly infestations caused ripe tomatoes to be banned for import into the United States in 1987.

The tomato collapse in Comayagua coincided with the collapse of the Asian vegetable industry in the Dominican Republic. The US Food and Drug Administration put an automatic detention on all imports from the Dominican Republic because of illegal pesticide residues, allowing them to detain shipments without physical examination. Detention on perishable products like fresh produce can lead to an unsellable result. The pest control problem prompted investors in Asian vegetable exports from the Dominican Republic to begin looking for new production sites and trading partners. One investor serendipitously had friends in the vegetable business in Comayagua and also in Homestead, Florida. Through relationships established in an Asian expatriate community in the Dominican Republic, a new network of trade was established between the United States and Honduras.

With the collapse of production in the Dominican Republic, Noburu Wataya, a Japanese Dominican businessman who was financing the export of Asian vegetables, consulted Toru Okada, an agronomist managing tomato production in Comayagua and a friend of Wataya's, on the feasibility of moving production to Honduras. Agricultural land and labor were available for the production of new crops following the tomato collapse. Okada and Wataya invited a Honduran exporter, Alonso Lopéz, to join in their venture.[4] Lopéz was a former president of the Camara de Comercio (Chamber of Commerce) of Comayagua and was familiar with the politics of export from Honduras. Yi Jen, the niece of an old friend of Okada's and Wataya's from the Dominican Republic, had just started her own import-export business in South Florida and was looking for new trading partners. Okada later recalled in an interview, "Between our combined experiences we had no problem getting permission from the USDA to export."

Honduran farmers had never grown Asian vegetables before, and although Okada was an agronomist, he had been working with tomatoes. Wataya brought one of his Dominican growers, Victor Reyes, to Comayagua to train Honduras farmers. The exporters needed to work directly with farmers to provide technical support, so the Honduran model of export developed differently from what had been the pattern in the Dominican Republic. Exports from the Dominican Republic relied on intermediaries both to buy from farmers and to sell to exporters; there was no room for intermediaries in Honduras.

Wataya and his partners began with two farmers growing Chinese okra, winter melon, Chinese eggplant, Thai eggplant, and bitter melon. They had trouble collaborating with farmers at first because the latter were reluctant to work with the new exporters. Farmers were afraid of not getting paid for crops already shipped, a practice that had precedence in export-oriented agriculture. But the marketing of Asian vegetables proved to be different; it was more stable. Yi Jen, who worked closely with Chinatown brokers, knew the market well and encouraged the production of crops in Honduras that were counterseasonal to other production sites or that were too labor intensive to grow in Florida to avoid market saturation. And the crops have a long harvest window. Chinese eggplant, fuzzy squash, bitter melon, and long squash are continually harvested over a period of several months, whereas tomatoes and onions, the most prominent commercial crops in Comayagua at the time, were harvested once a season. The national market for tomatoes had fluctuated wildly and growing this crop was a risky business for small farmers. The US market for Chinese vegetables proved to be more consistent.[5]

Contract farming had been present in Honduras since the 1970s, when the Honduran government required agro-industry to outsource at least part of their production. As a blanket policy covering all types of agricultural production, it had not been an effective policy. In cases where the firms could have grown crops more cheaply themselves, contract farmers were maltreated (Glover 1987). This history, and the history of agricultural booms and busts caused by overproduction, monocropping, and pest outbreaks in Comayagua, have created a backdrop of mistrust between export firms and farmers and was the reason that Okada and partners had difficulty recruiting farmers. They had to start producing on a company farm, but their idea was always to work with small farmers over large ones. They also did not want to grow crops exclusively on a company farm with hired labor. The firm chose the contract model of production because they recognized that they were introducing new crops to the valley and that they would need to provide technical assistance. They chose to work with small farmers because they felt there was more agronomic control by spreading their production sites out in small parcels. Contracting to small farmers would reduce the risk of crop failure; if there was an outbreak on one parcel it wouldn't affect all their production (which had happened with tomato and cucumber production in the past). By providing inputs to farmers, the firm also had more assurance that farmers' would comply with US pesticide regulations. A Honduran agronomist has made the argument that forced compliance with US pesticide standards in export agriculture has improved pesticide use in Comayagua.[6]

Between 1989 and 1992 the export of Asian vegetables grew from six hundred to three thousand boxes a week. A shift in transport from air to water helped this growth. A shipping container could be rented at Puerto Cortes on Honduras's north coast—a four-hour drive from Comayagua—and reach Miami 3.5 days after harvest. The shipping time was longer by water than by air, but the cost in freight was less than half: air freight cost fifteen to twenty-five cents a pound, whereas the cost by boat was five to seven cents a pound.

A change in the national regulatory environment further helped stimulate the growth of the Asian vegetable industry. In 1992, shortly after Asian vegetables were introduced to Comayagua, Honduras adopted la Ley para la Modernización y el Desarrollo del Sector Agrícola (the Agricultural Modernization Law). The law established a general framework for future agrarian policy, focusing mainly on economic and social development through the production and commercialization of basic grains, agro-exports, agro-processing, technology transfer, and credit. It deregulated the import of agricultural inputs, the import and subsidy of basic grains, and the production of commercial seed and eliminated taxes on agro-exports (Thorpe 2002) and had several immediate effects on the agricultural sector: deflation of basic grain prices, an increase in number of export firms, increased access to agricultural inputs and credit, and an increase in joint public and private programs for technology transfer.

In these respects, the Agricultural Modernization Law facilitated the development of contract farming of Asian vegetables in Comayagua. Export firms, Honduran government, and foreign development agencies collaborate to improve the production of Asian vegetables and have made valuable agronomic contributions. Production techniques were developed exclusively for the microclimates of Comayagua's production zones. Two exemplary practices are the production of seeds of various Asian cultivars by the Taiwanese Agricultural Mission in Comayagua and the grafting of a Chinese cultivar of eggplant to a native *Solanum* species root stock that is resistant to soil nematodes, a grave problem in many zones of the valley.

The introduction of Asian vegetables has been significant for the agricultural economy of the Comayagua Valley. In the entire country of Honduras there were fifteen agro-exporting firms in 2004.[7] Nine of these firms are located in Comayagua; of these, five contract with small farmers, and of the five, three export Asian vegetables. Between 1999 and 2005 Asian vegetable exports from Honduras increased from 10 million pounds to just over 47 million pounds. With an average rate of twelve cents a pound paid to farmers, the farm value of production was $5.64 million in 2004. Eighty-two percent of farmers interviewed for this book report a modest increase in earnings and material wealth from growing Asian vegetables. In addition, the financial benefits extend beyond the four hundred contracted farmers: including the administrative staff of the three exporting firms, employees at the packing plants, and hired farm laborers, the export of Asian vegetables from Comayagua employs approximately 5,370 people.

Firms and Farmers

Farmers in Comayagua engage with contract firms for several reasons: it allows them to receive a stable income, financing, and inputs and Asian vegetables offer the highest profit of commercially available crops. While most contract farmers in Comayagua have experienced improved incomes, profit alone should not be the sole determinant of achievement in a contract scheme. Farmers need to know that they are earning a representative portion of the business profit and are not being cheated by firm maneuvering (Porter and Phillips-Howard 1997). This is why it is essential to look at the power relationships between firms and farmers. The case of contracting in Comayagua presents a unique situation through which to compare the competition between firms for farmers and examine how this competition presents intra-industry alternatives that affect the social relations of production. Competition between firms leaves room for farmers to maneuver between firms.

By request of my informants, I am going to refer to the three export firms as Exporters 1, 2, and 3 in order to preserve anonymity. Exporter 1, the oldest firm, was formed in 1990 and has coexisted with Exporter 2 since 1994. Exporter 1 is content with its size and is not interested in further growth. Exporter 2, by contrast, is assertively growing. Their desire to grow has generated conflict with Exporter 3, which came to Comayagua in 2002 and is also trying to expand. Exporter 2 has aggressively engaged Exporter 3 in direct competition through pricing wars and improved service to farmers in order to win farmers' favor. Because of the limited extent of land suitable for Asian vegetables in Comayagua, firms are protective of their territory and have made concessions to keep farmers.

The stipulations of the contracts are largely the same between the three firms. The farmer promises to sell all his crop to the firm, follow the production guidelines of the firms' technicians, use pesticides approved by the United States Food and Drug Administration (FDA) and supplied through the firm, and authorize the firm to deduct the value of consumables received from the firm (plants, seeds, fertilizers, pesticides, cash advances) from the value of their purchased fruit. The firm promises to pay the farmer a set price on a set schedule (weekly or biweekly), purchase fruit for a set duration of the year, provide technical support and necessary inputs, and finally, reserve the right to determine "export quality fruit" and reject fruit considered unacceptable. The contracts of Exporter 2 detail a few other conditions: if farmers use chemicals not approved by the FDA, then they will be held responsible for any incurred loss; if they cannot pay off the initial financing, they guarantee their land; and if a crop is lost through natural disaster, they are still financially obligated to pay their debt for agro-inputs.

Exporter 3 changed their process of contracting to appease farmers. Interestingly, when Exporter 3 began to recruit new farmers they found many farmers unwilling to sign contracts. Mostly, this was because Exporter 3 would not offer to buy crops during the low season, as the other two firms do.[8] Exporter 3 waived the written contract for a verbal one with similar premises of credit extended to farmers for inputs and sole rights to purchase harvests. While in practice there is no difference between having written or verbal contracts, Exporter 3's compliance with farmers' requests was a gesture of goodwill.[9] The manager of Exporter 3 said that he hoped to have respectful relationships with farmers. As he saw it, the act of foregoing the written contract was a step in that direction. He is a resident of a farming village in the valley and several of Exporter 3's farmers told me that they were willing to give the firm a chance because the manager was a good guy.

As the willingness to discard the written contract implies, the irony of "contract" farming is that contracts are indeed a formality. Contracts have more symbolic than material meaning. No firm in Comayagua has ever used legal recourse to force compliance with a contract even though contracts are routinely breached. The breaching of contracts is significant because it generates mistrust between farmers and firms, one of the most systemic problems associated with contract farming. Farmers assert power in contracting schemes by dishonestly selling fruit to the highest bidder on the open market and firms tolerate this behavior because of other benefits, such as the mitigation of production risks, that contracting offers them. While the case is similar in Comayagua, the complicating factor is that if contracts are breached, it is with one of the other firms. There is no open market in which Asian vegetables can be bought and sold outside of the contract system. The sale of contracted vegetables to a competitive firm incites hostility between firms. Purchase price between firms varies and some farmers in Comayagua have been known to send portions of their harvest to another firm through a contracted friend. Also, firms in Comayagua have aggressively outpriced their competitors to entice farmers from other firms to contract with them, or to break their contract. An extreme example of this behavior is when Exporter 2 set up a shipping container in front of Exporter 3's packinghouse and offered the farmers of Exporter 3 higher prices in order to cajole farmers to break their contract.

Pricing is one reason why farmers switch firms. The second reason is the belief that firms reject harvested crops based on false quality claims. Some farmers believe that firms cull perfectly good fruit to pass the financial burden of market fluctuations or overproduction on to the farmer. For example, 40 percent of farmers who work with Exporter 2 report instances in which over 50 percent of their fruit was rejected, even up to 90 percent. Yet firms maintain that fruit is rejected only on the basis of quality. Firms retain the right to set quality standards and reject any fruit that does not meet their standards. It is up to the technician to relay the quality standards to the farmers. There are no grading scales linked to price variations for high-, medium-, or low-quality fruit. Blemished, overripe, or underripe fruit is simply discarded or fed to animals. Since there is no local market for Asian vegetables, piles of rotting Chinese eggplant (*berenjena china* in Spanish) and bitter melon (*cun de amor*) are common features on farms and roadsides.

Pricing and quality assessments are two features of contract farming that create power struggles between firms and farmers. Unfortunately, the social tensions surrounding these issues are often predicated on misconceptions. The market for Asian vegetables is highly competitive and problems of overproduction frequently depress prices. The average price of Chinese eggplant, for example, has fallen and risen five times between 1998 and 2005, although the price paid to farmers has remained the same. The overall increase in the wholesale price over this period has been only from thirteen to fifteen dollars for a thirty-five-pound box (equivalent to six cents a pound) (US Department of Agriculture 2006). Some farmers erroneously believe that selling prices keep up with inflation. One farmer felt discouraged that "the costs of production have gone up, but the price offered for eggplant has remained the same for seven years." While he blamed the export firm for garnering more profits than they were passing on to their farmers, there has actually been very little increase in the wholesale price of eggplant.

In terms of quality assessments, the rejection of vegetables based on false quality standards is a practice of intermediaries in New York that Asian vegetable farmers in Florida claim to be a problem as well. Because vegetables are bought on consignment, it is not unlikely that intermediaries reject produce that the market cannot absorb and pass the loss on to farmers as well as importers. It is probable that the Honduran export firms have similar problems with their buyers. There is no standardized system of grading fruit along the entire commodity chain, yet at the retail end in New York City there are many choices for differing levels of quality at respective prices. It is the wholesalers in New York that really set the quality standards and benefit from sorting the fruit according to the quality of their daily inventories.

The manipulation of quality standards by intermediaries, which is unverifiable and irreconcilable, is not the only issue at stake for improving farmers' faith in quality assessments. In looking more closely at the Honduran system for harvesting, sorting, weighing, and determining the final acceptable volume of export-quality fruit, there are inconsistencies in practice that confuse actual verses perceived harvest volumes. First, farmers do not have scales in the field, and they often pack boxes with less than the specified weight, causing the counts of boxes they drop off at the packinghouse to be higher than what they are paid for simply because they misjudged box weight. Second, some farmers tend to inadequately sort fruit in the field, sending poor-quality fruit to the packing plant. Third, the packing house of Exporter 2 is closed to farmers; the farmers cannot watch the packing process after they drop off their harvests, which creates distrust about how the process works. This may, in part, explain why farmers report the highest and most consistent rejection rates from Exporter 2. But transparency has been taken into consideration with the design of new packinghouses; Exporters 1 and 3 now have open packinghouses to allow farmers to watch the sorting of fruit, although farmers might have to wait hours to see their harvest be sorted and do not commonly wait.

It is critical to understand the culture of mistrust between firms and farmers that exists in contracting scenarios, a suspiciousness that is a continuation of a historical legacy between international capital and peasant farmers in Honduras (Stonich 1993). Honduran agriculture has been influenced by world systems since colonial times—when the Spanish didn't find much precious metal in the country, they turned to cattle and agriculture (Jansen 1998). Researchers have characterized two socially distinct sectors of producers that developed with relations between capital and labor in Honduras. One sector is capitalist producers and the other is semiproletarian producers (de Janvry 1981; Stonich 1993). This dualistic model stems from capitalist producers who have pushed peasants off fertile lands into more marginal ones and who depend on the cheap labor of individuals from the semiproletariat (who are subsidized by family labor in subsistence agriculture). In the contracting system in Comayagua, there is a blending of producer strategies and movement between income-generating activities, as well as an emergent middle sector of producers that make the two-sector model less relevant.

There is no clear line of precapitalist (traditional) and capitalist (modern) agriculture in Comayagua. It *is* clear that booms and busts, resulting from

monocropping, overproduction, depression of market prices, and pest outbreaks, have been common in the Comayagua Valley since the public promo-
tion of agricultural exports in the 1970s. Bankrupted firms and failed
cooperatives have left farmers skeptical and disinterested in organizing. But
production relations are generally improving as firms respond to farmers' needs
as they are expressed individually, and subsequently en masse. The action and
reaction on the part of firms and farmers illustrate that the practice of contract
farming is not subsumed by capital. It is a differential process whereby markets
and technology create room to navigate, or as Ploeg and Saccomandi (1995)
refer to it, "room to maneuver," and a differential class of farmers emerges. Production relations in Comayagua are dynamic and constantly evolving.

Navigating Contract Farming

Now that Asian vegetables have been in Comayagua for over twenty years,
farmers are well aware of this economic option. They do not passively accept
firms' suggestions to contract with them. On the contrary, they seek out the
firms because they have heard that Asian vegetables are profitable. Whereas
contracting for export is typically characterized as being more risky than growing for national markets, contracting Asian vegetables for export has proved to
be the least uncertain economic option in Comayagua.

Farmers of Asian vegetables come from a variety of economic backgrounds
and integrate contract farming into their household economies in different
ways (a listing of the demographic characteristics, land holdings, and views of
the farmers in the study sample can be found in table 11). While about half the
farmers who contract Asian vegetables had grown cash crops before, the other
half had grown only maize and beans, had been farm laborers, or had come
from other forms of work. This finding suggests that it is possible for laborers
and nonagriculturalists to become producers and for producers to diversify
their crops.

In order to contract with Asian vegetable firms, farmers must have access to
irrigable farmland and transport. This requirement is common in contracting
scenarios and sometimes favors more elite, landed classes over the landless
(Carletto et al. 1999; Goldín 1996). Contract farming in Comayagua, however,
is not limited to landowners, because there is a system for leasing farmland.
Thirty-five percent of contracted farmers cultivate rented land.

Firms find it advantageous to contact with small farmers in order to defray
labor and land costs (Key and Runsten 1999). Farmers who contract with Asian

Table 11 Socioeconomic characteristics of Honduran contract farmers

Variable	N	Mean	% Total	Min	Max
Land area cultivated in Asian vegetables (AV) (mz)	62	2.03	—	0.5	6.5
Total land area owned (mz)	30	4.89	45	0.5	36
Total land area rented (mz)	23	2	33	0.5	5
Total land area borrowed (mz)	14	1.14	21	0.5	4
Years farming AV under contract	69	4.5	—	1	14
Number of AV grown at same time	69	2	—	1	5
Grew other cash crops before AV	31	—	47	—	—
Grew crops only for home consumption before AV	21	—	32	—	—
Were a farm laborer before AV	7	—	11	—	—
Grow AV because they are more profitable	55	—	93	—	—
Grow AV because firms offer credit	4	—	7	—	—
Learned to grow AV from firm technicians	35	—	60	—	—
Learned to grow AV on own	15	—	26	—	—
Contract AV with a partner	30	—	48	—	—
Have switched firms or worked with more than one firm	32	—	56	—	—
Permanent hired laborers per mz	63	2.6	—	0	10
Temporary hired laborers in high season or harvest per mz	26	2	—	0	6
Family members work on farm for wages*	6	—	9	—	—
Family members work on farm for no wages†	25	—	36	—	—
Household size	55	5	—	1	12
Grow other cash crop in addition to AV	10	—	15	—	—
Grow crops for home consumption in addition to AV	32	—	47	—	—
Have other household income from nonfarm sources	21	—	42	—	—
Growing AV has increased income	40	—	82	—	—
Have invested profits in farm	17	—	25	—	—
Have invested profits in house	17	—	25	—	—
Have saved profits	7	—	10	—	—
Have invested profits in education	7	—	10	—	—
Want one's children to farm	19	—	32	—	—

Note: N equals the number of affirmative responses to each variable. Responses are expressed as mean, minimum (min) and maximum (max) or as a percentage of the total sample of contract farmers questioned (69 is the maximum, but the totals vary according to the number of responses obtained for each question); *AV* represents "Asian vegetables"; *mz* represents "manzanas" (0.7 hectares).

* *Family members* in this variable refers to mainly nonhousehold family members, such as brothers or cousins whom farmers partner with or hire, although one farmer had three sons working with him for wages.

† *Family members* in this variable refers to the contract farmers' wives who help during harvest and children who help on farms in almost all chores or only when they have off from school.

Table 12 Costs and returns of Asian vegetables

Reported earnings from eggplant in 2003–2004 of two farmers of Exporter 2

	Farmer 1	Farmer 2
Area cultivated	2 mz	2.5 mz
Cultivars	Chinese eggplant, nongrafted	Indian and Thai eggplant
Costs before production began (lps)	40,000	30,000
Production (boxes/cycle)	5,959	5,000
Gross income (lps)	380,000	320,000
Total costs (lps)	120,000	80,000
Net profit (lps, shared by two partners)	260,000	240,00
Net profit per person (USD)	**$7,222**	**$6,667**

Note: Production was reported as harvested boxes from the field, not the final, purchased amount. Gross income was calculated using the reported 80 percent pack rate and reported price, eighty lempiras (lps) per box. Lempiras are based on costs in 2004 and the conversion rate of eighteen lempiras to one US dollar.

vegetable firms must be able to provide a portion of the start-up capital. Export firms cover 45–60 percent of production costs prior to harvest. Farmers report that they need to invest 30,000–40,000 lempiras (US$1,667–2,222) before the first harvest. The national average monthly income for farmers in Honduras is 1,949–2,033 lempiras (US$108–113) (Secretaría de Agricultura y Ganadería 1999).[10] At this income level, farmers would need at least fifteen months of savings to invest into a crop (see table 12 for a breakdown of the costs of production). One way that farmers reduce their start-up costs is by contracting in partnership with others. Forty-eight percent of Asian vegetable farmers have a partner with whom they split costs, labor, and profits.

Labor is the most significant cost for a farmer. The labor investment per *manzana* (0.7 hectare) of land is quite substantial. On average, each contracted farmer works two *manzanas* and hires five full-time workers, plus four more part-time workers on harvest days. Laborers are paid wages. Farming Asian vegetables is not a family enterprise for about two-thirds of the sample. Twenty-five farmers reported that their children help them in most chores or when they are off from school; two have sons who work permanently on the farm for wages. However, brothers, cousins, or fathers and sons will often partner together on a contracted crop. Women often work in harvest, but they are generally not contracted farmers. No male farmer told me that his wife helps him on a regular basis, only occasionally to harvest crops. Wives work at home, run a small store (*pulpería*) out of their home, or hold other jobs to contribute to the household income.

It is not easy to organize the capital and labor it takes to start farming Asian vegetables, but contractual relations have changed to facilitate entry into production. Exporter 2 guarantees a standard cash advance per *manzana* of contracted land. Exporters 1 and 3 issue selective cash advances at the request of farmers. Managers of both firms recognize that cash is what farmers ask for most; cash is necessary to pay laborers until harvest time. While it is not part of the original contract, they will work out cash advances on a case-by-case basis on demand.

Cultivating Asian vegetables can be insecure in the low season from May to October. Exporters 1 and 2 purchase crops during both high and low seasons to keep their farmers' incomes steady in the low season, because farmers are disinclined to invest in contract farming if it is only a part-time opportunity. Exporter 3 initially wanted to purchase crops only during the high season because it is an easier time for the firm to guarantee sales. Exporter 3, however, has found that farmers are reluctant to work for them without the provision of a year-round market. The manager told me that they were working toward buying year round as they worked to secure their markets.

Firms maintain strict control over some production practices and not others. The firms retain the right to inspect and approve farmers' land for soil type and irrigation before contracting, and they do stand by this practice. Many zones of the valley have soil nematodes that can attack the roots of Solanaceous crops and, given this problem, farmers in these zones are required to use a grafted eggplant that is resistant to nematodes. Firms also require that farmers rotate crops to maintain soil productivity and reduce the chances of pest and disease outbreaks. They will not contract a farmer to grow the same cultivar two seasons in a row on the same parcel. The Asian vegetables fall into the Solanceae family (four varieties of eggplant) or the Cucurbitaceae family (six varieties of squashes and melons). Farmers rotate crops between these two plant families, or they rotate with maize and beans.

Outside crop rotation, irrigation, and soil type, control over production is more tenuous. The contracts state that farmers must adhere to technicians' advice, but Exporter 1 and 3 do not provide weekly assistance. Exporter 2, on the other hand, has a cadre of young technicians from a local school who make regular weekly visits to farmers. Still, I found much variation in the fertilizer and pest control measures reported by farmers. Almost all farmers use chemical fertilizers, pesticides, and fungicides (but not herbicides), although to various extents. The agricultural agencies that are working with Asian vegetable farmers are trying to encourage integrated pest management. They have made a few strides, but there is a long way to go to reduce chemical dependency in commercial agriculture.

Figure 18 Oxen are used to cultivate Chinese eggplant in between rows to remove weeds and aerate the soil. Sugarcane is planted around fields to protect crops.

Other cultural practices include crop barriers and windbreaks between parcels, incorporation of past crop residues, animal waste soil amendments, and tillage by oxen or by tractor, as well as no-till (see figure 18). Chinese eggplant, the most common crop grown, is also the most labor intensive since the fruit is prone to blemishes and misshapenness (both important quality measures). All crops need to be trellised and staked, but eggplant has to be carefully attended (see figure 19). New shoots should be plucked to encourage strong branches, one of the two axillary flowers should be plucked to encourage long and straight fruit formation, and leaves around the fruit need to be plucked to discourage the chafing of the rough leaves on the delicate skin of the fruit.

The presence of three Asian vegetable export firms in Comayagua provides farmers with a choice of firm to work with and the option to work with a new firm when their contracts expire. Movement between firms is common: 43 percent of farmers who had worked with Exporter 2 left them for Exporter 1, and 27 percent of Exporter 1 switched to Exporter 2. Seventy percent of farmers who began working with Exporter 3 came from the other two firms. Farmers have clear reasons for choosing firms, based on variation in the amount of credit for

Figure 19 Chinese eggplant is carefully managed by hand to allow fruits to grow long and straight.

inputs, cash advances, technical assistance, buying prices, and style of packing. Of the three firms, farmers were most loyal to Exporter 1. Although the prices that Exporter 1 pays are not the highest, Exporter 1 is reputed to be the most consistent in the percentage of harvest they purchase. Financial stability is considered of paramount importance and leads farmers to stay with Exporter 1. One farmer expressed, "Exporter 1 is more responsible with payment. If there is a problem in the market, they maintain their responsibility to purchase their farmers' harvests. The other firm [Exporter 2] plays with us to maintain a high level of production. If the market doesn't want it, they don't buy it."

Farmers had the most gripes about the buying practices of Exporter 2. This firm rejects the greatest percentage of fruit—there were reports of 90 percent of harvest being rejected. The advantage of Exporter 2, however, is that they offer the most consistent technical assistance. Finally, Exporter 3 offers the best prices, rejects little harvest, picks up fruit at the farm (a new practice in the contract system), and opened a packinghouse in a new location in the valley that is more convenient for farmers in that zone.

Exporter 3, as the newest firm, is looking to win over farmers and intentionally offers more advantages than do the other firms. Exporter 3 offers higher prices, on farm pickup, and lower rejection rates. Having fruit picked up on the farm is a big cost break for farmers. In addition, on-farm pickup extends the opportunity to grow Asian vegetables to farmers who do not own, or have access to, transport. Exporter 3 has also extended the opportunity to grow Asian vegetables to farmers in a new part of the valley. They opened their packinghouse in San Jeronimo, a thirty-minute drive from the city of Comayagua, where Exporter 1 and 2 maintain their packinghouses. Exporter 2 has responded to the presence of Exporter 3 by also offering on-farm pickup and by building a second packinghouse in San Jeronimo to compete for growers.

Asian vegetables have proved to be different from other cash crops that farmers in Comayagua have grown. When asked why they prefer Asian vegetables, 93 percent of farmers said it is because they are more profitable than other crops. These farmers agreed that tomatoes, onions, maize, and beans (other common cash crops) have volatile markets and are not profitable. Farmers grow maize and beans for home consumption, or as rotational crops, but have observed that the rising cost of agricultural inputs and gasoline, combined with the decline in prices of basic grains, make growing their traditional milpa crops fit only for home consumption, not for cash. Most farmers appreciate that two export firms provide the option to continue to plant Asian vegetables during the low season (May–October), or that they can choose to grow maize and beans during the low season, which happens to corresponds to the traditional first planting (*primera*) in early May and second planting (*postrera*) in late August.[11] Other farmers like that most of the Asian vegetables can sustain harvest for up to three or four months; grafted Chinese eggplant can produce continual harvest for six to eight months. This characteristic provides a much longer harvest season than that of tomatoes and also differs from the single harvest of basic grains. In general, farmers state that they feel more secure growing Asian vegetables because they can depend on a weekly paycheck for their continual harvests. Also, because there are thirteen cultivars to choose from, they can rotate crops and experiment with different cultivars. One farmer described his previous experiences and present situation thus: "I have a lot of experience with many crops, and the reality is that for me, *vegetales orientales* are the most profitable. The prices for tomatoes are very low, and the costs of production are very high. Also, there is a problem with the climate here. It is very hot, causing a lot of white fly! Tomatoes are not profitable. Now with *los orientales* each day I am a little more financially solvent. I still have a bill from the tomatoes!"

A veteran farmer of eighteen years had a similar perspective: "I have planted since 1976. I grew tomatoes from 1976 to 1982, and during this time I couldn't buy a shirt or a pair of pants. I was growing tomatoes! How terrible! And we weren't blind to needs of our children. We just couldn't raise ourselves up. *Vegetales orientales* are better. I am not going to say that they have considerably improved our lives, but at least they have helped our boys finish their studies. They are sustaining us."

While farmers have experienced gains, most have a very incomplete grasp of how much they spend and earn in a season, making it difficult to quantify earnings. Two farmers were able to discuss earnings from the previous year and can be used as a profit guide (see table 12). One farmer produced 5,959 boxes last season and made 260,000 lempiras (US$14,444) between him and his partner on two *manzanas*. Another farmer reported having 80,000 lempiras in costs for 1.5 *manzanas* and producing 250 to 300 boxes per week. This gave him and his partner a net income of US$6,667 for the six-month season. These are good earnings, especially considering that a professional agronomist in Comayagua earns around US$700 a month.

On the whole, farmers in Comayagua have shown that they have clear preferences for how their contracts are fulfilled, and because of the existence of three Asian vegetable contracting firms, they have been able to exercise agency, albeit limited, in the contracting system in Comayagua. An emergent class of farmers in Comayagua who are commonly referred to as *productores independentes* has further challenged the classic structure of the contract system and has redefined it according to their needs. These farmers are classified as independent because they do not receive credit, inputs, or technical assistance from the firms. They contract with firms only to guarantee the sale of their crops, and they maintain multiple contracts with more than one firm at a time, a practice otherwise heavily discouraged by the export firms. Female farmers were a part of this group; otherwise I did not encounter female contract farmers. It may seem that the independent farmers can be classified as typical capitalist growers that are middle to large sized and depend on hired labor, but none of the independent farmers whom I met fit this characterization. The sample size of this group is small (six) and further research would be needed to make verifiable conclusions. I mention the independent farmers here to further illustrate the point that firms are willing to forgo the classic contract model according to the needs of their contract farmers.

THE introduction of Asian vegetables as export crops in Comayagua has been a differential process in which changing markets and technologies leave room for farmers to navigate the contracting system. Farmers in Comayagua have taken an active role in shaping production relations to cope with incongruence in the contract system, frequently moving between export firms if they are unsatisfied with treatment by a firm. The limited extent of land that is appropriate for vegetable production in the Comayagua Valley promotes intense competition between export firms, so firms are willing to better serve farmers in order to retain them. Export firms have been successful in maintaining stability in the production and marketing of Asian vegetables. Prices do not fluctuate much and historical problems of overproduction and large-scale pest outbreaks have not plagued Asian vegetable production, likely because of the use of crop diversity and rotation. The opportunity to grow Asian vegetables has provided farmers a means of garnering more economic wealth and the promise of providing a better life for their children.

Issues of mistrust and perceived exploitation of farmers by firms stem from historical legacies of maltreatment of farmers by capital and the current political economic system in which contract farming is embedded. There are still fundamental barriers to social and economic growth for contracted farmers. Although farmers may not be completely powerless in contracting schemes, they remain divorced from their international markets with no control over price setting. Poor communication between exporters and small farmers leads to ambiguities in the contracting system that are misinterpreted by both firms and farmers, creating unnecessary tensions between contracting parties. Farmers, with no secure national market for Asian vegetables, or any other cash crops for that matter, remain dependent on contracting firms to market their crops. Indeed, contracting with export firms is the best option for farmers in Comayagua, but largely because there are few other market-oriented agricultural options.

The existence of alternatives to diversify on-farm income is considered fundamental for the long-term success of smallholders (Porter and Phillips-Howard 1997). The dependency of farmers on Asian vegetables may be a precarious situation. Although the industry has been growing and the market has remained stable for fifteen years since its inception, this niche market cannot grow indefinitely and competition from other points of production can increase. Fortunately, 62 percent of Asian vegetable farmers maintain other crops. For now, the success of Asian vegetables has led to diversification within the industry. Farmers are forcing firms to move away from written contracts, adjust their contracts, and amend their policies to allow farmers to work with more than one export firm at a time. These changes illustrate that firms are willing to respond to the changing demands of farmers. Many farmers have found room to navigate the industry, negotiating positive and negative experiences.

For rural development to be successful, there must be marketing alternatives for farmers. If there are means to produce and sell other crops, or sell the same crops to other venues, then labor organization is not the only means to achieve power over production relations. Areas where contract farming is implemented as a means of rural development are commonly those where cooperatives have failed, as in Comayagua, or in areas where social capital among farmers has weakened during colonial or military occupation. Instead of cooperative-led bargaining, the collective desires expressed by individuals in Comayagua became argument enough for firms to adjust their policies to attract farmers from their competitors. Competition between firms is healthy because distributors in Chinatown's food system are always looking to develop new relationships with exporters. Although the power relations between agri-business and small farmers are skewed, it is important to recognize that farmers are not passive actors. Their resistance, albeit individual and often fragmented, can be effective.

## CHAPTER 6

Chinese Food in American Culture

Asian fruits and vegetables might be considered specialty crops in American markets, but their presence in the United States has had a more profound impact on American culture than the characterization of specialty crops suggests. A unifying motivation for the production of Asian vegetables by the Floridian and Honduran farmers in Chinatown's food network is to make a living. Farmers agree that the crops they grow are not mainstream, but how they are understood, exactly, varies. The Chinese vegetable growers of Florida's Palm Beach and Hendry Counties did not see their crops as "niche" because they had no added value; they do not command a price premium at market. In fact, they are lower-grossing vegetable crops per acre than many others commonly grown in Florida. To Leo Cheng, the newest-generation Floridian grower, Chinese vegetables represent the "old way" of his father's business, and he desperately wanted to grow mainstream crops (lettuce!) for mainstream supermarkets. The Southeast Asian homegardeners in Homestead, Florida, on the other hand, specifically chose to grow the foods of their homeland and take pleasure in growing crops that no one, or few others, grow. They take pride in the fact that what they grow and how they grow make them unlike other farmers in their area. In Honduras, the suite of Chinese vegetables that are grown are commodities, in that they bring in cash, not sustenance. If exporters did not purchase their vegetables, this produce would rot or be fed to animals. Chinese vegetables have no place in the Honduran diet.

The agricultural products that I have described in this book thus far are results of environmental, social, and economic processes. It could be easy to see them as "alternative" products themselves, since I argue that practices I have observed involving their production and distribution are alternative to practices attributed to spatially extended agricultural networks. But the provisioning of these "alternative" food products has actually had a more widespread impact on American culture than in their simply supplying traditional foods of immigrant populations. Chinatown's food network has a great symbolic importance that is worth understanding. After touring Chinatown's produce markets and the production sites that supply them, this chapter turns toward the meaning that this ethnic food system has in the United States at large.

Demand for Chinese food is not as specialized as one might think; in fact, it has grown and diversified since the Chinese enclave in Manhattan developed in the late 1800s. The category *Chinese food* itself represents a diversity of styles of cooking reflective of the changing tastes of American diners as well as Chinese immigrants. Through its restaurants, Chinatown's food network serves the material needs of not only the ethnic enclave but also the United States' culinary imagination about what constitutes ethnic, foreign, and authentic foods. Shifting demand is an important driver shaping Chinatown's supply chains and while it is tempting to conclude that these chains are dependent on ongoing immigration to the United States from China, a look at the public image of Chinese food and restaurants in the enclave shows that patrons of Chinese restaurants and grocers are not only Chinese immigrants. Chinese restaurateurs have actively shaped the public image of Chinese food, working to appeal to the taste expectations of many kinds of Americans, cosmopolitan diners, and immigrants alike.

Ongoing immigration from East and Southeast Asia to New York has fueled the growth of Manhattan's Chinatown and led to the creation of satellite Chinatowns in Queens and Brooklyn. The foreign-born population no doubt supports the trade of ethnic groceries: Chinese Americans are characterized as culinary conservatives; while they experiment with new foods, they retain their traditional eating habits (Gabaccia 1998). Foodways are typically one of the last traditions to change during the process of acculturation in many groups of people, but given this conservatism, within one or two generations the children and grandchildren of immigrants typically reject the food habits of their parents and grandparents in favor of Anglo-Saxon-influenced American eating habits (Levenstein 2002). Nevertheless, Chinese Americans have been shown to retain traditional food habits over multiple generations, particularly if they can have access to traditional foods in nearby Chinatowns.

Non-Chinese populations support Chinatown's food network too. Chinatown markets, and especially the restaurants, serve all kinds of Americans from all walks of life. The Chinese restaurant trade developed in the late 1800s with an eye toward mainstream tastes, and willingly adapted recipes to suit diverse clienteles. Chinese restaurants continue to introduce and adapt regional and hybrid cuisines, shaping what constitutes Chinese food in the United States.

Restaurants in Manhattan's Chinatown and throughout the metro area are important members of Chinatown's food network, both as consumers of the fruits and vegetables the network supplies and as producers of food, flavors, and ambience in the small public space that is a restaurant. In this way, immigrant producers of food are important shapers of the cultural economy of eating and the taste of their compatriots' experiences that come to represent ethnicity to native and immigrant populations alike (Ray 2011). There is no one, commonly understood definition of *ethnic, foreign,* or *authentic* foods. Rather these categories are understood on a continuum of personal experience combined with cultural norms. By looking at the history of Chinese foodways in the United States, from the initial development of Manhattan's Chinatown in the second half of the 1800s to the cosmopolitan Chinese restaurants of Manhattan today, we can address the questions of what constitutes Chinese food in the United States, the role that Chinese restaurants play in defining Chinese food, and whom the restaurants serve. Through this analysis we can see how Chinatown's food network not only supplies the material needs of the enclave and immigrant populations but also plays a role in the public understanding of Chinese food and ethnicity in the United States at large.[1]

The Role of Food in Chinese Culture

Chinese immigrants developed a robust food system in New York because of the desire to preferentially feed their enclave during a time in which they were recipients of overt political antipathy. The first Chinese immigrants came to New York from California, where in the 1870s unemployment and hostility incited violence against them. The Chinese Exclusion Act was signed into federal law in 1882, limiting immigration from China to merchants and Chinese-born children of American-born Chinese men. This era of exclusion lasted until immigration reform in 1943, prompting shifts in the economic activities that Chinese pursued in the United States. Chinese sought self-employment as a move away from low-skilled work, with the food service industry gaining importance for this group through the first half of the twentieth century (Carter 2011).

It is no surprise that Chinese immigrants brought their food culture to the United States. In China, food is central to living a good life, and the sophistication, elaboration, and diversity of Chinese cuisine owe much to the unique importance of food in the social scheme of things (Anderson 1988). China's vast and diverse biogeography provides a rich array of wild and domesticated plant and animal species. Moreover, the country's position along the Silk Road trade network facilitated the incorporation of foods from the tropical vegetation of Southeast Asia and the ancient agricultural cradle of the Near East. China's geography provided for the cornucopia of edible biodiversity that the nation's inhabitants experimented with, and a social system developed to incorporate food into society, where it plays a strong role. Chinese enjoy life through food. They use food to mark ethnicity, holidays, events, and social transactions. It solidifies business deals, is shared during family gatherings, and is offered during religious ceremonies. Food is a powerful symbol of the good life; it is not only a source of nutrients but also a means of communication. It communicates ethnic solidarity, favor, indebtedness, and opulence. For Chinese, nothing is more important than eating: eating is an affair redolent of heaven (Newman 1999).

Chinese gourmetship was never morally restrained by religion, or even by communism in recent history. In fact, the most vigorous expression of resistance to government asceticism in mainland China is banquets (Anderson 1988). In Hong Kong, even trivial matters are reason for a feast. Chinese people defy an economic convention known as Engel's law, which states that as income rises the proportion spent on food decreases, and this is the norm in most of the world; low food costs relative to average income is considered a marker of a good standard of living. In Hong Kong, however, the opposite holds true—as people get richer, they spend a higher percentage of their income on food. Cantonese display this trend, as do individuals from Taiwan and Singapore. Chinese people spend more on food and drink per week than do people of any other culture (Newman 1999).

The freshness of food is very important to Chinese. As food distribution was beginning to centralize in Hong Kong in the 1970s, frozen fish, industrially raised meat, and wholesale vegetables were being imported from the mainland. People responded by growing their own vegetables. The observation that Chinese grow their own vegetables holds true for Chinese living in Boston in 1882, San Francisco, and New York City in the late 1800s (Newman 1999; Blasdale 1899; Beck 1898). This urban agriculture response was not rooted in the idealization of rural life as noble or in the idea that being close to the soil is transcendent, ideas that form the basis of urban agriculture movements in the United States today. These traditional Jeffersonian beliefs are not traditional in China. Chinese grew food to have the food they wanted.

Food is also seen as medicine in China. In studies in Taiwan and Hong Kong it was shown that at least 93 percent of cases of sickness resulted in altered diets as treatment (Anderson 1988). A traditional Chinese belief that underlies the use of food as treatment for illness is that some foods are strengthening and some are weakening. The humoral system of Western medicine practiced from the fifth to nineteenth centuries influenced Chinese nutritional medicine, holding that the human body is affected by heat, cold, wetness, and dryness. These qualities must remain in balance for people to be happy and healthy. Foods were characterized as hot (typically high-calorie or spicy foods like chili, ginger, pepper) or cool (low-calorie vegetables). Wet foods might be something that causes an allergic reaction, like shellfish (they are wet); by contrast, dry foods, like peanuts, leave the throat parched and scratchy. The heating/cooling dimension was much more important than the wet/dry, the former classifying certain foods and drinks as dangerously heating and to be avoided by those not in good health, some examples being fried and spicy food and alcohol. Milder heating foods are restorative and include ginger; ginseng; meats; red beans; and a few spicy-tasting vegetables, such as chrysanthemum leaves. Starch staples and white fish are neutral foods and are dietary mainstays. And cooling foods such as Chinese cabbages, green beans, radishes, and watercress, are routinely used as medicine or dietary aids. The humoral dimensions are supplemented by the concept of *pu*, meaning "strengthening," supplementing," or "patching up." Most high-quality animal proteins, as well as weird, anomalous, or aphrodisiac foods, are pu: sea cucumbers, bird's nests, deer antlers, shark fins, white tree fungus, abalone. These are just some examples of folk nutrition in China, ideas that have largely been abandoned with nutritional science but that still persist as a way to accommodate the facts of nutrition and folk classification of peasant societies. I have heard from many Chinese Americans that bitter melon is a cool food, and its extreme bitterness is good for one's health.

Chinese are committed to and united by good cooking and good food. There are many regional cuisines throughout China but with some commonalities that form a general understanding of what Chinese food is. Rice and other boiled grains form the base of the diet, followed by soybean products and vegetables. Meat used to be rare, except for the wealthy, and its present consumption is about half the US per capita rate, although it is on the rise in China (Larson 2012). Fish and eggs provide some protein, but grains and soy provide more. Beans and vegetables are eaten fresh and fermented, many greens half dried first, then fermented, differentiating Chinese fermentation methods from others.

Above all, the Chinese diet relies on rice. Food *is* rice in China—to eat is to eat rice (*fan* in Cantonese). An ordinary meal is rice with a topping (*sung, fan*). And the most common *sung* are greens, *ts'ai*. Chinese greens, or cabbages, are the most characteristic of the Chinese diet and most universally and abundantly used, apart from starch and soy staples. Rich in vitamins, minerals, and fiber and low in calories, they make a very nutritious part of the diet. The main forms of cabbages are *Brassica pekinensis*, the heading cabbages such as napa from north China, and *B. chinensis* (paak ch'oi, aka bok choy), from the south. *B. parachinensis* is the third category; these are the mustard greens, of which the stem buds and young leaves are eaten. *B. juncea* and *B. alboglabra* are also mustard green types (see appendix B for common names of Chinese vegetable species). The great diversity of Chinese cabbages make up the most iconic group of Chinese vegetables, with napa and bok choy reaching mainstream markets and the other varieties filling enclave produce stands year round.

Chinese Foodways in the United States

The role of food in China as social marker, as medicine, and in the everyday enjoyment of life underlies the construction of Chinese foodways in the United States. But as Chinese immigrants become a minority group within a mainstream culture, how do their foodways change? Chinese have been observed to retain their traditional food habits more strongly than other ethnic groups in the United States, a phenomenon Gabaccia (1998) refers to as "culinary conservatism." To some degree human beings across cultural lines are understood to be both simultaneously curious about new foods and deeply comfortable with traditional foods. However, some groups are more conservative than others. In the United States, Chinese and Italians share the particular distinction of holding on to culinary traditions during the process of cultural assimilation, even drawing ethnic pride from retained culinary traditions in generations subsequent to immigration (Levenstein 2002; Newman 1999). Chinese strongly maintain their way of eating because of the complex role of food in socialization, cultural traditions, and healing.

Access to traditional culinary items is a primary factor in retention of traditional Chinese eating habits in the United States. It has been repeatedly observed that Chinese Americans with convenient access to traditional Chinese food items retain their eating habits more than those who have to drive far distances or pay more for traditional foods. In a study of 102 Chinese immigrant mothers in New York City, Newman and Linke (1982) compared the food habits of the mothers living in a predominately Chinese community (Chinatown in Manhattan) with those in a mixed ethnic community in Queens. Both groups of mothers diversified their diets, but those in Chinatown changed their food habits less. Overall, the study participants retained traditional foods while incorporating other foods into their diets. They increased the frequency of different types of fruits and vegetables consumed, with an overall increase in meat and dairy. From eight food items (bok choy, Chinese kale, scallions, pork, congee, chicken, rice, and tea) consumed daily before immigration, the number increased to seventeen after immigration. Traditional foods such as kumquat, litchi, shark's fins, pigeon, and quail's eggs were still consumed after immigration. There was also a change in the social patterns of eating across both groups of Chinese mothers. Family togetherness at meals decreased and mothers and children, in place of grandparents, shopped for food, prepared meals, washed dishes, and set the table.

This study tells us that foodways change in the United States, but not why. It does suggest, however, that the maintenance of traditional diets is limited by time to prepare food at home and access to traditional foods. In a study of 399 Chinese immigrants living in Pennsylvania, Lu and Cason (2004) showed that the most common causes for why immigrants changed their eating habits were matters of convenience. The places where participants shopped changed; whereas previously, in China, food had been obtained from independent vendors in open air markets (67%), it was now bought in large supermarkets (83%) in Pennsylvania. Like Newman and Linke (1982), Lu and Cason (2004) found that consumption frequency in all food groups increased after immigration, with grain products being the first major category of change (substituting bread for rice) and dairy the second. But when eating out, half the participants would choose Chinese food because they believed it is healthy.

Traditional food availability is very important in making decisions about what to eat. Peng (2005) studied dietary acculturation in 105 Chinese students in Ohio at the University of Akron and found that traditional food availability was ranked as the second-most-important factor of food choice behind flavor. Akron had no specific Chinese food markets. Students had to drive to Cleveland for more choice and lower-priced traditional foods, which they did from time to time. An important consideration in the preference for traditional foods is that 87 percent of the student sample cooked at home to maintain cultural food habits. Peng notes that Chinese students have more cooking experience than other cultural groups but also that the financial constraints of being a student would prevent them from eating out.

Not only do Chinese in the United States hold on to traditional foods; also, the preparation of traditional foods for special events and holidays has been shown to increase with length of time residing in the United States. Immigrants in the United States more than five years had eating habits more similar to before immigration (Newman and Linke 1982). Similarly, in a study comparing women born in China to second- and third-generation Chinese American women, a higher percentage of the Chinese American women consumed Chinese food than foreign-born Chinese. The Chinese American women showed a strong ethnic identification with the foods of their culture, suggesting a renewed interest in heritage in generations after immigration (Spindler and Schultz 1996).

Dietary acculturation is the process of adopting eating patterns of the host country. It is a nonlinear, multidimensional, dynamic process whereby immigrants pick and choose which foods to retain, exclude, adopt, or replace when preparing traditional Chinese meals or American meals. Food traditions are the slowest to change through the process of acculturation (Spindler and Schultz 1996). Eating is done in the privacy of one's home, so is not subject to social pressures of the majority culture (Peng 2005).

Since the 1960s, Americans have become more interested in "foreign" foods, probably as a result of increasing travel, the changing structure of the American home, and renewed immigration. But in earlier periods, Americans' acceptance of foreign foods into domestic diets since English colonization is more checkered. Gabaccia (1998) argues for acceptance and celebrates the creolization of dishes in early America. Corn was added to the Dutch dish of hutespot, and African slaves in the Carolina Low Country adapted the southern rice dishes hoppin' John and pilaf. Levenstein (2002), on the other hand, sees American tastes as resolutely and narrowly Anglo-Saxon until Italians began arriving between 1880 and 1920 and influencing the Anglo-Saxon diet by introducing dishes (such as lasagna) that mixed meat, vegetables, carbohydrates, and dairy. Even then, Americans more willingly accepted *spaghetti italienne* as haute cuisine through the French interpretation so as not to associate it with the Italians who emigrated to the United States en masse—peasants from poverty-stricken southern Italy.[2]

The example of Chinese food is similar to that of Italian food in the United States in that several dishes were rapidly Americanized to suit American palates, differentiating a new style of Chinese American food from Chinese cuisine. But upon the arrival of Chinese food in the United States with the first Chinese laborers, it has always been a differentiated category, with food made for tastes and budgets along class, ethnic, and racial lines (Beck 1898). Mainstream Chinese American food such as chop suey and chow mein bears little resemblance to food from China. And Chinese food never became haute cuisine; it is most commonly served in inexpensive to moderately expensive restaurants today (Ray 2010). But segments of the American population, from the late 1800s to now, experiment with exotic Chinese foodstuffs. Asian vegetables have been introduced to the public by media tastemakers as something special to behold. As one *New York Times* reporter noted, "Crisp bunches of bok choy, their stems an unblemished white, their leaves dark green, can usually be found in D'Agostino markets, and tender stalks of Chinese broccoli show up in Balducci's in Greenwich Village. Purple-veined amaranth lurks at the Union Square Greenmarket" (Louie 1997). Chinese broccoli (gai lan), bok choy, and purple amaranth were present in Chinatown markets before they entered New York's gourmet marketplaces. The shift represents changing tastes and values about foreign foods, and exotic produce in general, but from history we see that "exotic" Chinese food has always been present in Chinatown and has been prepared in many different ways to appeal to immigrants as well as particular segments of the American population at large.

The counterintuitive finding that Chinese Americans increase their use of traditional foods with length of residency in the United States can be interpreted as active resistance to mainstream culture or as a result of the acceptance of some Chinese foods by mainstream culture. Chinese Americans don't necessarily have to choose Chinese food over American if Chinese food *is* American food. There is not enough evidence to explain definitively why the use of Chinese traditional foods has defied norms of dietary acculturation, and which foods over others have been retained or how their preparation may vary. But we do know that Chinese food is a diverse category, with some foods that satisfy tastes of immigrants, some that are part and parcel of the American dining-in and dining-out experience, and some that are on the edge of cosmopolitan culinary innovation and adventurous eating.

Dining in Chinatown

Chinese restaurants have much to do with introducing Americans to various styles of Chinese cooking. The restaurants of Chinatown are highly valued in New York City's culinary and cultural landscape. They provide a taste of home for many immigrant diners and gastro-tourism by subway for many kinds of New Yorkers. In times of distress, such as economic downturns post–September 11, 2001, and post–Hurricane Sandy in 2012, New Yorkers have rallied to save the restaurants, proclaiming the neighborhood the "last line of defense against a single, homogenous culture in Manhattan" (Wells 2012, D1). While this is clearly an overstatement, it suggests that New Yorkers should not want Chinatown restaurants to acculturate too much—just enough so they are appealing—but not to be static or too familiar. According to Wells's quote from his *New York Times* article, eating in Chinatown is akin to voting with one's fork, to borrow locavore termi-nology. What one is voting for, however, is cultural preservation in light of the gentrification of Manhattan. Ironically, enclave restaurants have actively con-structed the perceived authenticity of their cuisine for over one hundred years, not simply replicating what was done in China but creating a new Chinese experi-ence for Americans. So what, exactly, is being preserved?

The material and symbolic value of Chinatown's restaurants developed in tandem. The history of Chinese restaurants and Chinese food in the United States is a fascinating story, and one that is told well by several writers (Spiller 2008; Coe 2009; Yu 1987; Barbas 2003; Lu and Fine 1995; Lee 2009; Jung 2011). What history reveals is that twenty years after the first documented Chinese men were moving in around Mott Street in the 1860s, Chinatown's restaurants established themselves as a cultural attribute of New York City. Since the late nineteenth century, Chinese immigrants in the metropolitan area have depended on the restaurants to partake in Chinese society in the United States and retain their foodways. Chinese chefs and restaurant own-ers also self-consciously adapted foods to suit the tastes of a wider audience as a means of expanding their economic reach. Chinatown's restaurants served all kinds of people, capturing the imagination of Americans, as they still do.

In a *Cosmopolitan* article about New York's newly established Chinatown, Wong Chin Foo (1888) stated, "Nearly all Chinese in New York are 'high livers' in diet." This observation reflects the important role that food plays in Chinese society and within the society they were creating anew in New York. As soon as Chinese bachelors began arriving in Lower Manhattan, they set up groceries and restaurants to provision traditional foods. One of the first records of Chi-nese living in New York was from 1868, documenting that a man named Wah Kee opened a store that sold vegetables, dried fruit, and "curios." He also had a gambling and opium den upstairs (Spiller 2008). If Kee had a laundry and restaurant, his enterprise would have represented each of the most common business types in early Chinatown.

Chinese food establishments quickly proliferated in early Chinatown. There were over thirty Chinese groceries toward the end of the nineteenth century, mostly around Mott Street. Dwellers in Chinatown would often sleep and eat in the small quarters where they made their living washing clothes or selling imports. Their main staple was rice, fresh greens of some kind, and a bit of boiled pork or steamed fowl. Given the humble livelihoods of Chinese bache-lors, the Chinese sought out good food and conviviality at restaurants (Beck 1898).

Chinese men from a fifty-mile radius would descend on Chinatown's social restaurants often once a week on Sundays, the great congregating day. There was a menu for every budget. A first-class spread of fifty dollars for twelve people would include forty courses and would be feasted on for over two days. The cheapest spread for a formal dinner would be eight courses for eight dollars (Foo 1888). There were also places to eat a short meal, and again there was a menu for every budget: two dollars could buy a dish of shark's fins or bird's nests; seventy-five cents could buy fried chicken with balsam pear; twenty-five cents would buy sponge squash soup; and for a mere fifteen cents one could have chop suey, which at that time was a hash of offal and vegetables. For ten cents one could finish a meal with preserved litchi nuts or dragon's eyes (Beck 1898).

The exoticism of Chinese foodstuffs played on the fears as well as curiosity of New Yorkers. Contrary to urban legend, Chinese did not eat rats, cats, or puppies. Rather pork, duck, and Chinese vegetables were common foods (Beck 1898). Chinatown restaurants drew the attention of urban hucksters who would lead tours for urban adventurers seeking to experience New York City's underbelly. One particular restaurant, Mon Lay Won Company, at 24 Pell Street, assumed the nickname the "Chinese Delmonico's" after one of New York's most famous restaurants in order to draw tourists (Spiller 2008). In the 1880s there were at least five hundred Americans who regularly ate in Chinatown in Chinese fashion, with chopsticks and sharing family-style meals. Clearly media coverage about Chinatown was geared toward New York trendsetters, as we can see from Foo's 1888 *Cosmopolitan* article, but laborers and visitors from all walks of life also took meals in Chinatown. Of an average of $500 in daily receipts, about $200 came from white patrons, $275 from Chinese men, and $25 from African Americans (Beck 1898).

Chinese chefs developed dishes to appeal to American palates and restaurateurs learned to market ethnicity at the turn of the twentieth century. The development of chop suey as a distinctly Chinese American dish illustrates this point. In Cantonese cooking, chop suey is a hash of entrails, giblets, and vegetables. A recipe from 1888 included chicken livers and gizzards, pig's tripe, bamboo buds, fungi, and bean sprouts. It was adapted to American tastes by replacing the innards with meat, and odd vegetable matter with American vegetables. It was advertised as the favorite dish of a well-known Chinese envoy to the emperor, Li Hung Chang, who made a famous trip to New York in 1896. Restaurateurs capitalized on Li's reputation and the attention given to his trip to the United States to sell the dish and attract American clients (Yu 1987). It worked fabulously—by the 1920s chop suey restaurants were exploding out of urban enclaves across the country, and chop suey became a mainstay in the US culinary repertoire.

Chinese restaurants in the United States now make up an industry with over $17.5 billion annual sales, with 43,139 Chinese restaurants, which is more than the total number of McDonald's (about 13,000), Burger King (about 11,000), and Wendy's (about 6,900) domestic stores combined (Chinese Restaurant News 2012). There might be a Chinese take-out restaurant in every urban neighborhood and rural town in the United States, but it is not only because of the diaspora of Chinese immigrants from the city to the suburbs. Many Chinese believe that restaurant ownership is a means of obtaining the American dream. These restaurateurs have spread Chinese food all over the country for Americans to dine in—not solely for Chinese—making Chinese food ubiquitous. Chinatown's food cluster, with its kitchen supply stores, menu-printing companies, employment agencies, food manufacturers, and grocers, is connected to Chinese restaurants in the hinterland via private bus networks to ensure the flow of necessary goods and people between Chinatown and afar.

Today, the restaurant trade continues to be an economic engine in Chinatown, serving Chinese restaurateurs in suburban and rural outposts. Three sociological studies of Chinatown affirm the centrality of the restaurant industry to Chinatown's economy in the past two decades (Zhou 1992; Kwong 1996; Lin 1998). A report by a team at Hunter College estimates that almost one-quarter of all jobs in Chinatown are food related, within food manufacturing, wholesale distribution, kitchen and equipment supply, menu-printing companies, grocery stores, and restaurants. According to the New York State Department of Labor, there are 352 restaurants in Chinatown employing 6,243 people.[3] These numbers can be understood as a lower limit for the restaurant industry. Department of Labor data is inclusive for all establishments that have at least one paid employee and pay unemployment insurance. It does not include family members of the owner or employees off the books, which other researchers have found to be numerous in the restaurant industry (Jung 2011). Peter Kwong estimated that in 450 restaurants, there were fifteen thousand employees (Kwong 1996). Further, the Department of Labor data is reported by zip code, and Chinatown straddles several not included here.[4]

Small restaurants are the hallmark of ethnic enclaves, and Chinatown is no exception. The US Census Bureau reports the number of establishments by employee size class, showing that since 1998, 65–78 percent of restaurants in Chinatown had one to four employees. These data are estimated by survey collection, so they differ slightly from the Department of Labor data but show similar trends in total number of restaurants (see table 13). Restaurants in Chinatown

Table 13 Number of restaurants and dominant size
class of restaurants in Chinatown

Year	Number of establishments	1–4 employees (%)
2010	523	68
2009	474	68
2008	422	67
2007	408	65
2006	465	69
2005	444	73
2004	372	67
2003	315	66
2002	264	68
2001	575	78
2000	367	75
1999	224	68
1998	182	78

Source: Data is from the Country Business Patterns, US
Census Bureau.
Note: Numbers of establishments are shown for full-
and limited-service restaurants, cafeterias, and snack and
nonalcoholic beverage bars for zip code 10002.

rarely exceed nineteen employees, with only a handful of restaurants coming in
and out of the 50–99 employees size class in recent years. In 2006 one full service restaurant in the 100–249 employee size class emerges, with a total of two
reported in the last data year of 2010.[5]

The large restaurants in Chinatown are banquet halls serving the Cantonese and Fuzhounese communities from within the city as well as out of state.
They do simple business lunches, daytime dim sum, weddings, and private
nighttime banquets weekdays and weekends alike. Mondays are the big restaurant days for Fuzhounese, extending the weekend, and the New Year's season
from January to April is quite busy (Lin 1998). Dining in the banquet halls can
be a mark of having achieved a life dream for new immigrants. Restaurant
workers in the New York metro area make regular trips to Chinatown for personal supplies and aspire to have their own party at a banquet hall (Guest 2003).

The restaurants in Chinatown are part of the enclave economy, but it is inaccurate to characterize them as shielded by their ethnic base from the larger economy, just as it is inaccurate to view the food system itself this way. Formal and
informal alternative economies exist in Chinatown, but the enclave economy is
by no means isolated. Looking at the number of restaurants in Chinatown over

the past decade reveals a dramatic sensitivity to city and national economic trends. The events of September 11, 2001, illustrate this point. Lower Manhattan suffered from a lack of transportation and dearth of tourism after that day, and restaurants are particularly dependent on tourism. The number of restaurants in Chinatown declined by 54 percent, from 575 to 264, and has still not regained the pre-2001 total (see table 13). Restaurants in Lower Manhattan, including those in Chinatown, showed immediate response to the events of September 11 such as lowering price points on menus and offering more comfort food for regulars. Long-term strategic responses to regain business included privately sponsored events like Dine Around Downtown and the Tribeca Film Festival, as well as various Restaurant Weeks organized by NYC & Company (Green et al. 2004). Chinatown's first Restaurant Week as well as the tourism initiative Explore Chinatown were direct responses to the decline in tourism.

Tourists and other out-of-state patrons support Chinatown restaurants. From interviews with restaurants owners, McCormick et al. (2010) reported that Fuzhounese restaurant owners estimated the bulk of their regular clientele were Fuzhounese from Chinatown and from out of state, and some were other New York City residents and tourists. Cantonese restaurant owners estimated that a small percentage of their regular clientele were from out of state, most were from Chinatown, and the rest were other New York City residents and tourists. The difference between the Fuzhounese restaurants, which represent the most recent wave of immigrants from Fujian Province, and the Cantonese restaurants, which represent the original Chinese immigrants, is that there are more out-of-state Fuzhounese patronizing restaurants for celebrations. The banquet halls specifically serve ethnic Chinese, who make up 90 percent of their business (Zhou 1992). Also, out-of-state Fuzhounese restaurant owners and workers regularly visit Chinatown for personal and restaurant business within Chinatown's food industry cluster.[6] It is clear from both primary and secondary data that out-of-state residents, city residents, and tourists dine in Chinatown. Furthermore, its restaurants overwhelmingly support the area's wholesale and retail grocery trade, getting 90 percent of their supplies from retail or wholesale groceries in Chinatown (McCormick et al. 2010). Restaurants, then, are great consumers of Chinatown's produce, as well as the cheerleaders of it.

The Multiple Flavors of Chinese Restaurants

Chinese restaurants in New York City stretch from the Hudson to the East River, from Coney Island to the Whitestone Bridge, from Battery Park to City

Island. Suffice it to say that they are ubiquitous in the metropolitan area. Chinese restaurants are currently following two general culinary trends: hybridization and regionalization. Both trends reflect the shifting socioeconomic demographics of New York. Hybrid cuisine is a manifestation of cultural border crossing resulting from human migrations but presently is also an outcome of cosmopolitan tastes for unique culinary experiences. On the one hand, hybrid cuisines reflect unique personal histories and tastes of chefs and restaurant owners, and the desire to market one's menu to multiple ethnic groups. Chinese takeouts on the street corners of Upper Manhattan neighborhoods home to Latino immigrants feature fried plantains—*maduros* or *tostones*—to appeal to Puerto Rican and Dominican clients. The blending of Chinese and Hispanic culture is not new, as evident from the days of "chop suey and cha cha," in the 1940s and 1950s, but is a continual verification of the ethnic boundary crossing that Chinese restaurants have accomplished (Spiller 2008). In the borough of Queens, hybrid Chinese eateries abound: Chinese Guyanese in Jamaica, Chinese Jamaican in Rosendale, and Chinese Indian in Elmhurst offer specialties like jerk pork fried rice and curry-filled egg rolls. Chifa—Cantonese food with Peruvian ingredients—is a very popular cuisine developed by Chinese in Peru that can now be found in Jackson Heights (Remizowski 2010). It is unclear if these other hybrid cuisines are a result of the Chinese diaspora or because of adaptation of Chinese restaurateurs in New York to other minority groups in the city. This would be an interesting topic to explore further. But it does represent cultural blending.

Hybrid, or Asian-inspired, foods are also alive and well in New York City's trendy dining scene. *New York Magazine* declared 2012 the year of Asian hipster cuisine, remarking that its annual "Cheap Eats" issue was not an Asian edition, although it might seem so given the onslaught of "buzzy" openings of Asian-inspired restaurants by American cooks who found their calling through passion, not ancestry.[7] *New York Magazine* is hesitant to use the word *fusion* to describe this cuisine, perhaps because of the yuppie, faddish, and pricey associations that the concept of fusion cuisine congers up. The latest incarnations of Asian-inspired restaurants serve food that nonetheless is a combination of cultural traditions. The son of a Taiwanese restaurant owner opened a downtown place that takes culinary liberties with gua bao, a Taiwanese street food. Gua bao is traditionally a steamed white bun with stewed pork belly, pickled vegetable, crushed peanuts, and unrefined cane sugar crystal, but new twists are oysters for a po'boy influence or organic tofu for the environmentally conscious. Another new place that calls itself a noodle bar serves oxtail ramen soup with long beans and Chinese mustard greens, appealing to multiple ethnic sensibilities. Dale Talde, of

Top Chef season 4 fame, proudly opened an Asian American restaurant that serves an appetizer of shrimp wrapped in perilla leaf with bacon-tamarind caramel. For him, novel flavor combinations are all that matter, as for the chef at a West Coast Chinese restaurant who just opened an outpost on the Lower East Side that serves, in his words, weird Chinese food. Braised pea greens with Old Bay Seasoning and pumpkin broth—weird or Chinese vegetables meet Maryland crab, on Thanksgiving?

The list of hybrid dishes goes on and on, as a testimony to the culinary innovation that results from cultural mixing. But in these cases, elite tastemakers in the culinary world and in trendsetting media endorse hybrid cuisines. The three chefs discussed above publicly discuss their Asian heritage, but arguably their cuisine comes more from a cosmopolitan sensibility than from their heritage per se. For example, the chef Danny Bowien of Mission Chinese Food was born in Korea and raised by white parents in Oklahoma. The first time he ate Korean food was as a teenager in San Francesco (Martin 2012).

One thing remains the same in the history of Chinese restaurants in the United States. Chinese chefs, since the early twentieth century chop suey craze to the trendy hipster cuisine of 2012, have self-consciously tried to adapt their food to target audiences. A case in point comes from a sociological study of Chinese restaurants in Athens, Georgia, that found authenticity was not the primary goal of the restaurants. Whether restaurants were consumption oriented, characterized by efficiency, low price and informality, or connoisseur oriented, appealing to patrons with more time and money to spend and more experience with Chinese culture to inform their expectations, immediate satisfaction was the first goal, adherence to tradition the second (Lu and Fine 1995). Likewise, a regular patron of Chinese restaurants in Chinatown notes that for those in the know, many restaurants offer Chinese and American versions of the same dish, which one you receive dependent on whether you order in Chinese or English or if you ask for a particular preparation specifically. For example, the American version of egg foo young is a hash of eggs, while the Chinese version is an omelet (Lee 1995). Whether in a university town without a closed ethnic community, as is the case with Athens, Georgia, or in the largest Chinese enclave in the United States, many Chinese restaurants want to appeal to a broad clientele by diversifying their cooking styles.

Talde's comment on authenticity is "There's two kinds of cooks: good and bad."[8] In this view, innovative and transcendent flavor combinations are the dominant kitchen culture. Chefs should not feel beholden to great culinary traditions, and traditions themselves are more flexible than one might suppose. In this view, good Chinese chefs should cross cultural borders, recognizing traditional ingredients and preparations, but experimenting with new ones. This appears to have occurred with the Chinese diaspora all over the world, and cultural boundary crossing with food is part and parcel of the US story since colonial times. The introduction of new flavors—whether it is Mexican chilies to the Spanish colonized American Southwest, or the cabbage salad, coleslaw, of German settlers to Pennsylvania—depends on human migrations and cultural contact (Gabaccia 1998). This is not to say that experimentation was the norm in the United States, only that it occurred. Again, experimentation is tempered by culinary conservatism and the maintenance of traditional foodways.

In addition to the mixing of cultural traditions in restaurants, there is a parallel trend of the regionalization of restaurants. This is where Chinatown restaurants really shine, particularly now that there are immigrants from so many diverse regions of China and Southeast Asia. Diners can experience regional specialties in a restaurant atmosphere that symbolizes the culture from which the cuisine comes. This kind of experience informs diners' expectations of what constitutes authentic food. Food from Vietnam, Thailand, Malaysia, Yunnan, Taiwan, Hunan, Fujian, Sichuan, and Shanghai, in addition to Cantonese mainstays, can all be experienced in Chinatown. Shanghai soup dumplings, Fujianese chicken wing tips, northern Chinese breads, hand-pulled and knife-cut noodles from Lanzhou, and a Hunanese dish of red-cooked pork favored by Mao Zedong are examples of what one can discover (Spiller 2008).

Even restaurants that specialize in a particular regional cuisine can also actively manage to appeal to specific kinds of customers. Some restaurateurs are aware that the ambience they create is part of this experience and strategically deploy symbols to create subtle exoticism and authenticity. For example, a Vietnamese restaurant owner hangs signs in Vietnamese knowing that the absence of signs in English will appeal to an Anglo clientele (Hage 1997, referenced in Ray 2011).

Yunnan cuisine is an exemplar cuisine currently enjoying New York's dining spotlight. This is not based alone on migration of people from Yunnan; it results from cosmopolitanism associated with Yunnan cuisine in Chinese cities. Yunnan cuisine has come out of the shadows of Chinatown largely because it is enjoying a boom in Beijing and Shanghai. A Beijing restaurateur thought New Yorkers would love the food from this little-known part of southwestern China that borders Laos, Myanmar, Tibet, and Vietnam and so brought it to New York City. The only Yunnan cooking in New York used to be found in Sunset Park, Brooklyn's Chinatown, and was for immigrants rather than cosmopolitan diners. Now two new Yunnan-inspired restaurants have opened on the gentrifying edges of Chinatown in TriBeCa and the Lower East Side. When interviewed in the *Daily News*, the chef and owner of one new Yunnan restaurant expressed his philosophy on authenticity: "Chefs keep the authentic Chinese technique, but they bring in new ingredients or combinations. We have to modernize it. We shouldn't just create traditional Yunnan cooking because what you end up having is another Chinatown" (Lee 2012). Hybrid cuisine is seen as modern and Chinatown is associated with traditional cooking, even though history tells us that neither perception is accurate.

Over time, hybrid cuisines become traditions in their own right. At a Malaysian restaurant in Chinatown, Nyonya, named after ethnic Chinese ladies in Malaysia, they proclaim that they offer "the most authentic nyonya cuisine to the affluent palate of our American and Asian friends."[9] The term *affluent* in this proclamation seems to be an awkward translation, but it shows that the restaurateur's intent is to market a hybrid cuisine as traditional to customers from multiple ethnic backgrounds and of a similar, wealthy class.

Authenticity can also be associated with nostalgia in Chinatown, particularly in regard to Cantonese dim sum. A ninety-year-old tea parlor on Doyers Street, one of the narrow, curved lanes in Chinatown that evokes pre-automobile urban design, just underwent a restoration when a nephew of the previous owner took over. He wants to preserve the historical character of the restaurant— the 1920s vintage red booths and original tea bar—and also modernize the menu. His explicit goal is to provide a learning experience for his customers. Amid all the hybrid and new regional cuisines, he wants to make sure there is a restaurant that defines what traditional Cantonese dim sum is, while meeting modern expectations. If patrons want to drink Earl Grey while eating their taro root dumplings, then they will serve it (Sidman 2011). His responsibility as a public provider of a Cantonese food tradition is to oversee his restaurant in a historically accurate yet flexible way.

The past and present of Chinese restaurants in New York provide evidence that they do have material and symbolic importance in supporting Chinatown's food network and also defining the heterogeneous category of food represented by the term *Chinese food*. Restaurants enable cultural border crossing, acting as symbols of tradition and of acculturation. They introduce Americans to new regional cuisines and hybrid dishes. As a *New York Times* reporter said, Chinatown feels like a museum that gets new curators from time to time (Wells 2012). Whether it's a historical Cantonese tea parlor, a Fuzhounese banquet hall, or a noodle shop with urban sensibilities, there is always something old, new, and Asian inspired in Chinatown's restaurant world.

The Role of Chinese Restaurants in Shaping the "Ethnic" Experience

Hybrid cuisines can be dismissed as adulterations of pure tradition—abominations of postmodern, confused identities. The history of Chinese food in the United States shows that experimentation with "authentic" foods is hardly new; it is a recurring theme throughout our history. American history also shows that hybridization of Chinese food is not the result of adulteration from a more powerful American entity; it was not cultural subjugation. It was Chinese chefs initiating the transformation of their traditional cuisine in search of a wider market. Feeling the tension between clinging to traditional or familiar foods and the desire to experiment with new ones is a common human experience (Gabaccia 1998). Foods are concrete symbols of human culture and identity. Human beings cling to familiar foods because the latter are associated with every dimension of social and cultural life. When people want to celebrate their culture or themselves, they elevate their foods and demean others. When they want to express curiosity and tolerance and are willing to incorporate new cultural dimensions into their identities, they eat the other.

Being served ethnic food by members of a minority culture in a restaurant setting also maintains societal hierarchies consistent with the expectations of some members of the majority culture. Chinese restaurants in the United States began attracting American clientele in the early 1900s during times of political antipathy and exclusion towards Chinese. A Chinese waiter serving an Anglo diner in a Chinese restaurant can be perceived as consistent with the social hierarchy between members of a minority and a majority culture. The cost of the dining experience also plays a role in the larger experience. While there have always been a few high-priced Chinese restaurants in New York, Chinese food in the United States has still not reached the level of haute cuisine and won the cultural reverence that comes with that designation. In a survey of Zagat-rated Chinese restaurants in New York City in 2006, it was found that Chinese restaurants cluster in the group of most inexpensive ethno-national restaurants. Ray (2010) suggested that the expectation for the cost of ethnic dining is related to the association of that cuisine with poor immigrants. Because Chinese immigrants and subsequent generations in the United States have higher than average household incomes as well suggests that there are other factors at play, perhaps that deal with the place of Chinese in relation to Americans in the global political economy.

As much as Chinatown's restaurants are celebrated, there are generalized traits about them that the majority culture disfavors. The utilitarian atmosphere, the subpar service, and the possibility of trade in illegal food items like exotic animal parts and homemade fermented beverages are ridiculed, but tolerated.

The toleration might be because these traits are in line with expectations, or because they are simply understood in economic terms. You get what you pay for, and Chinatown restaurants are, and should be, cheap. Chinatown restaurants are loved because they serve diverse, and usually good-quality, food at low prices. This kind of value is portrayed in the media about the dining-out landscape in Manhattan as unparalleled and to be preserved. Atmosphere and service seem to be reasonable trade-offs to keep costs down in Chinatown.

There are other trade-offs as well. Chinatown has been mostly resistant to the gentrification that has swept over Manhattan in the past two decades, but the costs of this go deeper than run-down interior spaces and harried wait staff. Entering into the restaurant business is costly and uncertain, and few new restaurants in Chinatown last more that one year. Most restaurant workers who try to start their own restaurant fail. Competition is fierce and often leads to undercutting menu prices (cheap food!). Low prices translate into lower wages, longer hours, corner cutting with ingredients, and sacrifices on sanitation. Labor abuses in the restaurant industry are well documented (Kwong 1996; Guest 2003; Lin 1998). Restaurants provide dead-end jobs for vulnerable individuals when they are portrayed to Chinese immigrants as pathways to the American dream.

The story of a recent immigrant from Fuzhou pulled to the United States by the promise of economic opportunities in the restaurant and garment industries in Chinatown illustrates the problems with the Fuzhounese version of the American dream. After seeking political asylum in the US Virgin Islands and ending up in a children's home in Georgia, he found a sponsor so he could work in the United States and is saddled with a debt of three thousand dollars to his sponsor and twenty-eight thousand dollars to the snakeheads that brought him from China. He relates his situation:

> I've been working in restaurants, mostly doing deliveries on a bicycle. . . . I eat in the restaurant and live in the restaurant if I can. Otherwise I stay wherever I can find a place to lie down. Someday I hope to be a busboy, then waiter, then to reception, and then finally to open my own restaurant. Fuzhounese in America all have this hope. They don't speak English. They have huge problems with their legal status. So they dream of working their way up and someday owning their own restaurant.
>
> Guest 2003, 29

If working in a restaurant is a dead-end job for a Chinese immigrant, then unionization might be seen as a way to improve labor conditions. But labor organization has been mainly out of the mainstream and left to the enclave with its own unjust politics to deal with. The AFL/CIO Hotel and Restaurant Employees and Bartenders Union (Local 69) claimed that Chinese restaurants are too scattered, small, and costly to organize. Low job security, lack of benefits, long hours, and unwelcome chores encouraged Chinese restaurant workers to fight for unionization themselves, forming the Staff and Workers Association, a Chinatown-based voluntary association. This association has won some labor disputes by publicly shaming high-profile restaurant managers in Chinatown for labor abuses (Lee 2002), but still the Chinatown-based Restaurant Owners Association is much more powerful. Members have been identified as leaders of human smuggling networks that bring Fuzhounese undocumented immigrants—who become restaurant workers—to Chinatown (Kwong 1996).

HOMOGENIZATION of food culture through mass production is rife in the American food industry. Ethnic restaurants and alternative food economies fill the need to explore new cultures through food. The survival of ethnic culture in public life and the survival of ethnic restaurants are mutually constitutive. Ethnicity, like authenticity, is not an objective or fixed criterion; it is socially constructed and shifts with expectations of members of the ethnicity and majority culture (Lu and Fine 1995). Restaurants are one way that ethnicity is economically grounded and can become part of a marketing strategy. Chinese restaurant owners in the United States have been very conscious of their public ethnic identity, wanting to appeal to non-ethnics. The culinary traditions that Chinese restaurants present can be simultaneously exotic *and* familiar to mainstream culture, and appeal to multiple segments of the population. Different, yet desired to be eaten. The strategy of Chinese chefs has been to modify traditional foods to make the unfamiliar seem appropriate, comfortable or enticing, playing with the notion of authenticity (Lu and Fine 1995). That which is perceived as authentic Chinese food is actually locally constructed. It is more common to see Chinese restaurants in urban Chinatowns serving food that Chinese immigrants prefer than it is in suburban and working-class neighborhoods without an immigrant population to support them. In urban areas of cultural or artistic capital, cosmopolitan takes on Chinese food appeal to expectations for an innovative dining experience. Chinatown restaurants in urban enclaves have the ingredients they need at hand and have a more diverse clientele. Chinese restaurants outside ethnic enclaves might cater to a more generalized American palate, but they still are symbols of ethnicity along the continuum of factors that shape the concept.

Restaurants in Chinatown help maintain traditions of first and subsequent generations of immigrants; they provide much of the demand for ethnic groceries in the enclave, maintain networks of trade, and provide jobs and paths for upward socioeconomic mobility for some immigrants. It is clear that restaurants play a large role in expanding the influence of Chinatown's alternative food network.

## CHAPTER 7

Chinatown's Food Network and New York City Policies

Chinatown in Lower Manhattan is a unique place—its vibrancy, culture, and commerce breathe life into every edifice, every sidewalk, and every street corner that it occupies. Other Chinatowns in Boston, Philadelphia and San Francisco, even in Flushing, Queens, seem tame and contained in comparison. Manhattan's Chinatown rambles from indoors onto the streets and across its old boundaries into what had been Little Italy and the Jewish Lower East Side.

Life in Chinatown also rambles into other unlikely places. Farmers in South Florida and central Honduras make their livelihoods from the vegetables that characterize Asian cuisines. These cuisines have made their way from East Asia to New York City through a consistent stream of immigration over the past fifty years. Chinese restaurateurs and chefs consciously adapted Chinese foods to the palates of diverse constituencies, making Chinese food one of the United States' most widely embraced ethnic cuisines. People, plants, and culinary traditions crisscross borders in this truly globalized world. On the streets of Chinatown, global processes collide to form something that cannot be designed or remade elsewhere. Chinatown's story is a personal one, full of a cast of actors who leveraged their particular life histories to create something unique.

However unique Chinatown is, there are lessons to be drawn from its way of sourcing and distributing both exotic and ordinary fresh fruits and vegetables. Urban planners and those involved with food systems should take note of the decentralized distribution model that Chinatown uses and the importance that the geographic proximity of food manufacturing and wholesale and retail sectors has for economic development. The current association of "quality food" with high prices and urban development with residential and retail upscaling has led to greater socioeconomic stratification within cities and within American food culture. The disparity in food environments between wealthy and low-income neighborhoods has become an important issue for study and for political action. The correlation between low-income census tracts, lack of full service supermarkets, and rates of obesity is well documented and has given rise to the concept of the "food desert" (Ver Ploeg et al. 2009). The causal links between food access, food choice, and diet-related diseases are much harder to establish, but many municipalities have developed programs and policies to incentivize increased availability of fresh fruits, vegetables, and other whole foods in food deserts, with New York as one example of a large city that has taken action to improve access to healthy foods. However, most incentives and metrics for determining "healthy" food availability are geared toward supermarkets, not small-scale independent food retailers like those that dominate in Chinatown.

Chinatown's food system provides a model that is culturally and socioeconomically inclusive, supports small business, provides market outlets for small and middle-sized farms that have been marginalized from national and international markets, and supports agricultural practices that use crop diversity rather than monocropping. Independent food retailers can be more responsive to the needs and demands of neighborhood residents and can include more diverse kinds of producers than supermarkets that have centralized supply chains and management structures and prefer to source from high-volume producers. Local and regional government officials interested in crafting policies to create more sustainable food systems should learn from the retail and wholesale distribution structure of Chinatown's food system, whose organization enables an affordable supply of fresh fruits and vegetables and includes small-scale and regional producers.

Food Policy in New York City

Food policies and programs initiated by New York City government have been changing rapidly in recent years, with significant efforts put forward to reduce food related illnesses and promote healthy eating. In 2007 Mayor Michael Bloomberg established the Office of the Food Policy Coordinator in order to oversee the efforts of city agencies working to improve access to healthy food. Historically the city's hunger-prevention efforts were not integrated with their attempts to promote healthy eating, but now the Office of the Food Policy Coordinator is working to increase access to food support programs, improve the healthfulness of meals served by city programs, and promote healthy food retail and demand.

Although hunger and nutrition are key drivers of the city's food politics, so are jobs, education, and environmental concerns. In a span of a several years, different city offices have released numerous food-related policy reports, which use a food systems framework to integrate the city's effort to better manage production, distribution, consumption, and waste. In 2009, the office of the Manhattan borough president, Scott Stringer, released the document *Food in the Public Interest: How New York City's Food Policy Holds the Key to Hunger, Health, Jobs, and the Environment*.[1] This report emerged from a conference of over six hundred food advocates, community activists, social service providers, and policy makers hosted by the Borough President Stringer in 2008 with Columbia University's School of International and Public Affairs, Earth Institute Urban Design Lab, and Office of Environmental Stewardship. The call to action in the report is framed by the increase of obesity and its associated health risks in New York City, particularly in low-income, black, and Latino communities, and the recommendations are far reaching. They include the reduction of hunger, a local foodshed analysis, an increase in market options for regional farmers, the development of "food enterprise zones" in food desert neighborhoods, nutrition education campaigns, and increased staffing at the Office of Food Policy.

Also in 2009, Stringer released two other reports explicitly focused on improving the city's food retail environment: *FoodStat: Measuring the Retail Food Environment in NYC Neighborhoods* and *Planning for Healthy Neighborhoods: Including Food Infrastructure in the City's Environmental Review*.[2] These two reports seek policy changes to draw attention to environments with insufficient food retail by initiating a simple metric system of neighborhood assessment and to require "healthy food infrastructure" to be added as an assessment category within the city's environmental quality review process. The idea is that if a proposed development project might displace healthy food retailer, distribution site, or urban agriculture site, a full environmental impact statement would be needed. *FoodStat* calls for the adoption of a neighborhood-by-neighborhood assessment of food environments using a simplified measure that divides the total number of bodegas (convenience stores) and fast food restaurants, by the total number of supermarkets and produce vendors. This measure is supposed to represent the ratio of unhealthy food options to healthy food options in a neighborhood.

These reports were followed by the 2010 release also by Stringer of *FoodNYC: A Blueprint for a Sustainable Food System*, which emerged from the "NYC Food and Climate Summit," held at New York University in December 2009.[3] This report is meant to build on *Food in the Public Interest* and uses a more explicit environmental framing to emphasize many of the same policy recommendations. This time the call to action involves climate change, population growth, greenhouse gas emissions, and asthma, but supporting local and regional food production and procurement, and the wider topic of economic development through food, are still at the heart of the discussion. An addition here is the reduction of food waste. There was also a request to the mayor's office to take up food in its sustainability plan. This recommendation came to pass in 2011 when Mayor Bloomberg added a section on food to PlaNYC, a comprehensive effort encompassing twenty-five city agencies to create a sustainable New York. Again, the policy recommendations of PlaNYC focus on local and New York State food procurement, waste reduction, and the increase in access to fresh fruits and vegetables in underserved neighborhoods.[4]

The list of policy reports and recommendations from city offices goes on. In 2010, New York City Council Speaker Christine Quinn unveiled *FoodWorks: A Vision to Improve New York City's Food System*.[5] The New York City Department of Health, Department of City Planning, and the New York City Economic Development Corporation conducted a study in 2008: *Going to Market: New York City's Neighborhood Grocery Store and Supermarket Shortage*.[6] Both documents use the causes of health and the environment as rationale to support more local food production and distribution and more evenly situated supermarkets throughout New York. City laws and programs have been put in place to these ends. Local Law 52 of 2011 establishes baseline food metrics, the campaign Shop Healthy NYC aims to improve fresh food offerings at bodegas, and the FRESH (Food Retail Expansion to Support Health) program focuses on food access. The emphasis on supermarkets as a linchpin of healthy food distribution in low-income neighborhoods and support for local food production and procurement remain steady; local laws have established financial and zoning incentives to attract supermarkets and facilitate urban agriculture projects.

There is a remarkable absence of discussion about ethnic food systems in New York's neighborhoods and the challenges and opportunities of these alternative food systems. Communities of color are more often seen as being in need than as producers of food systems in their own right. They are not seen as the producers of food cultures that are revered in cosmopolitan eating circles and that influence mainstream tastes. How ethnic food systems work needs to be understood and supported.

Reports, plans, and initiatives that touch on food distribution represent political strides that can direct the use of city resources to make great improvements in the food system. The case of Chinatown's food system can be instructive in these efforts and should not be overlooked. In particular, two structural features of Chinatown's food system are relevant to current policy discussions: decentralization and clustering. Removing wholesale businesses from integrated residential and commercial neighborhoods should not be standard practice. The city's emphasis on removing wholesale food operations from across the city and centralizing it in the South Bronx is detrimental to small, independent food enterprises. The wholesale food sector is key to the viability of producers, retailers, and restaurants, and its locations matter. There is also a theoretical orientation that I believe should be inherent in policy rationale: a sustainable food system is one that is embedded locally and globally, simultaneously, with neither economic sphere being privileged over the other.

Supporting Decentralized Food Distribution

One of the most important features of Chinatown's food system is the proximity of wholesalers to retailers. The existence of wholesalers in the neighborhood enables Chinatown's micromarket structure to exist: over eighty-five retail vendors sell two hundred different types of fresh fruits and vegetables. The storefront and makeshift vendors need to be close to the refrigerated storage that the wholesaler provides. They also rely on their wholesalers for delivery of produce. The bare-bones nature of produce retail sales keeps the cost of produce low for the consumer. No fancy temperature- and humidity-controlled displays are needed. Produce is kept fresh because deliveries are small in quantity and frequent. The use of electricity for refrigeration and delivery trucks is cut out of the retail end, reducing infrastructure and operating costs and the capital investment needed to get into produce retail. With this system, the quality and freshness of produce remains high.

This distribution model stands apart from the city-supported prevalent one: the use of Hunts Point Food Distribution Center, one of the largest such centers in the world. This facility is located on a 329-acre site in the Hunts Point neighborhood of the South Bronx and contains the New York City Terminal Market, with over forty produce vendors; the Hunts Point Cooperative Market, with over fifty meat and poultry processors and distributors; the new Fulton Fish Market, with about thirty-five wholesale seafood dealers; and the Wholesale Greenmarket, with about twelve farmers, from New York and New Jersey. All told, the center houses over eight hundred industrial businesses, produces twenty-five thousand jobs, and generates over three billion dollars in revenue. Ironically, all this activity takes place in a neighborhood riddled with poverty and crime. Half the residents of Hunts Point live below the poverty line and 60 percent are unemployed. Drug use, drug sales, and prostitution are rampant.

Hunts Point Food Distribution Center is clearly not a community-revitalization project, but the stark economic difference between the activities within the center and the situation outside it represents a lost opportunity to use food distribution and processing as a way to support a community and a region. Each of the city's food policy documents mentioned above calls for the renovation of Hunts Point Terminal Produce Market, without giving thought to other places that could host wholesale produce distribution in a way that integrates community jobs and food needs on the retail end. Paradoxically, city initiatives to promote access to fresh fruits and vegetables focus only on the retail end.

The lack of integration between the retail and wholesale distribution efforts is something that needs reconsidering. Chinatown's food system shows how the proximate integration of wholesale and retail supports a dynamic, entrepreneurial system of food exchange. Imagine if other communities were integrated so that neighborhoods could have more robust food markets. There could be Mexican produce markets in East Harlem; West African produce markets in Central Harlem; South Indian produce markets in Jackson Heights, Queens, and Murray Hill in Manhattan. There could also be wholesalers who deal exclusively in local and regional goods that are located in neighborhoods where restaurants and produce retailers would benefit from such a facility.

One of the goals of the City Council's *FoodWorks* and Borough President Stringer's *FoodNYC* is to improve food distribution in New York City through infrastructure enhancements, technological advances, alternative transportation, and integrated planning, with a focus on updating and expanding Hunts Point Terminal Market. One of the strategies offered in *FoodWorks* to achieve this goal is to transform the Hunts Point Distribution Center into a hub for citywide food system improvement. While this statement of purpose can be interpreted in many ways, the use of the word *hub* invokes a set of meanings that have been swirling around in the world of food system reform and is receiving a good deal of support from the United States Department of Agriculture. The working definition of *regional food hub* in use by the USDA but not yet officially endorsed by the agency is "a centrally located facility with a business management structure facilitating the aggregation, storage, processing, distribution and/or marketing of locally and regionally produced food products" (Barham 2011).

The objectives of a regional food hub are to expand market opportunities for farmers; to create jobs; and to improve access to fresh, healthy foods for consumers. These objectives are very much in step with each of the city's food policy documents, but it would be a mistake to consider Hunts Point Distribution Center the only place to become a food hub. Remember the mantra of

Chinatown's food system, "Location, location, location." The location of Hunts Point would limit its utility in a way that would not transform the city's food distribution system.

Stringer's *FoodNYC* recognizes that many restaurateurs and grocers find it difficult to make regular trips all the way to Hunts Point to procure foods. This problem of distance is a limitation on the effort to establish a wholesale farmers' market there and on proposals to recommend finding city-owned property in other boroughs. It would make a lot of logistical sense to locate a wholesale market more proximate to the buyers who would support it.

Supporting Ethnic Food Clusters

Chinese cuisine is a beloved part of New York City's food landscape. Whether Hunan, Szechuan, or Cantonese, comfort food or three-star Michelin cuisine—New York City has historically been a test bed for new Chinese dishes as well as a showcase for traditional ones. Succulent soup dumplings, crispy Peking duck, and savory scallion pancakes are revered as mainstays, and wacky offshoots such as Reuben spring rolls and General Tso's monkfish tempt taste buds and stimulate the imagination.

Once Chinese immigrants started to settle in the notorious Five Points area of Manhattan in the later part of the 1800s, it did not take long for New Yorkers of all kinds to become curious about the foods of China. By the turn of the twentieth century ambitious Chinese restaurateurs were opening Chinese restaurants north of the Chinatown neighborhood to cater to non-Chinese clienteles. Now Chinese cuisine is a feature of tourism campaigns and media dedicated to food culture.

After the events of September 11, 2001, Chinatown experienced an economic downturn. The Lower Manhattan Development Corporation worked with NYC & Company, the city's official tourism marketing organization, to launch Explore Chinatown, a campaign to reinstate Chinatown as a visitor destination. Chinatown's eateries and food markets are a key part of this campaign: the website Explore Chinatown (www.explorechinatown.com) featured the "Ultimate New York Chinese Food Glossary" in 2011. The glossary contains references, stories, and pictures of Chinese foods, food establishments, and restaurateurs and was compiled by the popular blog *Eater*, which in 2011 hosted its first "Chinese Food Week" to feature people and food from the world of Chinese cuisine in New York City and to provide a platform for readers to weigh in with their restaurant recommendations. The city's tourism organization also features Chinatown restaurants specifically. In 2012, during the twentieth annual New York City Restaurant Week, Chinatown had its own Restaurant Week, when three-course dinners were offered by participating restaurants for $18.88.

Chinatown restaurants are the cheerleaders of Chinatown's food system: they dazzle diners and showcase the exotic foods sold on the surrounding streets. The restaurants also anchor a unique and important industry feature, Chinatown's food cluster. This was identified in a 2009 study by Hunter College's Urban Planning studio; the cluster includes restaurants, restaurant and kitchen supply stores, food distributors and wholesale companies, food manufacturing companies, restaurant business consultants, and food related-businesses such as printing and employment services that directly support the food cluster. The researchers found that the food cluster could comprise up to 23 percent of all jobs in the Chinatown area and draws dollars regularly from not only Chinatown residents but also others from throughout New York City and up and down the East Coast (McCormick et al. 2009, 1). Like the produce wholesalers in Chinatown, other food industry businesses provide unique services within the East Coast metropolis.

Clusters are an interesting geographic phenomenon because they challenge the concept that place does not matter in the new global economy. They are inherently place based; they are physical concentrations of interconnected companies and associated institutions in a particular field and arise because they increase the productivity with which companies can compete by leveraging local assets. Clusters demonstrate that comparative advantage can lie with the knowledge, relationships, and ambitions of local places. In an increasingly complex and dynamic world economy, geographic, cultural, and institutional proximity provides companies with special access, closer relationships, better information, powerful incentives, and other advantages that are difficult to tap from a distance (Porter 1998). The entrepreneurs of Chinatown's food cluster, like those of its food system, which extends to Florida and Honduras, use their relationships, cultural knowledge, language skills, and access to unique forms of information to develop competitive, widely reputable businesses.

Ethnic neighborhoods throughout urban areas are often distinguished by the unique foods and cuisines they offer and that make them tourist destinations. It is even possible that ethnic neighborhoods of past waves of immigration retain their ethnic identities through the food-related businesses that remain long after the first- and second-generation immigrant residents have left. One iconic New York City neighborhood that has maintained a successful base of restaurants, grocers, and food manufacturers is Arthur Avenue, the "Little Italy of the Bronx." Visitors from all over the metropolitan area and beyond go there to enjoy New York's Italian cultural heritage, which remains in the businesses around Arthur Avenue even though Italian residents have long left the neighborhood.

An anchor for the food cluster around Arthur Avenue is the indoor retail marketplace that was established by Mayor Fiorello La Guardia to clear the streets of pushcart vendors. This is one of four remaining marketplaces established by La Guardia. To revitalize the four markets and establish a new one in the former Fulton Street Fish Market at South Street Seaport, in 2010 the City Council initiated the program NYers 4 Markets. Pike's Place Market in Seattle is an inspiration to the markets program. With two hundred year-round businesses, 190 craftspeople and one hundred farmers who rent table space by the day, and countless street performers and musicians, Pike's Place sees ten million visitors a year and is dubbed "the Soul of Seattle." Market revitalization is included in the City Council's plan FoodWorks, as part of the strategy to generate growth and employment in the food manufacturing sector.

Cluster-development initiatives are an important new direction in economic policy that need to be considered in urban food system planning. The neighborhood is the marketplace—the marketplace does not exist just within the physical confines of a designated indoor space. The food cluster approach would offer a means of supporting the nonretail parts crucial to any food system. In Chinatown, retail grocery stores make up only 19 percent of the number of businesses in the food cluster. Wholesale, manufacturing, and service providers are crucial to the success of retailers. Proximity reduces transport costs, redundancy in infrastructure, and easily accessible supplies. It facilitates small business, the development of relationships, and knowledge formation about consumer demands and market trends—the very attributes that make the Chinatown food system competitive and flexible in long-distance trade. Geographic clustering also facilitates service to more distant customers. Restaurant equipment, menu printers, and kitchen supply distributors in Manhattan's Chinatown report that up to 80 percent of their customers are from out of state; Fujianese restaurants report that 40–70 percent of their customers are from out of state, especially to host banquets for special occasions (McCormick et al. 2009, 17). Chinatown is the place to shop and dine not only because of the specialized products that are offered but also for the variety and competitive prices.

Although the location of Chinatown contributes to the success of the food cluster, it also presents many challenges. Escalating rents and real estate taxes have burdened small business owners. One business owner interviewed by McCormick and her team said that his rent was three thousand dollars a month in 2000 but had been six thousand dollars since 2008. The burden of the real estate tax, a portion of which was passed on to him by the building owner, rose from eight hundred in 2000 to ten thousand dollars in 2008. The encroaching gentrification of SoHo and the Lower East Side is in part to blame. The growing population of New York City at large is also a contentious issue, sparking many debates about how New York is going to accommodate the projected one million new residents by 2030. In the years after Mayor Bloomberg took office in 2002, he rezoned one-fifth of New York City. Upzoning, or allowing for more dense development, is concentrated around transit-rich areas, and downzoning is being used in more car-centered areas of the city—but it is also being employed to preserve the character of some streets and neighborhoods (Kazis 2010). Chinatown activists are fighting to downzone Chinatown to preserve stable rents for its many low-income residents, as well as its small businesses. A group of real estate developers want to see more high-rises along Canal Street because it is Chinatown's main thoroughfare, but opponents argue that Chinatown's economy is driven by small businesses, and if those die, Chinatown's economy goes with it (Troianovski 2010).

Indeed, Chinatown's food cluster is made up of small businesses and, conservatively, provides 23 percent of the enclave's jobs. Fifty-four percent of food manufacturing, 75 percent of wholesale businesses, 72 percent of retail operations, and 61 percent of full-service restaurants have no more than four employees (McCormick et al. 2009, 4). These businesses have given Chinatown the reputation of being the preeminent place to go for all things related to Asian food and cooking. They attract clients from all along the East Coast. In the produce sector, the small businesses situated in Chinatown provide market access to myriad farmers abroad so that they have more choices about how to make their livelihoods. All this demonstrates that Chinatown holds significance both within and beyond its boundaries, making it a place to recognize and support.

Locally and Globally Embedded Food Systems

Chinatown's food system is powerfully rooted in its place and is simultaneously dependent on global flows of goods, people, and knowledge. It is a transnational community of immigrants that provisions ethnic goods and services desired by city residents, tourists, and businesspeople from the city and beyond. Its food system is composed of small-scale firms that form an industry cluster in Chinatown and make it anomalous in the context of the dominant food retail sector controlled by big business.

The urban dimensions of Chinatown's food system—its proximity, concentration, knowledge, and buzz—facilitate the system. They create social norms and codes of conduct that facilitate learning and innovation. But exclusive face-to-face interaction and the development of local practices can also undermine a system by leading to rigid conventions. Thus, the argument can be made that firms thrive when they are rooted in a dynamic local community while also making and sustaining global lines of communication that bring in new ideas and practices.

As in Chinatown, much is happening in new urban food economies. In Toronto, where food manufacturing is its second-largest industry because of the presence of Pepsi, Nestlé, Kellogg's, and Kraft, a so-called creative food economy is booming. Organic, specialty, and ethnic food producers, processors, distributors, and retailers—small and midsized enterprises—are the fastest-growing sector of the food industry. The motivation behind the new food companies forming in Toronto can be attributed to the urban experience, which includes homegrown attributes and those that are brought to the city by a great diversity of people from around the world. Problems of hunger, poor nutrition, and restricted access to fresh food are factors propelling the creative food economy, as is the hotbed of ideas generated by public agencies and nonprofits. But among the most salient features of Toronto's creative food economy is the social inclusion that is fueled by the city's cultural diversity. Creative or otherwise, alternative food economies such as organic and artisanal foods suffer from the reputation (and practice, in some cases) of being for elitist consumers. By focusing on the role of diversity as a means for social inclusion, researchers observed that ethnic food establishments in Toronto provide an opportunity to explore and experiment with other ways of living, like a "gateway to humanity." This can be means to move past simply tolerance or celebration of others to understanding and validation of others (Donald and Blay-Palmer 2006, 191).

The alternative food networks of Toronto and Chinatown demonstrate that the concept of embeddedness has economic and social meanings. When referring to alternative food networks, in which farmers' markets and community-supported agriculture have been the stars, social embeddedness is inherently invoked by a transaction that cuts out the intermediary and puts the farmer and consumer face to face. The ideal assumed through this kind of transaction is that social relations will develop and somehow trump what is otherwise an antisocial economic transaction (possibly one that supports environmental degradation and labor injustices). The idea of knowing one's farmer has gained much resonance in the American consciousness and is a powerful way to garner support for farmers, woefully undersupported members of the economy. It is a mistake, though, to conflate only these kinds of market transactions with social ties. As Chinatown's food system shows us, all kinds of markets are suffused with embeddedness. Trust and social connection do not distinguish local from global food systems (Hinrichs 2000). Spatial and social relations can be conflated. Social injustices can exist in the local sphere; likewise, social embeddedness can exist in the global sphere. Hinrichs goes so far as to warn that sentimental assumptions about face-to-face interactions must be tempered with self-interest and a clear view of prices, ideas that the market espouses that are not necessarily morally negative but are important to successful business. Trust and compassion can also make their way into the market in the form of forgiveness for late payments and acceptance of undesirable prices, actions that abound in the trade of Asian fruits and vegetables between farmers and distributors. The social ties between farmers and distributors lubricate the wheels of the market and soften the form of exchange.

There are many reasons to turn political focus from global to local sourcing of food. But Chinatown's food system reminds us about what we might be overlooking in the transition. It also challenges us to question the attributes of a food system that are worth fighting for and ask whether geographic scale is the best way to discern the "good" from the "bad." Chinatown is a unique marketplace for foods that are simultaneously exotic and traditional, new and old. It is the place to shop for peoples of Asian descent and it is a center of tourism in New York City. The success of its food industry cluster and its food system at large is important to understand and to recognize within the discussion of the future of New York City's food politics.

WE must accept that choosing between local and global trade is not an either-or situation. New York City in particular does not have the luxury of making such a decision. It needs both global and local trade to feed its over eight million residents. There are too many people in the city for the agricultural land around New York to support (Peters et al. 2008). This does not mean that we should let the theory of comparative advantage govern our food systems and that we should accept the decline of agriculture in the New York region. We should be promoting urban agriculture and agricultural development adjacent to urban areas. It would be, and has been, foolish not to. The social movements that have led to real change in how cities feed themselves through farmers' markets, community-supported agriculture, and rooftop and community gardens is incredibly exciting and beneficial to society.

Nevertheless, New York City, as well as other urban centers with large and heterogeneous populations, will have to keep sourcing food from outside their regions. The model of Chinatown's food system offers some ideas about how to do it in unconventional yet old-fashioned ways. The decentralized model of produce retail and wholesale is how cities used to supply their food. Street peddlers and greengrocers were integral parts of urban commerce, particularly in immigrant neighborhoods where the food trade offered obtainable jobs and entrepreneurial opportunities for people with limited English-language skills or questionable legal status. The hawkers and gawkers were part of the New York City that Jane Jacobs made a case for saving in her 1961 classic, *The Death and Life of Great American Cities.*

The process of bringing life back to city streets through food has been in full swing in New York City. Food trucks sell anything from cupcakes to tacos, and street carts laden with fruits are popping up in neighborhoods with limited access to fresh foods. Of course, the vendors of the city's mainstays, hot dogs, soft pretzels, and candied nuts, still abound. Festivals devoted to artisanal food and the city's farmers' markets revitalize public spaces, provide access to healthy foods in places otherwise bereft of options, and support grassroots food cultures. These initiatives mesh well with the structure of Chinatown's food system, where food life never left the city streets. Chinatown's food system might find much appreciation in a city so devoted to food as New York, but it might also provide ideas for ways that New York can support ethnic food systems and global embeddedness in a meaningful way. It is time for local politicians to assert what kind of food landscape they want to retain or remake.

Conclusion

DIVERSITY AND DYNAMISM IN GLOBAL MARKETS

Chinatown's food network is a result of global and local processes. The produce brokers who supply Chinatown have been building connections between markets in New York City, Boston, and Philadelphia to production points around the northeastern metropolises and the year-round growing climates of Florida, California, Mexico, Central America, and the Caribbean. But who makes whom in this network of exchange? Do urban markets determine the production practices and economic opportunities of farmers in whatever far-flung place they exist? Or does the place of production—its particular geography—shape the makeup of the urban market?

The relationship between cities and their ever more distant hinterlands has always been complex. Cities are economic powerhouses whose markets are desired by rural producers of all kinds, not just agriculturalists. Labor and land costs, trade agreements, and market opportunities shape what is grown where. Yet how agriculture is organized in any place is very much attributable to geography.

When an urban consumer picks up a bunch of litchis, a Chinese eggplant, or a bag of baby bok choy in Chinatown, that consumer benefits from a supply network that shapes agriculture in distant places. Supply networks are also shaped by the particular places they connect. The land use histories, labor relations, real estate markets, and capital investments of agricultural production sites influence what is grown and how, and who the growers are. If it weren't for immigration from Asia to New York City, and the work of ethnic restaurants to popularize Asian foods, the Floridian and Honduran farmers would not be growing tat soi or fuzzy squash. Likewise, if it weren't for the drained Everglades or the irrigation canals built off the Rio Humuya and the Pan-American Highway in Comayagua, those Floridian and Honduran farmers would not be growing anything for New York City, or any other, markets. This is how the particularities of a place and global processes are mutually constitutive—they influence each other.

We can gain insight into a global network of trade by following the commodity chain from the vendor at the corner of Canal and Mulberry Streets to a backyard homegarden outside Miami or to a small farm in the Comayagua Valley of Honduras. We should ask how this network of trade challenges ideas about what constitutes a global food system. Aspects of it are what one might expect of a global food system, as prescribed by neoliberal reforms: chemical-intensive production practices, contract farming, cutthroat brokers, and long-distance transport from farm to market. Not coincidentally, these conventions of a global food system represent the very aspects of food systems that are seen as problematic and in need of reform by its critics. What about the unexpected features of Chinatown's food system: the use of crop diversity on farms, the inclusion of small farmers and homegardeners, the socially embedded relations between farmers and brokers, the small steps of resistance of Honduran contract farmers to improve their contracts with exporters, and the bustling food economy of Chinatown? Are these also representative of a global food system, and if they are, might they be worth perpetuating?

There are over two hundred fresh fruits and vegetables for sale in Manhattan's Chinatown year round. Old and new Chinese immigrants, as well as Vietnamese, Thai, Malaysian, Cambodian, Laotian immigrants, make a living within Chinatown's food system. Countless other first-, second-, and multigeneration Americans patronize Chinatown's shops, street vendors, and restaurants. The cultural heterogeneity of the system is iconic of New York City. The makeup of the cosmopolitan dining experience depends on ethnic diversity of foods and their producers. The abundance, freshness, and cost of produce in Chinatown are unrivaled in the city. Where else can you get a pound of baby bok choy or Chinese eggplant for a dollar?

Chinatown markets offer an outstanding variety of good-quality products for outrageously low prices. In order for a marketplace that comprises many small vendors and a great diversity of products to be steadily supplied throughout the year, a dynamic, flexible network of production and distribution must be in place. The marketing channels that deliver the variety and volume of products to Chinatown are constantly growing and changing. Entrepreneurs continually enter and leave the system and continually look for new suppliers and products. Because of this dynamism and competition, successful farmers and brokers are constantly experimenting with new products and new places. In this era when offshore sourcing of produce is the dominant trend, Chinatown brokers do not shy away from global trade. Instead they use their social networks to develop new trade relations. The globalization of Chinatown's food system has resulted from the actions of multiple individuals, in a bottom-up rather than a top-down fashion.

Chinatown's food system exemplifies an alternative form of globalization that some scholars call globalization from below, globalization from the margins, and transnational urbanism (Glick Schiller 1999; Basch et al. 1994; Appadurai 1996; Smith 2001). As a process it is not something extrinsic to daily life, or imposed by regulatory bodies, but rather is a result of new spatial arrangements made by individuals. Globalization, in this sense, is the means of conducting business over widening distances and distended social relations. As Smith points out, "Specific collectivities—local households, kin networks, elite fractions, and other emergent local formations—actively pursue such strategies as transnational migration, transnational social movements or transnational economic or cultural entrepreneurship to sustain or transform resources, including cultural resources, in the face of the neoliberal storm" 2001, 167.

Chinese immigrant entrepreneurs have indeed transformed their cultural and economic resources in a way that has led to globally distended networks of trade. What remains exceptional is that they have done so in a way that mimics and interacts with dominant systems of food trade, while also remaining outside of them.

Ethnic Entrepreneurship in the Global Marketplace

There are several contributing factors that begin to explain Chinatown's food system as it exists today. Overseas Chinese have seen entrepreneurship as a traditional path to success (Kwong 1996). Chinese Americans dominate the Chinese food sector in New York City, from the supply of ingredients to preparation and service. The ethnic character of the food products, as well as the community in which they are sold (Chinatown), characterize the system as separate from society at large. "Ethnicity" shields these businesses from takeover by American agribusiness and grocery corporations. Because Cantonese- and Mandarin-language skills and Chinese identity are needed within Chinatown to supply the retail end of this system, Chinese brokers control market access. Non-Chinese are involved at other points along the commodity chain, such as in farming and exporting from Florida and Latin America, but trustworthy relationships with Chinatown brokers are necessary for long-term success. Relationships were formed through shared ethnicity and kinship and through friendship. People found partners through business associations, community and religious organizations, and former employment.

Extreme competition, particularly on the retail end, keeps companies within the system from getting too big. It also keeps quality high but prices low. In Manhattan's Chinatown alone there are ninety produce vendors and twelve wholesalers. In a race to keep up with competition, wholesalers look for ways to expand and make new contacts. Many "new" entrepreneurs have got their start by working for others in the system and have learned the business through an informal structure of apprenticeship. Other entrepreneurs are family members who opened an independent branch of the family business at a different point in the commodity chain, or are children who have inherited the family business. Still other entrepreneurs look to friends and associates for potential business partners. Seventy-one percent of the actors in the network of trade between Honduras, Florida, and New York came into the network through a social contact, and 61 percent of the actors in the network trade with people with whom they have a social tie. Trust can be very elusive, however; it is not guaranteed through shared ethnicity or the other types of social relations we have seen. Successful farmers and distribution firms are constantly negotiating their business relationships, extending and intertwining the social networks that unite those involved in Chinatown's food system.

The social networking aspect of Chinatown's food system is critical to its success, and while business relations are not bound by shared ethnicities, a range of East and Southeast Asian ethnicities that become lumped into the category *Asian* by non-Asians, has become a definitive feature of the system to people outside it. Insiders use the perception of ethnicity, language, and the barriers created by defining ethnic differences to keep control of their industry.

One outcome of seeking out new trade partners and keeping up with global economics is the inclusion of new production locations in the system. Disparate natural and political environments have become subject to the same economic fluctuations as a result of participating in the global marketplace. The mixing of people in very different political-economic situations through global markets often perpetuates social inequities and creates winners and losers. In Chinatown's food system the same entrepreneurs manage various production locales, leading to some complementary rather than antagonistic practices between farmers. The crops produced in Florida complement the seasons in the New York area, and the crops produced in Honduras complement the Florida crops. Small farmers benefit from the marketing infrastructure that exists because of the volume of produce imported and supplied by large growers. The small, highly diverse farmers in Florida (the Southeast Asian homegardeners) do not survive *in spite of* large area growers and international growers; they survive *because* of them. One of the main reasons why small farms cannot survive as markets grow more distant is that they have to "get big or get out." But China-towns across the United States and Canada, the main markets of these farmers, are home to a diverse mix of Asian immigrants from cultures that typically eat many types of fruits and vegetables. The market itself is so varied that there is room for all sorts of specialty growers.

Crop Diversity in the Global Marketplace

The research for this book has shown that the vast diversity of products sold in China-town present many opportunities for crop diversity to be used. My market study in Chinatown reveals that the over two hundred fresh fruits and vegetables are sold in low frequencies across the marketplace. Consumers want a small volume of a great variety of products. In order to serve this market, distributors in Chinatown's food system deal in a varied assortment of fruits and vegetables, and they like to source their inventories through a few farmers. Both large and small growers in Florida have told me that their buyers want to be able to buy an entire inventory of products from one farm. The preference of buyers for "one-stop shopping" forces farmers to maintain diverse crop inventories.

While agricultural research and extension today generally dismiss biodi-verse agriculture and the trend around the world has been crop specialization and monocropping with increased commercialization, the farmers studied for this book have shown that diversity can be used for economic gain and that it is worthwhile to maintain noncommercial crops on the farm for other ecological, social, and cultural benefits. These farmers prefer growing multiple crops because diversity gives them more economic stability and reduces pest pres-sures. Because prices are always fluctuating, some crops may turn out to be less or more profitable than expected. Also, pest and disease outbreaks, extreme weather events, and shifting consumer demands can quickly lead to crop fail-ures. Maintaining a diverse inventory helps minimize overall loss.

The importance of the flexibility that comes with dealing in smaller vol-umes of many crops rather than larger volumes of fewer crops is a factor that has led exporters in Honduras to contract small growers rather than use the model of a plantation-style farm managed by the export company. One exporter told me that he works with small growers because "the agronomic risks of farming are so high that it is better to manage smaller parcels of land so that if there is damage, the entire plantation is not damaged." In the Comayagua Val-ley there were many booms and busts in export agriculture caused by overpro-duction and pest and disease epidemics. But for the decade and a half that

Asian vegetables have been produced there, production has been stable. The introduction of Asian vegetables to the valley has provided over four hundred farmers with a reliable income and has lead to better agronomic practices there. The stability of Asian vegetables developed into a project worthy of investment by national and international agencies. Hondurans are proud of what they have accomplished with the production and export of Asian vegetables and they have held international workshops to present their case as a development model for other Central American countries. There is still much work to be done to improve the production of Asian vegetables in Comayagua, but its successes cannot be overlooked.

Power in the Global Marketplace

The final finding revealed in the book is that spatial expansion of agricultural trade networks alone does not result in the concentration of power along commodity chains. While Chinatown's food system has become increasingly international in scope, expansion is not due to consolidation or buyout of enterprises at the level of production or distribution. Social ties are used to form trade alliances, but firms are individually owned and operated. Competition causes firms to continually enter and leave the system, and it also drives innovation in the system. As we can see from the discussion above, there is room for many types of farmers as well as varied approaches to producing Asian fruits and vegetables.

All the actors in the system echoed the difficulty of dependency on global markets: they are unsure of what the future will bring. This sentiment is encapsulated in the greeting that Johnny Li gave me on my second visit to his farm in Florida. He said, "Good thing you came to visit us this year. We might not be here next year." Anxiety about the future seems to be a prerequisite of farming, but relying on markets subject to great political and economic fluctuations that are out of one's control exacerbates anxieties. Being part of a global system of trade means that one needs to constantly negotiate one's situation and learn to overcome new challenges. Astute monitoring of the market, using the tools at hand, and thinking innovatively are necessary skills for success in global markets. These are the skills that I have identified in the successful farmers and distributors I interviewed for this book. The only way to cope with change is to embrace it.

Chinatown's food system is largely dependent on emigration from East Asia to the United States. Few fruits and vegetables have mainstream appeal, even with the success of Americanized Chinese dishes like chop suey and chow mein. Since the 1960s immigration rates have been steadily increasing, so that Chinese immigrants are one of the fastest-growing groups in New York City. But with China's rapid economic growth and slowing outmigration it is uncertain what the immigration rates of the future will be and how the production of Asian vegetables in the Americas will be affected. While the supply of Asian fruits and vegetables to ethnic restaurants is clearly important in the construction of public ethnic identities and the production of food cultures, we simply do not know the material importance that restaurants have in Chinatown's food network. How much food do they purchase, and what types? Who dines in these restaurants and what do they order? These questions would make for an excellent basis for more research.

The contested, global agro-food systems controlled by a handful of powerful multinational corporations and institutions may dominate food sales (Burch and Lawrence 2007; Magdoff et al. 2000; Weis 2007). They are not the only global food systems, however; alternatives exist. Certain forms of global trade, rather than leading to simplification and loss of diversity, can help preserve traditions as well as foster innovation. Small-scale firms can thrive without inevitable cooptation or appropriation by larger, more powerful global giants. Variety and diversity can exist in a food system at competitive prices, without the sophisticated rhetoric and added value of popular forms of alternative food networks, such as organic and fair trade, that many people are unaware of, disenfranchised from, or completely skeptical of. Chinatown's food network shows us that alternatives can be found in the everyday lived experience of people leveraging the capital and skills that they have to create new economies.

Far from leading to consolidation of ownership and homogenization of practice, Chinatown's food network shows that the interstices of the dominant global food system are filled with diversity and dynamism. Alternative economic practices can exist as practices in their own right, not only as relics of a past era (McCarthy 2006; Goodman et al. 2012). The very nature of how food is produced and supplied to consumers is so varied and complex that we cannot presume to know all its manifestations. Chinatown's food network shows us that alternatives may be present within existing markets and distribution networks, that they don't need to be created from scratch.

Immigrant food systems that have not been explored in this context might have more to show. The contribution of immigrants to the economy and culture of their host countries, as well as abroad, cannot be underestimated. The innovations they bring to globally complex systems, such as those of food, deserve attention from researchers and policy makers. Immigrant food systems remind us that there is no monolithic global food system, and that globally distended networks of trade can also be locally embedded, blurring the lines between dichotomies such as local and global and conventional and alternative agriculture.

APPENDIX A
PRODUCE VENDORS IN CHINATOWN

Retail Markets

#	Market type	Market name[a]	Address	Fruit/veg/both/SEAH[b]
1	storefront	Choi Kun Heung Inc.	111 Chrystie St.	V
2	storefront	Subway	254 Grand St.	B
3	storefront	Tan My My Market Inc.	253–259 Grand St.	B
4	store	Sieu Thi Viet Nam	247 Grand St.	B; SEAH
5	storefront	United E Group	240 Grand St.	V
6	store	Grand Star Lotto	242 Grand St.	F
7	storefront	Hanging Longan	232 Grand St.	B
8	cart	Long Luffa	233 Grand St.	V
9	cart	Washing Fuzzy Melon	231 Grand St.	V
10	cart	Large Longan	223 Grand St.	F
11	storefront	Wing Fat	221 Grand St.	B
12	cart	Afei	217 Grand St.	longan/litchi[c]
13	storefront	Yue Fung	206 Grand St.	B
14	storefront	Sweet Valley Fruit and Vegetable	207 Grand St.	B
15	storefront	Sweet Valley Fruit and Vegetable	205 Grand St.	V
16	storefront	GV Trading (was Sweet Valley)	146 Mott St.	longan
17	table	GV Trading (S end)	144 Mott St.	B
18	table	temp1	142 Mott St.	B
19	table	temp2	140 Mott St.	B
20	table	temp3	138 Mott St.	V
21	table	temp4	136 Mott St.	V
22	table	temp5	134 Mott St.	V
23	cart	temp6	132 Mott St.	B

#	Market type	Market name[a]	Address	Fruit/veg/both/SEAH[b]
24	storefront	temp7	130 Mott St.	F
25	table	Optical	203 Grand St.	B
26	cart	temp8	149 Mott St.	V
27	cart	temp9	147 Mott St.	V
28	store	New Au Jang Market	141 Mott St.	B
29	store	Shing Hing Trading Co.	139 Mott St.	B
30	table	Tai Chong Meat Market	128 Mott St.	B
31	store	WK Vegetable Co.	124 Mott St.	V
32	storefront	Won Chueng Fish Market	131 Mott St.	V
33	storefront	Won Chueng Fish Market (S side)	131 Mott St.	V
34	storefront	Tung Lay Meat Market	124 Mott St.	V
35	table	Martha's Best	125 Mott St.	mango, longan
36	storefront	Farmer's Market	121 Mott St.	V
37	makeshift	pre-construction veggies	110 Mott St.	V
38	makeshift	pre-construction fruit	108 Mott St.	F
39	cart	Longan	90 Mott St.	longan
40	cart	Abacus	89 Mott St.	longan
41	cart	Vita Soy	185 Canal St.	B
42	cart	Mou Cheng Optical	184 Canal St.	longan, litchi
43	cart	Chase Cart	178 Canal St.	longan
44	cart	Hoho	71 Elizabeth St.	longan
45	store	Mee Li Fruit and Vegetable Co.	56 Elizabeth St.	B
46	cart	BEA Pitaya	94 Mulberry St.	F
47	cart	BEA	92 Mulberry St.	F
48	cart	Taipan Bakery	200 Canal St.	F
49	cart	Taipan Bakery II	202 Canal St.	V
50	cart	Chinatrust I	93 Mulberry St.	F
51	cart	Chinatrust II	91 Mulberry St.	V
52	store	Thuan-Nguyen Trading	84 Mulberry St.	SEAH
53	store	Asia Mart-Thai and Indonesian	71 1/2 Mulberry St.	V
54	storefront	Han May	73 Mulberry St.	B
55	store	Sung Hung Lee	79 Bayard	B
56	store	Bangkok Center Grocery	104 Mosco St.	SEAH
57	storefront	Lung Hing Fruit and Veg. Corp	120 Walker St.	B

#	Market type	Market name[a]	Address	Fruit/veg/both/SEAH[b]
58	cart	Four Season	226 Canal St.	F
59	cart	Non-Chinese	152 Centre St.	F
60	cart	Nice Cart	153 C Centre St.	V
61	cart	Canal St. Station	153 D Centre St.	F
62	cart	Starbucks	241 Canal St.	F
63	cart	Chinese	250 Canal St.	longan/litchi
64	cart	HSBC	252 Canal St.	longan
65	cart	Longan	226 Canal St.	longan
66	cart	fish corner	224 Canal St.	longan/litchi
67	cart	M+F Fish	214 Canal St.	longan
68	cart	Music and Gifts	210 Canal St.	F
69	cart	Jackfruit and Horns	208 Canal St.	F
70	cart	ATM	200 Canal St.	B
71	cart	Peking	198 Canal St.	F
72	cart	Bamboo	196 Canal St.	B
73	storefront	Number One Long Hing Market Inc.	17 East Broadway	F
74	storefront	Number One Long Hing Market Inc.	17 East Broadway	F
75	storefront	Number One Long Hing Market Inc.	17 East Broadway	F
76	storefront	Sun Tung Wui Market Inc.	37 East Broadway	B
77	storefront	Sun Tung Wui Market Inc.	37 East Broadway	F
78	storefront	New Lung Hing Market	51 East Broadway	B
79	storefront	Lou Cheng Market Inc.	57 East Broadway	B
80	storefront	Hu Xin Vegetable and Grocery	107 East Broadway	B
81	store	Hong Kong Supermarket	109 East Broadway	B
82	storefront	HK Man Polo	291 Grand St.	longan/litchi
83	storefront	AA Meat Market, Inc.	288 Grand St.	B
84	storefront	Evergrand Trading Inc.	272 Grand St.	B
85	storefront	G.S. Food Market Corp.	250 Grand St.	B
86	storefront	Tai Fortune Food Market Corp	162 Grand St.	B
87	storefront	Tin Tin	121 Bowery	B
88	supermarket	Dynasty Supermarket	78 Elizabeth St.	B
89	indoor market	Deluxe Food Market	79 Elizabeth St.	V
90	outdoor market	Confucius Plaza	25 Bowery	B

Wholesale Markets

#	Market type	Market name	Address	Borough
1	Wholesale	Double Green	141 Chrystie St.	Manhattan
2	Wholesale	Finast Produce	119 Chrystie St.	Manhattan
3	Wholesale	New Son Yeng	69 Washington Ave.	Brooklyn
4	Wholesale	World Farm	429 Broome St.	Manhattan
5	Wholesale	Lau and Son Produce	252 Kent Ave.	Brooklyn
6	Wholesale	Bally Wholesale	Brooklyn	Brooklyn
7	Wholesale	Dai Sing / Tay Shing Corp.	1 Allen St. and Division St.	Manhattan
8	Wholesale	Top Green Farm	14 Allen St.	Manhattan
9	Wholesale	East Trading	130 Division St.	Manhattan
10	Wholesale	Lau and Son	57 Kenmare St.	Manhattan
11	Wholesale	Five Brothers	356 Broome St.	Manhattan
12	Wholesale	Jaya Produce	5 Roebling St.	Brooklyn

Note: Data were collected from 2004 to 2006.

[a]Market names are the names that appear on the storefront where the market is located. In cases where there is no name, the market is given a descriptive name.

[b]*SEAH* refers to "Southeast Asian herbs."

[c]Some vendors sell particular fruits only when they are in season.

APPENDIX B
FRESH FRUIT, VEGETABLES, AND HERBS SOLD IN CHINATOWN

Common name	Botanical family	Latin binomial	Availability	Production site in the book[a]
amaranth, green	Amarathaceae	*Amaranthus sp.*	Aug. through Sept.	
amaranth, red	Amarathaceae	*Amaranthus tricolor*	Feb. through Nov.	
apple, Gala	Rosaceae	*Malus domestica*	Feb., Mar., July	
apple, lady	Rosaceae	*Malus domestica*	Nov., Dec., Apr.	
apple, Macintosh	Rosaceae	*Malus domestica*	year round	
apple, Red Delicious	Rosaceae	*Malus domestica*	Nov. through July	
apples, Granny Smith	Rosaceae	*Malus domestica*	Dec., May, June	
arrowhead	Alismataceae	*Sagittaria sp.*	Dec. through Jan.	
asparagus	Liliaceae	*Asparagus officinalis*	year round	
atemoya	Annonaceae	*Annona cherimola x Annona squamosa*	Oct., July	Florida homegarden
avocado	Lauraceae	*Persea americana*	year round	Florida homegarden
bamboo shoots	Poaceae	*Phyllostachys spp.*	Mar. through May, Aug. through Oct.	Florida homegarden
banana	Musaceae	*Musa spp.*	year round	Florida homegarden
banana flower	Musaceae	*Musa spp*		Honduras, Florida homegarden
banana, Thai	Musaceae	*Musa spp.*	year round	Honduras, Florida homegarden

165

Common name	Botanical family	Latin binomial	Availability	Production site in the book[a]
basil, hoary	Lamiaceae	*Ocinum americanum*	Mar., May through Oct.	Florida homegarden
basil, holy	Lamiaceae	*Ocimum tenuiflorum*	Nov. through July	Florida homegarden
basil, Thai	Lamiaceae	*Ocimum basilicum*	year round	Florida homegarden
bean sprouts, mung	Fabaceae	*Vigna radiata*		
bean, hyacinth	Fabaceae	*Lablab purpureus*	Aug. through Sept	Florida homegarden
bean, lablab	Fabaceae	*Lablab purpureus*	Aug.	Florida homegarden
bean, string	Fabaceae	*Phaseolus vulgaris*	year round	
bean, winged	Fabaceae	*Psophocarpus tetragonolobus*	July	Florida homegarden
beans, dark green long	Fabaceae	*Vigna unguiculata sesquipedalis*	year round	
beans, light green long	Fabaceae	*Vigna unguiculata sesquipedalis*	May through July	Florida homegarden
blackberry	Rosaceae	*Rubus spp.*	Feb., May, June	
blood orange	Rutaceae	*Citurs sinensis*	Jan.	
blueberry	Ericaceae	*Vaccinium spp.*	Dec., July	
boxthorn, Chinese	Solanaceae	*Lycium chinense*	May through Oct.	
broccoli	Brassicaceae	*Brassica oleracea (Italica group)*	year round	
broccoli, Chinese, gai lan	Brassicaceae	*Brassica oleracea var. alboglabra*	year round	Florida
burdock	Asteraceae	*Arctium lappa*	year round	
cabbage, Korean flat	Brassicaceae	*Brassica oleracea*	year round	
cabbage, long napa, chihili	Brassicaceae	*Brassica rapa subs. pekinensis*	Oct. through April	Florida
cabbage, napa	Brassicaceae	*Brassica rapa subs. pekinensis*	year round	Florida
cabbage, Taiwan	Brassicaceae	*Brassica rapa*	year round	Florida
caltrops	Trapaceae	*Trapa bicornis*		
cantaloupe	Cucurbitaceae	*Cucumuis melo var. cantaloupensis*	Feb. through Oct.	
carambola, star fruit	Oxalidaceae	*Averrhoa carambola*	Oct., Mar. through June	Florida homegarden

Common name	Botanical family	Latin binomial	Availability	Production site in the book[a]
carrot	Apiaceae	*Daucus carota*	year round	
carrot, white	Umbelliferae	*Arracacia xanthorrhiza*	May	
cassava	Euphorbiaceae	*Manihot esculenta*	Mar., June	Florida homegarden
cauliflower	Brassicaceae	*Brassica oleracea var. botrytis*	year round	
celery	Umbelliferae	*Apium graveolens*	year round	
celery, Chinese	Umbelliferae	*Apium graveolens*	year round	Florida, Florida homegarden
celtuce	Asteraceae	*Lactuca sativa var. asparagina*	Oct. through Dec., Apr. through June	
cha ohm	Fabaceae	*Acacia pennata*	Aug. through Oct., June	Florida homegarden
chayote	Cucurbitaceae	*Sechium edule*	year round	
cherimoya	Annonaceae	*Annona cherimola*	Oct., Nov.	
cherry	Rosaceae	*Prunus avium*	Jan., May through July	
chestnut, water	Cyperaceae	*Eleocharis dulcis*	Aug. through May	
chestnut	Fagaceae	*Castanea sativa*	Oct. through Jan.	
chi' pluh	Piperaceae	*Piper lolot*	Jan., May	Florida homegarden
chive flowers	Liliaceae	*Allium tuberosum*	year round	Honduras, Florida, Florida homegarden
chive leaves	Liliaceae	*Allium tuberosum*	year round	Honduras, Florida, Florida homegarden
chives, yellow	Liliaceae	*Allium tuberosum*	Jan. through Feb.	Florida
choy sum, flowering	Brassicaceae	*Brassica rapa subs. chinensis*	Oct. through July	Florida
choy sum, yu	Brassicaceae	*Brassica rapa subs. parachinensis*	April through Dec.	Florida
choy tips, bok	Brassicaceae	*Brassica rapa subs. chinensis*	year round	Florida
choy tips, yu	Brassicaceae	*Brassica rapa subs. parachinensis*	April through Dec.	Florida
choy, AA	Asteraceae	*Lactuca sp.*	year round	Florida
choy, baby bok	Brassicaceae	*Brassica rapa subs. chinensis*	year round	Florida

Common name	Botanical family	Latin binomial	Availability	Production site in the book[a]
choy, baby Shanghai	Brassicaceae	*Brassica rapa* subs. *chinensis*	year round	Florida
choy, bok	Brassicaceae	*Brassica rapa* subs. *chinensis*	year round	Florida
choy, Shanghai	Brassicaceae	*Brassica rapa* subs. *chinensis*	year round	Florida
choy, taku	Brassicaceae	*Brassica rapa* subs. *chinensis*	Aug. through Jan.	Florida
choy, yu	Brassicaceae	*Brassica rapa* subs. *parachinensis*	April through Jan.	Florida
chrysanthemum leaves	Asteraceae	*Chrysanthemum coronarium*	Aug. through May	Florida
cilantro	Apiaceae	*Coriandrum sativum*	year round	Florida, Florida homegarden
clementine	Rutaceae	*Citrus reticulata*	Jan.	
coconut, immature	Arecaceae	*Cocos nucifera*	year round	Florida homegarden
coconut, mature	Arecaceae	*Cocos nucifera*	May	Florida homegarden
coriander, Vietnamese	Polygonaceae	*Polygonum odoratum*	year round	Florida homegarden
cucumber	Cucurbitaceae	*Cucumis sativus*	year round	
culantro	Apiaceae	*Eryngium foetidum*	year round	Florida homegarden
curry leaf	Rutaceae	*Murraya keonigii*	Feb., Mar., May, Oct.	Florida homegarden
durian, frozen	Bombacaceae	*Durio zibethinus*	year round	
eggplant, Cambodian	Solanaceae	*Solanum melongena*	June	Florida homegarden
eggplant, Chinese	Solanaceae	*Solanum melongena*	year round	Honduras, Florida, Florida homegarden
eggplant, Indian	Solanaceae	*Solanum melongena*	July through April	Honduras, Florida homegarden
eggplant, Japanese	Solanaceae	*Solanum melongena*	July through April	Honduras
eggplant, Thai	Solanaceae	*Solanum melongena var. depressum*	July through April	Honduras, Florida homegarden
figs	Moraceae	*Ficus carica*	Aug. through Jan	
galangal	Zingerberaceae	*Alpinia galanga*	year round	Florida homegarden
garlic	Liliaceae	*Allium sativum*	year round	
giap ca	Sauraceae	*Houttuynia cordata*	Oct. through July	Florida homegarden

Common name	Botanical family	Latin binomial	Availability	Production site in the book[a]
ginger	Zingerberaceae	*Zingiber officinale*	year round	
gourd, bird house	Cucurbitaceae	*Lagenaria siceraria*	July through Sept.	
grape, green	Vitaceae	*Vitis sp.*	year round	
grape, purple	Vitaceae	*Vitis sp.*	year round	
grape, red	Vitaceae	*Vitis sp.*	year round	
grape, Concord	Vitaceae	*Vitis sp.*	July through Oct.	
grapefruit	Rutaceae	*Citrus paradisi*	Oct. through July	
guava, Thai	Myrtaceae	*Psidium guajava*	April through Sept.	Florida homegarden
horseradish tree, drumstick	Moringaceae	*Moringa oleifera*		Florida homegarden
jaboticaba	Myrtaceae	*Myrciaria cauliflora*	Aug. through Nov.	
jackfruit	Moraceae	*Artocarpus heterophyllus*	April	Florida homegarden
jicama	Fabaceae	*Pachyrhizus erosus*	year round	
jujube	Rhamnaceae	*Ziziphus jujuba*	Aug. through Oct.	Florida homegarden
June plum	Anacardiaceae	*Spondias dulcis*	Aug.	Florida homegarden
kiwi	Actinidiaceae	*Actinidia deliciosa*	year round	
kohlrabi	Brassicaceae	*Brassica oleracea var. gongylodes*	Feb. through Nov.	Florida
kudzu	Fabaceae	*Pueraria lobata*	year round	
kumquat	Rutaceae	*Fortunella spp.*	Nov. through Jan.	
leek	Liliaceae	*Allium porrum*	Oct. through Nov., Mar through May	
lemon	Rutaceae	*Citrus limon*	year round	
lemongrass	Poaceae	*Cymbopogan citratus*	year round	Florida homegarden
lettuce, green leaf	Asteraceae	*Lactuca sativa var. crispa*	year round	
lettuce, iceberg	Asteraceae	*Lactuca sativa var. capitata*	year round	
lettuce, long pointed	Asteraceae	*Lactuca sp.*	Oct. through Nov.	
lily bulb	Liliaceae	*Allium sp.*	Oct. through Nov., Jan. through June	
lime	Rutaceae	*Citrus aurantifolia*	year round	Florida homegarden

Common name	Botanical family	Latin binomial	Availability	Production site in the book[a]
lime leaves, Kaffir	Rutaceae	Citrus hystrix	year round	Florida homegarden
lime, Kaffir	Rutaceae	Citrus hystrix	May through Feb	Florida homegarden
litchi	Sapindaceae	Litchi chinensis	May through Aug.	Florida homegarden
longan	Sapindaceae	Dimocarpus logan	Aug. and Oct.	Florida homegarden
loquat	Rosaceae	Eriobotrya japonica	May through Nov.	Florida homegarden
lotus root	Nymphaceae	Nelumbo nucifera	year round	
mah ohm	Scrophulariaceae	Limnophila aromatica	year round	Florida homegarden
malanga, dasheen	Araceae	Xanthosoma sagittifolium	year round	
mango, Haitian	Anacardiaceae	Mangifera indica	Feb. through June	
mango, Tommy Atkins	Anacardiaceae	Mangifera indica	year round	Florida homegarden
mango, unripe	Anacardiaceae	Mangifera indica	Feb. through Sept.	Florida homegarden
melon, Chinese bitter	Cucurbitaceae	Momordica charantia	year round	Honduras, Florida, Florida homegarden
melon, green striped	Cucurbitaceae	Cucurbita moschata		
melon, honeydew	Cucurbitaceae	Cucumis melo var. inodorus	Feb. through July	
melon, Thai bitter	Cucurbitaceae	Momordica charantia	year round	Honduras
melon, white bitter	Cucurbitaceae	Momordica charantia	Oct., July	
melon, winter	Cucurbitaceae	Benincasa hispida	year round	Florida, Florida homegarden
mustard leaves, Chinese loose	Brassicaceae	Brassica integrifolia	Feb. through July	Florida, Florida homegarden
mustard, Chinese heading, gai choy	Brassicaceae	Brassica juncea	year round	Florida
nectarine	Rosaceae	Prunus persica	year round	
okra	Malvaceae	Abelmoschus esculentus	year round	
okra, Chinese	Cucurbitaceae	Luffa acutangula	year round	Honduras, Florida, Florida homegarden

Common name	Botanical family	Latin binomial	Availability	Production site in the book[a]
okra, Thai	Cucurbitaceae	*Luffa aegyptiaca*	Mar. through Oct.	Honduras, Florida homegarden
onion, red	Liliaceae	*Allium cepa*	year round	
onion, white	Liliaceae	*Allium cepa*	year round	
orange	Rutaceae	*Citrus sinensis*	year round	
pan leaves	Piperaceae	*Piper betel*		Florida homegarden
papaya, large	Caricaceae	*Carica papaya*	Feb. through Nov.	Florida homegarden
papaya, small	Caricaceae	*Carica papaya*	Oct through July	Florida homegarden
papaya, unripe	Caricaceae	*Carica papaya*	year round	Florida homegarden
pea tips, snow	Fabaceae	*Pisum sativum var. macrocarpon*	year round	
pea, snap	Fabaceae	*Pisum sativum var. macrocarpon*	Aug. through Mar.	
pea, snow	Fabaceae	*Pisum sativum var. macrocarpon*	year round	
peach	Rosaceae	*Prunus persica*	June through Oct.	
peanut	Fabaceae	*Arachis hypogaea*	year round	
pear	Rosaceae	*Pyrus communis*	year round	
pear, brown Asian	Rosaceae	*Pyrus serotina*	year round	
pear, golden Asian	Rosaceae	*Pyrus serotina*	year round	
pear, large green Asian	Rosaceae	*Pyrus serotina*	Aug. through Jan.	
pepper, green bell	Solanaceae	*Capsicum annuum var. grossum*	year round	
pepper, long hot	Solanaceae	*Capsicum annuum var. annuum*	year round	
pepper, red bell	Solanaceae	*Capsicum annuum var. grossum*	year round	
pepper, Thai chili	Solanaceae	*Capsicum annuum*	year round	Florida homegarden
perilla, tia to	Lamiaceae	*Perilla frutescens*	July through Sept.	Florida homegarden
persimmon, conical	Ebenaceae	*Diospyros kaki*	Nov. through Dec.	Florida homegarden
persimmon, flat	Ebenaceae	*Diospyros kaki*	Oct. through Jan., April through June	

Common name	Botanical family	Latin binomial	Availability	Production site in the book[a]
pineapple	Bromeliaceae	*Ananas comosus*	Nov. through July	
pithaya	Cactaceae	*Hylocereus undatus*	June through Nov.	Florida homegarden
plum, oval purple	Rosaceae	*Prunus salicina*	July through Oct.	
plum, round purple	Rosaceae	*Prunus salicina*	July through Sept.	
plum, yellow	Rosaceae	*Prunus salicina*	July through Sept.	
pomegranate	Punicaceae	*Punica granatum*	Oct. through Jan.	
pomelo	Rutaceae	*Citrus grandis*	Aug. through Mar.	Florida homegarden
potato	Solanaceae	*Solanum tuberosum*	year round	
pumpkin, cheese	Cucurbitaceae	*Cucurbita maxima*	Mar. through June, Sept. through Nov.	
pumpkin, Japanese	Cucurbitaceae	*Cucurbita maxima*	year round	
radish, Chinese daikon	Brassicaceae	*Raphunus sativa var. longipinnatus*	year round	Florida
radish, large green	Brassicaceae	*Rapahanus sativus var. longipinnatus*	year round	
rainbow plant	Lamiaceae	*Elsholtzia ciliate*	May	Florida homegarden
rambutan	Sapindaceae	*Nephelium lappaceum*	July through Aug.	
sapote, black	Ebenaceae	*Diospyros dignya*	Oct., July	Florida homegarden
scallion	Liliaceae	*Allium cepa*	year round	
shallot	Liliaceae	*Allium cepa*	year round	
soursop	Annonaceae	*Annona muricata*		Florida homegarden
soybean	Fabaceae	*Glycine max*		
spearmint	Lamiaceae	*Mentha spicata*	year round	Florida homegarden
spinach	Chenopodiaceae	*Spinacia oleracea*	year round	
spinach, Malabar or Ceylon	Basellaceae	*Basella alba*	year round	Florida homegarden
spinach, water	Convolvulaceae	*Ipomoea aquatica*	April through July	Florida homegarden
squash, butternut	Cucurbitaceae	*Cucurbita moschata*	Nov.	

Common name	Botanical family	Latin binomial	Availability	Production site in the book[a]
squash, fuzzy	Cucurbitaceae	Benincasa hispida var. chien-gua	year round	Honduras
squash, long	Cucurbitaceae	Legenaria siceraria	year round	Honduras, Florida homegarden
star apple	Sapotaceae	Chrysophyllum cainito		Florida homegarden
strawberry	Rosaceae	Fragaria ananassa	Jan. through Sept.	
sugar apple	Annonaceae	Annona squamosa	June through Aug.	Florida homegarden
sugarcane	Poaceae	Saccharum officinarum	Dec.	
sweet corn	Poaceae	Zea mays	Aug. through Sept.	
sweet potato shoots	Convolvulaceae	Ipomoea batatas	year round	Florida homegarden
sweet potato, orange skin	Convolvulaceae	Ipomoea batatas	year round	
sweet potato, white skin	Convolvulaceae	Ipomoea batatas	year round	
tamarind	Caesalpiniaceae	Tamarindus indicus		Florida homegarden
tangerine	Rutaceae	Citrus reticulata	Oct. through May	
taro, eddoes	Araceae	Colocasia esculenta	year round	Florida homegarden
tomato	Solanaceae	Lycopersicon esculentum	year round	
tun, taro petiole	Araceae	Colocasia gigantea	year round	Florida homegarden
watercress	Brassicaceae	Nasturtium officinale	year round	
watermelon	Curcubitaceae	Citrullus lanatus	Feb. through July	
wax jambu	Rosaceae	Syzyguim samarangense	Oct., May	Florida homegarden
zucchini	Cucurbitaceae	Cucurbita pepo	year round	

Note: Data were collected from 2004 to 2006.

[a] Sites refer to those described in the book, with Florida referring to the farms in Hendry and Palm Beach Counties and Florida homegardens referring to those in the Homestead area of Miami-Dade County.

APPENDIX C
FOOD PLANTS FOUND IN SOUTHEAST ASIAN HOMEGARDENS IN MIAMI-DADE COUNTY, FLORIDA

Use	Latin name	Khmer	Vietnamese	Thai	Lao	English
herb	Acacia pennata	cha om	keo	cha om		acacia
veg	Allium tuberosum	slak katjhai	he		pak pen	flowering chives
herb	Alpinia galangal	mt daeng	rieng	khaa	khaa	galangal
herb	Anethum graveolens		thia la	pak chi lao	pak si	dill
fruit	Annona cherimola x Annona squamosa		na			atemoya
fruit	Annona muricata	tiep banla	mang cau xiem	ma thurian	mak khiap	soursop, guanabana
fruit	Annona squamosa		na	noina	khieb	sugar apple, annona
veg	Apium graveolens		can tay	khuen chai	pak si sang	Chinese celery
fruit	Artocarpus heterophyllus	khnao	qua mit	ka noon	mak mi	jackfruit
fruit	Averrhoa carambola	pla-ay spoeu	qua khe	ma fung	mak feuang	carambola, star fruit
herb	Azadirachta indica	sa dao	sau dau	sa dao	sa dao	neem leaves
herb	Barringtonia acutangula		loc vung	chik	ka don	cut nut, wild almond
veg	Basella alba var. rubra		mong toi	pak ptang	pak pang	Ceylon or Malabar spinach
veg	Benincasa hispida		bi dao			fuzzy melon
veg	Brassica integrifolia		cai ngot	pakkat khieo plee		mustard leaf
other	Canaga odorata		ngoc lan tay			ylang ylang
veg	Capsicum fruitescens	mate hel	ot	prik	piik thai	chile pepper

Use	Latin name	Khmer	Vietnamese	Thai	Lao	English
fruit	Carica papaya	pla-ay lehuang	trai du du	ma lakaw	mak huong	papaya
herb	Cassia siamea		muong xiem or muong den		key lek	glutinous soup herb
herb	Centella asiatica	trachiek kranh	rau ma	bua bok; pak nok		pennywort
other	Cestrum nocturnum		da ly huong			night jasmine
fruit	Chrysophyllum cainito		vu sua			star apple, caimito
fruit	Citrus aurantifolia		chanh ta	ma nao	mark nao kiao	lime
fruit	Citrus grandis		buoi	som o	mak kiang ny ai	pomelo
herb	Citrus hystrix	kraunch soeut	chanh sac, truc	bai makrut	kok mak khi hout	Kaffir lime
veg	Coccinia grandis		bat	tamlueng	thum nin	tindora
fruit	Cocos nucifera	dong	dua	ma phrao	mark phao	coconut
veg	Colocasia esculenta		cu khoai so	bak ha maruni	thoune	taro stem
veg	Cyamopsis tetragonoloba		cau			guar, cluster bean
herb	Cymbopogon citratus	culs la kray	xa	ta krai	si khai	lemongrass
fruit	Dimocarpus longan	pla-ay min	nhan	lamyai	mak lam nyai	longan
fruit	Diospyros dignya		thi			black sapote
fruit	Diospyros kaki		hong	lhok phub; phlap chin	mak phueang	persimmon
herb	Elsholtzia ciliata		rau kinh gio'i			rainbow plant, Vietnamese mint
fruit	Eriobotrya japonica		nhot tay			loquat
herb	Coriander sativum	vann sui	ngo tay; mui tau	pak chi	pak hom pom	cilantro, coriander leaf
herb	Eryngium foetidum	chi bonla		pak chi farang	hom pen	culantro, saw tooth herb
herb	Glinus oppositifolius		rau dang			glinus
herb	Houttuynia cordata	diep ca	rau giap ca	kau tong	pa kau tong	Chinese lizard tail, fishwort, heartleaf
fruit	Hylocereus undatus		thanh long; tuong lien			dragon fruit, pithaya
veg	Ipomoea aquatica		rau muong	pak boong	pak bong	water spinach

Use	Latin name	Khmer	Vietnamese	Thai	Lao	English
veg	Ipomoea batatas	damlo ng chvie	rau lang	man thet	man kew	boniato or potato leaf
veg	Lablab purpureus		dau van; bach bien	thua paep	mak thua paep	hyacinth, Indian bean
veg	Lagenaria siceraria	khlook	bau	naam tao	namz taux	long squash
herb	Limnophila aromatica	ma om	rau om, ngo om	cha yang		rice paddy herb
fruit	Litchi chinensis	pla-ay koo lain	vai	linchi	mak lin chi	litchi, lychee
veg	Luffa acutangula	ronoong chrung	muop khia	buap	mak noi/loi	Chinese okra
veg	Luffa cylindrica	ronoong muul	muop huong	buap hom	mak bouap	Thai okra, smooth luffa
herb	Marsilea crenata		rau deu rang		pak van	water clover
fruit	Mangifera indica	pla-ay mukhot	xoai	mamuang	mark muang	mango
veg	Manihot esculenta		la mi, khoai mi	mansampalang	bay man ton	yuca leaf
fruit	Manilkara zapota	pla-ay kom ping riedj	hong xiem	lamut farang	lamud	sapodilla
herb	Mentha piperita	ci poho	bac ha	bai saranai	pak hom	peppermint
herb	Mentha spicata		cay bac ha luc			spearmint
veg	Momordica charantia	mreah	kho qua; muop dang	mara khinok	mak khao	bitter melon
other	Morinda citrifolia			yo baan	ba yall	noni, awl tree
herb	Moringa oleifera	daem mrom	cay cai ngua	ma rum		horseradish tree, drumstick
herb	Murraya keonigii		cari; nguyet quoi	bai karee	khi be	curry leaf
fruit	Musa spp.	cheek namva	chuoi	kiew hom	mak kuay	banana
herb	Ocimum americanum	thjee		mang lak	pak etu	hoary or white basil
herb	Ocimum basilicum	ju liang vong	hung que	bai horapa	pak etu	Thai basil
herb	Ocimum tenuiflorum	mareh preuw	e tia: e do; hoang nhu tia	bai gaprow	pak etu holy	holy basil
herb	Pandanus odorus	taey	dua thom, la dua	bai toey	bai toey	pandan leaf, sweet leaf, fragrant screw pine

Use	Latin name	Khmer	Vietnamese	Thai	Lao	English
veg	*Parkia speciosa*			ga teen; sator		cabi bean
herb	*Perilla frutescens*		tia to	nag mon	nga chien chin	perilla, balm mint
fruit	*Persea americana*	avokaa	trai bo	awokhado	mak avocado	avocado
veg	*Phyllostachys sp.*		mang			bamboo shoot
herb	*Piper betle*		trau khong	phulu	pu	pan leaf
herb	*Piper lolot*	chi' pluh	la lot	cha plu	la lot, pak ileut	pepper leaves
herb	*Polygonum odoratum*	chi krassang tomhom	rau ram	pak chi wietnam	pak payo	Vietnamese coriander
fruit	*Pouteria campechiana*		qua trung ga			egg fruit, canistel
fruit	*Psidium guajava*	trapaek sruk	oi	farang	mak si da	Thai guava
veg	*Psophocarpus tetragonolobus*	prapiey	dau rong	thua phuu	mak thua phou	wing bean, asparagus bean
herb	*Sauropus androgynus*		rau ngot	pak wan	pak wan	sweet leaf bush
veg	*Sesbania grandiflora*	angkiedei	so dua	dok khae, khae ban	dok khae	white flower
veg	*Solanum melongena*	traap veing	ca tim	mak heva muang	mak kheau	Chinese eggplant
veg	*Solanum undatum*		ca phao	mak heva	khun	Thai eggplant
veg	*Solanum torvum*		ca hoang; ca nong	mak hua puang	puang	cherry eggplant, pea eggplant, turkeyberry
fruit	*Spondias dulcis*	mokak	qua coc	makok	kook hvaan	June plum
fruit	*Syzyguim samarangense*	man	roi, man	chom phuu		wax jambu
fruit	*Tamarindus indicus*	am peuhl	me chua	mak kham	mak kham	tamarind
veg	*Trichosanthes dioica*					parvar
veg	*Vicia faba*					valor or Indian broad bean
veg	*Vigna sesquipedelis*	sang dek khoua	dau dua	tua fak yao	mak thoua frang	long bean
fruit	*Ziziphus jujuba*	pla-ay poo tree e	tao ta	phutsa cheen	mak ka than	jujube

Note: Data were collected from 2003 to 2005.

APPENDIX D
RESEARCH METHODS

The global commodity chain approach was used as an organizing concept to select field sites for this project. I chose the GCC approach for its original intent to understand the integration of processes over geographical areas (Hopkins and Wallerstein 1986). The fruit and vegetable markets in Manhattan's Chinatown are supplied by many places, many more than appropriate for the scope of this book, so I conducted preliminary research to determine which sites could be combined most meaningfully. South Florida was selected because of its long-held importance as a source of winter fruits and vegetables for the United States, its climactic potential for tropical and subtropical crops, and its significance as a distribution center for Latin American products. Honduras was selected for its novelty in the production of Asian vegetables and because entrepreneurs in Florida have been involved in organizing export from Honduras. Thus the ecological, economic, and social attributes of these locations, in addition to their involvement in the Asian fruit and vegetable commodity chain, were considered for site selection.

In order to answer the questions presented in this study, a multifaceted, interdisciplinary approach was required. The methodology of this project combines anthropological and ecological techniques of data collection and analysis and generated qualitative and quantitative data. It follows methodologies used in leading international in situ conservation projects (Jarvis et al. 2000; Zarin et al. 1999). The primary data are supplemented with quantitative marketing and pricing data drawn from government and industry sources.

Semistructured interviews were used with market owners, packer/exporters, farmers, and government and nongovernment agricultural workers in all sites. Farmer interviewees were selected through the help of agricultural extension agents and exporting firms in Honduras. All packers and distributors were contacted for interviews. Farmers' fields in Florida were mapped and sampled for cultivated plant species and percentage coverage. Observations from preliminary research in addition to the concept of agrodiversity (Brookfield et al. 2002) were used to guide the development and analysis of structured interview questions. The research methods used in this book will be described for each field site: New York City, South Florida, and Central Honduras.

1. Market Research in Manhattan's Chinatown

Market research was designed following methods described by Anthony Cunningham (2001) in *Applied Ethnobotany: People, Wild Plant Use, and Conservation*. My market methods are outlined in table 14. Archival research was done to gather historical information on Chinatown's food system and market composition and Chinatown markets were visited over the course of four years, 2002–6. First, complete market inventories were done to generate a list of fresh fruits and vegetables sold in Chinatown and a list of markets that sell fresh fruits and vegetables. Markets were typified according to their infrastructure (store, storefront, cart, table) and were mapped.

In order to describe the species composition and seasonal variation of Chinatown markets, I conducted market inventories between 2004 and 2006. I developed a stratified sample of seventeen markets (about 20 percent of the total) to represent the proportion of market types in the sample. For example, there are street vendors who specialize in vegetables and others in fruits, and some stores carry a full inventory, while others just carry herbs. I conducted inventories on a monthly basis, supplemented by weekly visits during summer months to capture the impact of seasonal fruits on the market. I recorded the presence and absence of species, varieties of fruits and vegetables, new products seen, and prices.

2. Distributor Interviews in Chinatown and South Florida

All distributors of Asian vegetables were contacted for interviews; some through referrals from others in the business, and others not. Interview questions addressed marketing strategies, access to market information, use of networks and credit arrangements, forms, and frequency and quality of communications

Table 14 Chinatown market survey methods

Method	Question	Information obtained	Detailed method
Archival	Since when have Chinese fruits and vegetables been sold in New York?	Historical data on the farming of Chinese vegetables—years, products, farmers, farming methods, acres of production	Journals (*Econ. Bot.*), Rutgers and Cornell Cooperative Extension
	How has the variety of fruits and vegetables changed in the past several decades?	Composition of products sold now and at available times in the past	United States Department of Agriculture
	How are markets distributed in Chinatown? Do they change over time?	Market number, location, and typology	Complete market inventories
Market inventories	What are retail product prices?	Price per pound, can interpret dynamics of supply and demand according to seasonal changes in price, competition between production locations, market competition	Monthly inventories based on stratified market sample according to market type and location
	What is the seasonality of products?	Product availability per month	Monthly inventories based on stratified market sample according to market type and location
	What products are sold in the largest quantities? Smallest?	Quantity determined by amount and availability	Monthly inventories based on stratified market sample according to market type and location
	What is the diversity of products sold between and within months?	Diversity of fresh fruits and vegetables available over time	Shannon diversity index, relative frequencies of products, and evenness were calculated for each month

between packers and farmers within and between sites. Information was collected on the initiation and development of interviewees' businesses, use of kin and personal connections, the regulatory trade environment, and their perceptions of risks and trends in produce marketing. I worked with a few individuals throughout the project to understand the temporal variation and pressures of marketing and how they affect business relations. Some interview questions were structured so to collect numerical and other parametric data that could be statistically analyzed, other questions were used to gather ethnographic detail.

3. Farmer Interviews and Cultivated Plant Diversity Surveys in Florida

The ethnographic tools of interviews, life histories, and direct observation where used to shape the connections between farmers and their production systems, as well as between their past experiences and present situation. Consistency was obtained through multiple visits to sites, follow-up interviews, interviews with additional household members, and cross-referencing information through informal conversations with informants. I made four visits to Florida between 2003 and 2006, producing three months of fieldwork in total. For one of those months I lived at a tropical fruit grove in Homestead, where I had many occasions for informal conversations and observations. During my visits, it became clear that most farmers studied for this book were part of the same marketing channels and often did business together; further, their families were part of a social community that in some cases were rooted in the past but also united by professional and religious events.

In addition to farmers and their families, agricultural extension agents and researchers who work in the community were interviewed for background

Table 15 Interview questions for distributors

Quantitative	Qualitative
How long have you been selling Asian vegetables?	What did you do before this business?
	Why and how did you start this business?
Do family members work in the business with you? If so, how many?	What is your ethnicity?
	Why do you deal in Asian fruits and vegetables?
How many employees do you have?	Is ethnicity, kinship, or friendship important in building trust in your business relationships?
How many products do you sell?	If not, then how do you build trust?
What percentage of your business comes from which products?	What is the role of secure business relations in the success of your business?
How many boxes do you sell per day?	What gives your business a competitive advantage?
What percentages of your products come from which places?	How do you find farmers?
	How do you control quality?
How many farmers do you work with?	What changes have you seen in industry since you began?
	What is the future of produce marketing?

Table 16 Sample interview questions for farmers

Quantitative	*Qualitative*
How long have you been growing Asian vegetables?	Why and how did you start farming?
Do family members work on the farm with you? If so, how many?	How did you/do you learn new methods of farming?
How many employees do you have?	What did you do before farming?
How many products do you grow?	Why do you grow Asian fruits and vegetables?
What percentages of your business come from which products?	What is your ethnicity?
How many boxes do you sell per day?	Is ethnicity, kinship, or friendship important in building trust in your relationship with distributors?
What percentages of your products go to which places?	If not, then how do you build trust?
How long have you been selling to New York City?	What is the role of secure business relations in the success of your business?
How many distributors do you work with?	How do you find distributors?
How many acres/hectares do you farm?	Where do you get your seed? Do you experiment with new varieties?
How many do you own/lease?	What is the role of crop diversity on your farm?
	How do you irrigate, fertilize, and control pests?
	What gives your farm a competitive advantage?
	How do you control quality?
	What changes have you seen in industry since you began?
	What is the future of farming?

information on the historical and current agricultural situation. A list of Southeast Asian farmers was compiled through the Miami-Dade Agricultural Extension and the Farmers' Service Association in Homestead. Chinese vegetable growers were identified for Palm Beach and Hendry Counties through the respective county extension offices. Initial contact with farmers was made by phone, and interviews and farm visits were subsequently scheduled. Farmers were asked to recommend other farmers who grew similar crops and farmed in similar ways to increase the potential sample. Of twenty-eight potential Southeast Asian farmers, all were contacted. Some refused to be interviewed, and others could not be reached. Ten were successfully interviewed, most of these twice, and their farms were surveyed, and so are included in this book. All three Chinese vegetable farmers in Palm Beach and Hendry Counties were interviewed twice. Secondary data was gathered from the USDA Agricultural Census, the Miami-Dade Land Retention Study, the University of Florida's Institute for Food and Agricultural Sciences publications, and other research conducted in the area.

In order to quantify cultivated plant diversity, the technique of participatory mapping was used. Farmers or members of their households would lead me around their farm identifying plants, plant uses, and cropping zones while I recorded observations in a sketch map. Complete inventories were carried out to document plant diversity, abundance, and location. Tree crop and woody shrub abundance were recorded as the total number of individuals; abundance of herbs was recorded as percentage cover.

For the purposes of understanding farm-level practices, their relation to market changes, and their economic and ecological impacts, data was collected on three principle areas of agrodiversity (Brookfield et al. 2002): (1) biophysical diversity—soil type, rain, temperature, biodiversity; (2) management diversity—site preparation, irrigation, planting material, cropping patterns, rotations, weeding, pests, harvest, processing, storage, soil fertility, fallows; and (3) organizational diversity—farmer/household census, education, experience, land tenure, land use history, land use interventions, catastrophic events, off-farm employment, equity, food security, labor, transport, marketing. Some interview questions were structured to collect numerical and other parametric data that can be statistically analyzed; other questions were used to gather ethnographic detail.

4. Farmer and Exporter Interviews in Comayagua, Honduras

I conducted fieldwork in Honduras in September–November 2004. Introductions to the three exporting firms of Asian vegetables were facilitated by scientists from Zamorano; the Pan-American School for Agriculture; and FHIA, the Honduran Foundation for Agricultural Research, which is located in Comayagua. Technicians at each exporting firm escorted me to the farmers' fields for interviews. I worked with a research assistant to interview the farmers. We conducted interviews with 15 percent of each firm's farmers, which totaled about sixty interviews and the managerial staff of two of the three exporting firms.

The same guiding principles used in Florida were used to structure interview questions, but more specific questions were added to address the situation of contract farming in Honduras. These interviews were much more structured and formal than my interviews in New York and Florida. Farmers rarely strayed from the questions posed, and because we were making the interviews on the technicians' schedules, there were time constraints that impeded informal conversation. If I were to continue conducting research with this group of farmers, I would select a smaller sample to make return interviews in the evenings when the farmers are at home, more relaxed, and with more time. The benefit of visiting farmers with the firm technicians is that I was able to repeatedly see the interactions of the farmers with the technicians to understand the type of assistance farmers receive from the firms. While in Honduras I lived in Lejamani, a farming village twenty kilometers outside the city of Comayagua. I was also given office space at the FHIA office, and so I had many opportunities to make causal observations and have informal conversations about agriculture in the area.

I also conducted interviews with many agricultural professionals from around Honduras and around Central America. I attended a four-day workshop in Comayagua, which took place October 5–8, 2004, on the export of Asian vegetables. The workshop was sponsored by the Honduran secretary of agriculture and ranching, the Taiwanese embassy, and the Central America Bank for Economic Integration. The event brought together professionals from all around Central America to showcase the Asian vegetables produced in Comayagua and discuss challenges and successes. An importer from Homestead, Florida, whom I had previously interviewed, attended the event. This workshop, along with interviews with employees of the Center for the Development of Agribusiness (CDA), Organismo Internacional Regional de Sanidad Agropecuaria (OIRSA), the International Center for Tropical Agriculture (CIAT), the Honduran Foundation of Agricultural Research (FHIA), the Directorate of Agricultural Science and Technology (SAG-DICTA), the Mission to Agriculture of the Republic of China (MtCH), the Center for Agricultural Development (CEDA), and Zamorano provided invaluable background information for this book.

NOTES

Preface

1. The Global Commodity Chain framework asserts that international trade is increasingly organized by enterprises spread throughout the global economy. These enterprises make strategic decisions about the position of the chain in the market, exclusion and inclusion of actors, and division of functions along the chain at a global level. Networks of actors and their relationships are considered important for durability of the commodity chain, information sharing, and learning (Gereffi et al. 1994).

Introduction

1. The production of nontraditional agricultural export (NTAEs), also known as high-value exports, is an economic development strategy prevalent in Latin America. NTAE refers to those products that: (1) were not traditionally produced in a particular country for export (traditional exports are soybeans, sugar, bananas, and coffee); (2) were traditionally produced for domestic consumption but are now exported; (3) are traditional products now exported to a new market. NTAEs are generally high-value or niche products. Fresh fruits and vegetables and fair trade coffee are examples of NTAEs (Thrupp 1995).

2. The Agricultural Marketing Service of the United States Department of Agriculture used to collect volume data for products traded at the Hunts Point Terminal Market. Fred Teensma, the national reporting technology manager at the service, confirmed that they have not collected volume data for Hunts Point Terminal Market past 1998.

3. The city of New York built Hunts Point Terminal Market in 1967 to centralize and organize distribution. It is located in the South Bronx, in a very accessible location for most trucking routes. In a conversation in November 2002, Bob Lewis, chief marketing representative of the New York State Department of Agriculture and Markets, expressed his belief that the market is popular and well used.

4. Phil Howard (2003) has analyzed organic food brands introduced or acquired by the top fifty global food processors. An updated (February 2014) visual representation of these findings can be viewed at https://www.msu.edu/~howardp/organicindustry.html.

5. Greenmarket Farmers Markets are coordinated by GrowNYC. Current listings of markets can be found at http://www.grownyc.org/greenmarket/ourmarkets. Just Food coordinates CSAs in the city. Current listings can be found at http://www.justfood.org/csa/.

6. Regulation theory is based on Marxist-inspired ideas that attempt to relate changes in labor practices and forms of industrial and social organization to wider economic developments and the changing relations between nation-states and, more recently, transnational corporations.

7. More about Cittaslow can be found at http://www.cittaslowusa.org/.

Chapter 1 Greengrocers and Street Vendors

1. US Department of Labor's Covered Employment and Wages data (2000, 2007), cited in McCormick et al. 2010, 5–7.

2. For more about the integration of Chinese food in American society, see chapter 6.

3. The interview was conducted at the farm in Peconic, Long Island, on August 2, 2002.

4. The manager at a Chinese wholesale firm in Lower Manhattan, an immigrant from Taiwan, told me how she and her husband were able to get a loan to purchase land in New Jersey because she told the bank that "she knows the market and what it takes to be successful." She commented that there are many Chinese going into farming in New Jersey, some with more success than others.

5. Sang Lee Farms gave up growing for Chinatown markets in favor of producing baby vegetables and heirloom tomatoes for their farm stand and elite restaurants (see chapter 3). Another farmer of Chinese vegetables in New Jersey stopped growing them to open a winery.

6. There are many examples, among them *Asian Vegetables: From Long Beans to Lemongrass; A Simple Guide to Asian Produce Plus 50 Delicious, Easy Recipes*, by Sara Deseran and Richard Jung; *Asian Greens: A Full-Color Guide*, by Anita Loh-Yien Lau; and *The Asian Grocery Store Demystified*, by Linda Bladholm.

7. Cantonese was the first predominant dialect in Chinatown. It is still common, as is Mandarin and, more recently, Fukien (also romanized as Fujian).

8. Appendix B lists all fresh produce items sold in Chinatown and what time of year they are commonly found.

9. See http://florawww.eeb.uconn.edu/acc_num/200600008.html.

10. Florida growers are experimenting with cultivars that bloom at other times throughout the year and applications of potassium chlorate to produce year-round fruit. In 2009, Taiwanese export of fresh longan to the United States was approved by the USDA, increasing the supply of fruit on the market in the United States and causing fear of competition among Florida growers. The Taiwanese fruit, however, are subject to cold storage regulations during shipping and are of lower quality than the Florida fruit, giving the Florida growers an advantage.

Chapter 2 The Social Network of Trade

1. China is a state that within in borders has many nationalities and ethnicities that are culturally, linguistically, and geographically distinct. Taipei recognizes nine major indigenous groups in Taiwan and Beijing recognizes fifty-five, including the majority Han, on the mainland (see Hutchings 2001, 127–31). Furthermore as Chinese emigrate, they gain further ethnic distinctions such as Malay Chinese or Thai Chinese. These are very important distinctions, but for the case of comparing Chinatown's food system to other systems, the ethnicity of Chinese in the American context is sufficient.

2. Interview conducted with farmer in Florida on May 3, 2005.

3. For more on this subject, see Zhou 1992; Kuo 1977; Kwong 1996, 1997; Lin 1998; Wong 1988; Guest 2003. For a more general history of the Chinese in the United States, see Kwong and Miscevic 2005.

4. For a good review of the ethnic enclave model as it pertains to Chinatown in Manhattan, see Guest 2003, 37–44.

5. Pseudonyms are used for all the individuals discussed from this point on in the book.

6. Interview conducted in Homestead, Florida, on August 20, 2003.

7. Interview conducted in Boynton Beach, Florida, on April 3, 2004.

8. Information gathered on June 30, 2005, at www.sangleefarms.com.

Chapter 3 Okeechobee Bok Choy

1. The South Florida Water Management District's website is a good source of information on BMPs and stormwater treatment areas, as mandated by the Everglades Forever Act: http://www. sfwmd.gov.

2. The Everglades Forever Act further mandates that specific water control districts located in the EAA that previously discharged north to Lake Okeechobee divert their discharges south through use of stormwater treatment areas and BMPs.

3. For more information about the Managed Growth Tier System in Palm Beach County, see http://www.co.palm-beach.fl.us/pzb/planning/mgplanning/mangrow.htm.

4. Johnny Li's story, and Leo Cheng's and Jack Varney's below, are told through the eyes of the farmers themselves, as they were conveyed to the author during fieldwork. The descriptions are not meant to be a critique or an endorsement of the farmers and their farming techniques but are meant to give the reader a sense of who they are and the decisions they face as farmers in South Florida.

5. I interviewed former Palm Beach County extension agent Ken Schuler on April 28, 2005, and current Palm Beach County extension agent Darrin Parmenter on April 26, 2005, in Florida.

Chapter 4 Bringing Southeast Asia to the Southeastern United States

1. Quoted from interview with homegarden farmer in Homestead, Florida, on August 13, 2003.

2. The actual number of the Asian homegarden-type farms in southern Florida is difficult to quantify. The significance of this group of farms is better understood qualitatively. All interviewed individuals agreed that there has been a steady increase in Asian-operated farms, although ethnic distinctions reported within the broad category *Asian* vary among interviewees. USDA's agricultural census of 2007 counted 169 Asian-operated farms in Miami-Dade County, up from 103 in 2002 and 32 farms in 1987. From this category it is not possible to know what type of farms they are. Mary Lamberts at the UF/IFAS Miami-Dade Extension provided working phone numbers for eight farmers growing Asian specialty products and Marta Berrones at the USDA Farm Service Agency in Homestead provided a list of an additional twenty Asian growers whom she knew to grow "ethnic" crops. Of these twenty farmers, nine had phone numbers that were no longer in service. Yuncong Li of the Tropical Research and Education Center in Homestead reported in an interview that there were twenty Asian growers, three of whom regularly came to meetings. The most striking number of farmers growing specialty Asian products quoted by a farmer and distributor that are part of my sample is sixty to seventy. But this number includes full- and part-time farmers, wild-plant collectors, and Asian as well as Mexican and Cuban farmers. It also includes farms outside Miami-Dade County, as far north as Atlanta.

3. Quoted from an interview with farmer on August 20, 2003, in Homestead, Florida.

4. Miami-Dade County Department of Planning and Zoning commissioned an agriculture and rural area study in order to "retain the agriculture and rural land uses through the enhancement of the economic viability of commercial agriculture in Miami-Dade County." A sixteen-member Citizens Advisory Committee advised the county and consultants throughout the study; for its results, see http://www.miamidade.gov/planzone/ag/agras_home.asp.

5. The Fruit and Spice Park in Homestead houses a living collection of over five hundred species and varieties of tropical fruits. It is open to the public and acts as the "face" of tropical fruit production in the area. It often hosts cultural and educational events, many aimed at promoting awareness of the fruits grown in southern Florida.

6. Interview with commercial fruit grower in Homestead, Florida, on February 20, 2004.

7. For tabulated statistics from 1960–90 US census reports, see http://www.census.gov/population/www/documentation/twps0029/tab03.html.

8. The acreages reported here are based on estimates given in interviews by Carlos Balerdi, tropical fruits extension agent, Miami-Dade County Cooperative Extension Service, on July 30, 2003, and by Jonathon Crane, tropical fruit crop extension specialist, Tropical Research and Education Center, on August 1, 2003.

9. In addition to furnishing this information in interviews that I conducted with him, the Filipino American farmer was featured in an article by Noel Vietmeyer about South Florida's new bounty, titled "Exotic Edibles Are Altering America's Diet and Agriculture," published in 1985 by *Smithsonian Magazine.*

10. The precedent of five-acre zoning is now under much contestation as developers are fighting for subdivision rights to construct housing units. The dividing line between five-acre zoning and subdivision is 184 Street. To the west is the agricultural land, and to the east, where the Florida Turnpike and US Route 1 are easily accessible, there is beginning to be more suburban-like development.

11. Quoted from an interview on August 10, 2003, in Homestead, Florida.

12. Quoted from an interview on February 6, 2004, in Homestead, Florida.

13. Quoted from an interview on February 15, 2004, in Homestead, Florida.

14. Quoted from an interview on February 20, 2004, in Homestead, Florida.

15. For more information on underutilized vegetables in Thailand, see http://www.fao.org/docrep/004/ac145e/AC145E02.htm.

16. As mentioned previously in this book, the citrus canker eradication program in Florida is operating under the "nineteen-hundred-foot rule." If canker was found on Kaffir lime or pomelo trees, which are also found in homegardens, all citrus within a nineteen-hundred-foot radius would have to be removed.

17. For more information on underutilized species around the world, see Pareek et al. 1998.

18. Quoted from interview on February 13, 2004, in Homestead, Florida.

19. Interview on February 16, 2004, in Miami, Florida.

20. Quoted from interview on February 13, 2004, in Homestead, Florida.

21. Quoted from interview on August 15, 2003, in Homestead, Florida.

22. *Solanum torvum* is considered an invasive species and is on the Florida State as well as federal noxious weed list.

23. Quoted from interview on February 13, 2004, in Homestead, Florida.

Chapter 5 Growing Asian Vegetables in Honduras

1. During my field research in late summer of 2004, 573 hectares of Asian vegetables were in cultivation. Asian vegetables include chive flowers; chive leaves; Indian, Chinese, Japanese, and Thai eggplant; Chinese and Thai bitter melon; fuzzy squash; long squash; and Chinese and Thai okra. Other export crops contracted to outgrowers in Comayagua are slicing cucumber and tabasco and jalepeño peppers, accounting for another 570 hectares. Company-owned and -operated farms dominated export vegetable production, accounting for 1,630 hectares.

2. The term *small farmers*, which will be used interchangeably with *smallholders*, can be problematic, since its definition varies. I am using the terms to refer to farmers who own or cultivate fewer than five hectares.

3. For a more explicit history of export agriculture in Comayagua as well as Honduras, see Imbruce 2006; Macías Barrés 1998; and Clapp 1994.

4. Pseudonyms are used for those associated with the export of Asian vegetables. Quotes are from interviews. Noburu Wataya was interviewed on November 15, 2004; Toru Okada on

October 20, 2004; Alonso López on November 10, 2004; and Victor Reyes, mentioned below, on September 20, 2004.

5. All observations made on the production and marketing of Asian vegetables discussed in this chapter were made by the author over the course of four months of fieldwork in Honduras, from September to November 2004 and in July 2005, and four years of fieldwork, from 2003 to 2006, in New York.

6. Personal communication with Alfredo Rueda, associate professor of crop protection at Zamarano, the Pan-American School for Agriculture in Honduras, August 25, 2004.

7. Personal communication from Andy Medlicott, director of the Centro de Desarrollo de Agronegocios (Agribusiness Development Center) in Honduras, September 15, 2004.

8. Asian vegetables have a high and low season in Honduras in response to competition from production locations in North America during the summer months. The high season in Honduras is in the winter, November through April, but crops can be grown all year round.

9. Roy 1972 (referenced by Glover 1984) defines contract farming as those arrangements that specify conditions of production or marketing in either written or oral form. I am following this definition and characterizing Exporter 3 as following the contract model through use of oral contracts because in practice both farmers and the firm view their arrangement as contractually bound, although more on a "gentlemen's agreement." Exporter 3, as the new firm, has worked harder to build personal relations with farmers.

10. Pricing estimates are based on costs in 2004 and the conversion rate of eighteen Honduran lempiras to one US dollar.

11. *Primera* and *postrera* plantings correspond to the rainy season, which has a bimodal period of heavy rains, although many people say that the *postrera* has been dry in the past few years and that the seasons are changing.

Chapter 6 Chinese Food in American Culture

1. Many more people eat Chinese food than shop in Manhattan's Chinatown; this chapter, through a review of secondary literature, shows the significance of Chinatown's food network within food culture at large, exploring the cultural significance of Chinese dining experiences in the United States and how they originated. Restaurants have great material importance to Chinatown's food network. The volume of fresh produce that restaurants consume, how they drive demand for certain products, and how they source their products and form relations with their suppliers are all topics that deserve more attention through primary research. The pursuit of these kinds of inquiries would greatly enhance our understanding of the role of supply chains in the making of cuisines, consumption patterns, and eating habits.

2. Rachel Lauden (2013) argues in *Cuisine and Empire: Cooking in World History* that dried pasta was in fact not commonly eaten in Italy until it was mass produced. Dried pasta was too expensive for 80 percent of the people in Italy through the 1930s (277).

3. Data is from 2012 for the zip code 10002 and includes the North American Industry System Classification code 7225 for full-service and limited-service restaurants, cafeterias, buffets, and snack and nonalcoholic beverage bars.

4. This data is from zip code 10002, where the majority of Chinatown lies.

5. US Department of Commerce, U.S. Census Bureau for zip code 10002 between 1998 and 2010 (http://censtats.census.gov/cgi-bin/zbpnaic/zbpdetl.pl).

6. Chinatown's food industry cluster is explained in chapter 7.

7. See http://nymag.com/restaurants/cheapeats/2012/ and Weedman 2012.

8. See Talde's comments in Weedman 2012 at http://newyork.grubstreet.com/2012/07/asian_hipster_cuisine.html.

9. See http://www.ilovenyonya.com/.

1. The report was downloaded on August 7, 2013, from http://mbpo.org/uploads/policy_reports/FoodInThePublicInterest.pdf.

2. These reports were downloaded on August 7, 2013, from http://www.foodsystemsnyc.org/files/Stringer_2009_FoodStat-Measuring%20the%20Retail%20Food%20Environment%20in%20NYC%20Neighborhoods.pdf and http://www.mbpo.org/uploads/policy_reports/mbp/Food_CEQR_Paper_NEW.pdf

3. The report was downloaded on August 7, 2013, from http://urbanomnibus.net/redux/wp-content/uploads/2010/02/foodnyc.pdf

4. For progress on PlaNYC, see http://www.nyc.gov/html/planyc/html/home/home.shtml.

5. The report was downloaded on August 7, 2013, from http://council.nyc.gov/downloads/pdf/foodworks1.pdf.

6. The report was downloaded on August 7, 2013, from http://www.nyc.gov/html/misc/pdf/going_to_market.pdf.

REFERENCES

Ackerman-Leist, Philip. 2013. *Rebuilding the Foodshed: How to Create Local, Sustainable, and Secure Food Systems*. White River Junction: Chelsea Green Publishing.

Allen, Patricia. 1993. *Food for the Future: Conditions and Contradictions of Sustainability*. New York: John Wiley and Sons.

Allen, Patricia, Margaret FitzSimmons, Michael Goodman, and Keith Warner. 2003. Shifting Plates in the Agrifood Landscape: The Tectonics of Alternative Agrifood Initiatives in California. *Journal of Rural Studies* 19:61–75.

Altieri, Miguel A., and Clara Nicholls. 2005. *Agroecology and the Search for a Truly Sustainable Agriculture*. Mexico City: United Nations Environment Programme. http://www.agroeco.org/doc/agroecology-engl-PNUMA.pdf.

Anderson, Eugene N. 1988. *The Food of China*. New Haven: Yale University Press.

Angel-Peréz, Ana Lid Del, and Martín Alfonso Mendoza. 2004. Totonac Homegardens and Natural Resources in Veracruz, Mexico. *Agriculture and Human Values* 21:329–46.

Appadurai, Arjun 1996. *Modernity at Large: The Cultural Dimensions of Globalization*. Minneapolis: University of Minnesota Press.

Barbas, Samantha. 2003. "I'll Take Chop Suey": Restaurants as Agents of Culinary and Cultural Change. *Journal of Popular Culture* 36 (4): 669–86.

Barham, Jim. 2011. Regional Food Hubs: Understanding the Scope and Scale of Food Hub Operations. USDA Marketing Service. www.ams.usda.gov.

Basch, Linda, Nina Glick Shiller, and Cristina Szanton-Blanc. 1994. *Nationals UnBound: Transnational Projects and the Deterritorialized Nation-State*. New York: Gordon and Breach.

Baucum, L. E., and R. W. Rice. 2009. *An Overview of Florida Sugarcane*. Document SS-AGR-232. Gainesville: Florida Cooperative Extension Service, Institute of Food and Agricultural Sciences, University of Florida.

Beck, Louis. 1898. *New York's Chinatown: An Historical Presentation of Its People and Places*. New York: Bohemia.

Blasdale, Walter. 1899. *A Description of Some Chinese Vegetable Food Materials and Their Nutritive and Economic Value*. US Department of Agriculture, Office of Experiment Stations, bulletin 68. Washington, DC: Government Printing Office.

Bonnano, Alessandro, Lawrence Busch, William Friedland, Lourdes Gouvia, and Enzo Mingione. 1994. *From Columbus to Con-Agra: The Globalization of Agriculture and Food*. Lawrence: University Press of Kansas.

Bradshaw, Ben. 2004. "Plus C'est la Meme Chose? Questioning Crop Diversification as a Response to Agricultural Deregulation in Saskatchewan, Canada." *Journal of Rural Studies* 20:35–48.

Brookfield, Harold, Christine Padoch, Helen Parsons, and Michael Stocking. 2002. *Cultivating Biodiversity: Understanding, Analysing, and Using Agricultural Diversity*. London: ITDG.

Burch, David, and Geoffrey Lawrence. 2007. *Supermarkets and the Agri-food Supply Chains*. Northampton, MA: Edward Elgar.

Busch, Lawrence, and Carmen Bain. 2004. New! Improved? The Transformation of the Global Agrifood System. *Rural Sociology* 69 (3): 321–46.

Buttel, Fred. 1992. Environmentalization: Origins, Processes, and Implications for Rural Social Change. *Rural Sociology* 57 (1): 1–27.

Carletto, Calogero, Alain de Janvry, and Elisabeth Sadoulet. 1999. Sustainability in the Diffusion of Innovations: Smallholder Non-traditional Agro-exports in Guatemala. *Economic Development and Cultural Change* 47:345–69.

Carter, Susan B. 2011. America's First Culinary Revolution, or How a Girl from Gopher Prairie Came to Dine on Eggs Fooyung. In *Economic Evolution and Revolution in Historical Time*, ed. Paul W. Rhode et al., 419–46. Stanford: Stanford University Press.

Cheng, Andria. 2014. Wal-Mart, Wild Oats Aim to Disrupt the Organic Food Industry. *Market Watch*, April 10.

Chinese Restaurant News. 2012. Top 100 Chinese Restaurants to Be Announced November in New York. http://www.c-r-n.com/jin_e/contentlist.aspx?catid=300566012.

Clapp, Roger A. 1994. The Moral Economy of the Contract. In *Living under Contract: Contract Farming and Agrarian Transformation in Sub-Saharan Africa*, ed. Peter D. Little and Michael J. Watts, 78–94. Madison: University of Wisconsin Press.

Coe, Andrew. 2009. *Chop Suey: A Cultural History of Chinese Food in the United States*. New York: Oxford University Press.

Conway, Gordon. 1997. *The Doubly Green Revolution: Food for All in the Twenty-First Century*. London: Penguin Books.

Cook, Ian. 1994. New Fruits and Vanity: Symbolic Production in the Global Food Economy. In *From Columbus to Con-Agra: The Globalization of Agriculture and Food*, ed. Alessandro Bonnano, Lawrence Busch, William Friedland, Lourdes Gouvia, and Enzo Mingione, 232–50. Lawrence: University Press of Kansas.

Crane, Jonathan H., Richard J. Campbell, and Carlos F. Balerdi. 1993. The Effect of Hurricane Andrew on Tropical Fruit Trees. *Proceedings of Florida State Horticultural Society* 106:139–44.

Cunningham, Anthony. 2001. *Applied Ethnobotany: People, Wild Plant Use, and Conservation*. Sterling, VA: Earthscan.

de Janvry, Alain. 1981. *The Agrarian Question and Reformism in Latin America*. Baltimore: Johns Hopkins University Press.

Degner, Robert L., S. M. Moss, and W. David Mulkey. 1997. *Economic Impact of Agriculture and Agribusiness in Dade County, Florida*. Gainesville: Florida Agricultural Market Research Center, Institute of Food and Agricultural Sciences, University of Florida.

Degner, Robert L., Thomas J Stevens, and Kimberly L. Morgan, eds. 2002. *Miami-Dade County Agricultural Land Retention Study*. Gainesville: Florida Agricultural Market Research Center, Institute of Food and Agricultural Sciences, University of Florida.

Dolan, Catherine, John Humphrey, and Carla Harris-Pascal. 1999. Horticulture and Commodity Chains: The Impact of the UK Market on the African Fresh Vegetable Industry. Mimeo, Institute of Development Studies, University of Sussex.

Donald, Betsy, and Alison Blay-Palmer. 2006. The Urban Creative-Food Economy: Producing Food for the Urban Elite or Social Inclusion Opportunity? *Environment and Planning A* (38): 1901–20.

DuPuis, E. Melanie. 2002. *Nature's Perfect Food: How Milk Became America's Favorite Drink.* New York: New York University Press.

DuPuis, E. Melanie, and David Goodman. 2005. Should We Go Home to Eat?: Toward a Reflexive Politics of Localism. *Journal of Rural Studies* 21 (3): 359–71.

Foo, Wong Chin. 1888. The Chinese in New York. *Cosmopolitan* 5:297–311.

Friedmann, Harriet. 1993. The Political Economy of Food: A Global Crisis. *New Left Review* 197:29–57.

Gabaccia, Donna. 1998. *We Are What We Eat: Ethnic Food and the Making of Americans.* Cambridge, MA: Harvard University Press.

Gereffi, Gary, and Miguel Korzeniewicz, eds. 1994. *Commodity Chains and Global Capitalism.* Westport, CT: Greenwood Press.

Glick Schiller, Nina. 1999. Who Are These Guys? A Transnational Reading of the U.S. Immigrant Experience. In *Identities on the Move: Transnational Processes in North America and the Caribbean Basin*, ed. Liliana Goldin, 15–43. New York: Institute for Mesoamerican Studies.

Gliessman, Stephen R. 1997. *Agroecology: Ecological Processes in Sustainable Agriculture.* Chelsea, MI: Ann Arbor Press.

——. 2007. *Agroecology: The Ecology of Sustainable Food Systems.* 2nd ed. New York: CRC Press.

Glover, David J. 1984. Contract Farming and Smallholder Outgrower Schemes in Less-Developed Countries. *World Development* 12:1143–57.

——. 1987. Increasing the Benefits to Smallholders from Contract Farming: Problems for Farmers' Organizations and Policy Makers. *World Development* 15:441–48.

Goldín, Liliana. 1996. Economic Mobility Strategies among Guatemalan Peasants: Prospects and Limits of Traditional Vegetable Cash Crops. *Human Organization* 55:99–107.

Goodman, David. 2003. The Quality "Turn" and Alternative Food Practices: Reflections and Agenda. *Journal of Rural Studies* 19:1–7.

Goodman, David, E. Melanie Dupuis, and Michael Goodman. 2012. *Alternative Food Networks: Knowledge, Practice, and Politics.* New York: Routledge.

Goodman, David, and Michael Watts, eds. 1997. *Globalizing Food: Agrarian Questions and Global Restructuring.* New York: Routledge.

Gottwald, Tim R., James H. Graham, and Tim S. Schubert. 2002. Citrus Canker: The Pathogen and Its Impact. *Plant Health Progress.* http://www.apsnet.org/publications/apsnetfeatures/Pages/citruscanker.aspx.

Green, Claudia G., Pat Bartholomew, and Suzanne Murrmann. 2004. New York Restaurant Industry: Strategic Responses to September 11, 2001. *Journal of Travel and Tourism Marketing* 15:63–79.

Greller, Andrew M. 1980. Correlation of Some Climate Statistics with Distribution of Broad-leaved Forest Zones in Florida, U.S.A. *Bulletin of the Torrey Botanical Club* 107 (2): 180–219.

Grossman, Lawrence S. 1997. *The Political Ecology of Bananas: Contract Farming, Peasants, and Agrarian Change in the Eastern Caribbean.* Chapel Hill: University of North Carolina Press.

Guest, Kenneth J. 2003. *God in Chinatown: Religion and Survival in New York's Evolving Immigrant Community.* New York: New York University Press.

Guptill, Amy, and Jennifer Wilkins. 2002. Buying into the Food System: Trends in Food Retailing in the US and Implications for Local Foods. *Agriculture and Human Values* 19:3–51.

Guthman, Julie. 2004. *Agrarian Dreams: The Paradox of Organic Farming in California.* Berkeley: University of California Press.

Hage, Ghassen. 1997. At Home in the Entrails of the West: Multiculturalism, "Ethnic Food," and Migrant Homebuilding. In *Home/World: Space, Community, and Marginality in Sydney's West*, ed. Helen Grace et al., 99–153. Annadale, NSW: Pluto.

Hamilton, Sarah, and Edward F. Fischer. 2005. Maya Farmers and Export Agriculture in Highland Guatemala. *Latin American Perspectives* 32 (5): 33–58.

Harvey, David. 2012. *Rebel Cities: From the Right to the City to the Urban Revolution.* New York: Verso.

Hendrickson, Mary, William D. Heffernan, Philip Howard, and Judith Heffernan. 2001. Consolidation in Food Retailing and Dairy. *British Food Journal* 103 (10): 715–28.

Hinrichs, C. Clare. 2000. Embeddedness and Local Food Systems: Notes on Two Types of Direct Agricultural Markets. *Journal of Rural Studies* 16 (3): 295–303.

——. 2003. The Practice and Politics of Food System Localization. *Journal of Rural Studies* 19:33–45.

Hinrichs, C. Clare, and Thomas A. Lyson, eds. 2007. *Remaking the North American Food System: Strategies for Sustainability.* Lincoln: University of Nebraska Press.

Hopkins, Terence K., and Immanuel Wallerstein. 1986. Commodity Chains in the World-Economy prior to 1800. *Review* 10 (1): 157–70.

Howard, Philip. 2003. Consolidation in Food and Agriculture: Implications for Farmers and Consumers. *California Certified Organic Farmers Magazine* 21 (4): 2–6, http://www.ccof.org/pdf/mag_w0304.pdf.

Hutchings, Graham. 2001. *Modern China: A Guide to a Century of Change.* Cambridge, MA: Harvard University Press.

Ilbery, Brian, and Ian Bowler. 1998. From Agricultural Productivism to Post-productivism. In *The Geography of Rural Change*, ed. Brian Ilbery, 57–84. London: Longman.

Imbruce, Valerie. 2006. From the Bottom-Up: The Global Expansion of Chinese Vegetable Trade for New York City Markets. In *Fast Food/Slow Food: The Economic Anthropology of the Global Food System*, ed. Richard Wilk, 163–80. Berkeley, CA: AltaMira.

Immigration and Naturalization Service. 1988. *Statistical Yearbook, 1950–1988.* Washington, DC: US Department of Justice, Immigration and Naturalization Service.

Instituto Nacional Estadístico. 2000. Anuario Estadístico. Secretaría del Despacho Presidencial, República de Honduras.

International Noni Communication Council. 2005. Retrieved June 15, 2005, from http://www.incc.org/index.php.

Jackson, Wes. 2011. *Consulting the Genius of a Place: An Ecological Approach to a New Agriculture.* Berkeley, CA: Counterpoint.

Jacobs, Jane. 1961. *The Death and Life of Great American Cities.* New York: Vintage.

Jansen, Kees. 1998. *Political Ecology, Mountain Agriculture, and Knowledge in Honduras.* Amsterdam: Thela.

Jarvis, Devra, Bhuwon Sthapit, and L. Sears, eds. 2000. *Conserving Agricultural Biodiversity In Situ: A Scientific Basis for Sustainable Agriculture.* Rome, Italy: IPGRI.

Jones, Ashby. 2009. Making Sense of the Whole Food/FTC Antitrust Settlement. *Wall Street Journal*, March 6.

Jung, John. 2011. *Sweet and Sour: Life in Chinese Family Restaurants.* N.p.: Yin and Yang Press.

Kazis, N. 2010. Shaping the Next New York: The Promise of Bloomberg's Rezonings. *StreetsBlog NYC*. http://www.streetsblog.org/2010/02/18/shaping-the-next-new-york-the-promise-of-bloombergs-rezonings/>.

Key, Nigel, and David Runsten. 1999. Contract Farming, Smallholders, and Rural Development in Latin America: The Organization of Agroprocessing Firms and the Scale of Outgrower Production. *World Development* 27:381–401.

Kiong, Tong Chee, and Yong Pit Kee. 1998. Guanxi, Xinyong, and Chinese Business Networks. *British Journal of Sociology* 49:75–96.

Kirby, D. 1998. "Temporary" Stalls Look Too Permanent, City Says. *The New York Times*, August 23.

Kloppenburg, Jack, John Hendrickson, and G.W. Stevenson. 1996. Coming into the Foodshed. *Agriculture and Human Values* 13:33–42.

Knight, R. J., Jr. 2001. The lychee history and current status in Florida. *Proc. I Int. Symp.on Litchi and Longon*, ed. H. Huang and C. Menzel, 41–44. Acta Hort. 558. ISHS 2001.

Konefal, Jason, Carmen Bain, Michael Mascarenhas, and Lawrence Busch. 2007. Supermarkets and Supply Chains in North America. In *Supermarkets and Agri-food Supply Chains: Transformations in the Production and Consumption of Foods*, ed. David Burch and Geoffrey Lawrence, 270–90. Northampton, MA: Edward Elgar.

Kumar, B.M., and P.K.R. Nair. 2004. The Enigma of Tropical Homegardens. *Agroforestry Systems* 61:135–52.

Kuo, Chia Lung. 1977. *Social and Political Change in New York's Chinatown: The Role of Voluntary Associations*. New York: Praeger.

Kwong, Peter. 1996. *The New Chinatown*. Rev. ed. New York: Hill and Wang.

——. 1997. *Forbidden Workers: Illegal Chinese Immigrants and American Labor*. New York: New Press.

Kwong, Peter, and Dusanka Miscevic. 2005. *Chinese America: The Untold Story of America's Oldest New Community*. New York: New Press.

Lamberts, Mary L. 2005. Specialty Asian Vegetable Production in South Florida. In *Vegetable Production Handbook for Florida, 2004–2005*, ed. S.M. Olson and E. Simonne. Gainesville: University of Florida IFAS Extension.

Larson, Janet. 2012. Meat Consumption in China Now Doubles That in the United States. Earth Policy Institute, Plan B Updates. http://www.earth-policy.org/plan_b_updates/2012/update102.

Lauden, Rachel. 2013. *Cuisine and Empire: Cooking in World History*. Berkeley: University of California Press.

Lee, Jennifer. 2009. *The Fortune Cookie Chronicles: Adventures in the World of Chinese Food*. New York: Twelve.

Lee, Joanne. 1995. What Is Real Chinese Food? *Flavor and Fortune* 2 (3): 17, 21.

Lee, Josephine. 2002. A Picket Line with History. *Village Voice*, January 2. http://www.villagevoice.com/2002-01-22/news/a-picket-line-with-history/.

Lee, Patty. 2012. Banana Blossom Time: Yunnan Cuisine Comes to Manhattan at Tribeca's Lotus Blue. *New York Daily News*, April 22. http://www.nydailynews.com/life-style/eats/yunnan-cuisine-manhattan-thanks-tribeca-lotus-blue-article-1.1063628.

Levenstein, Harvey. 2002. The American Response to Italian Food, 1880–1930. In *Food in the USA: A Reader*, ed. Carole Counihan, 75–90. London: Routledge.

Lin, Jan. 1998. *Reconstructing Chinatown: Ethnic Enclave, Global Change*. Minneapolis: University of Minnesota Press.

Little. Peter, and Michael Watts, eds. 1994. *Living under Contract: Contract Farming and Agrarian Transformation in Sub-Saharan Africa*. Madison: University of Wisconsin Press.

Louie, Elaine. 1997. Familiarity Breeds Affection for Asian Vegetables. *New York Times*, October 15. http://www.nytimes.com/1997/10/15/dining/familiarity-breeds-affection-for-asian-vegetables.html.

Lu, Nan, and Katherine Cason. 2004. Dietary Patter Change and Acculturation of Chinese Americans in Pennsylvania. *Journal of the American Dietetic Association* 104:771–78.

Lu, Shun, and Gary Alan Fine. 1995. The Presentation of Ethnic Authenticity: Chinese Food as Social Accomplishment. *Sociological Quarterly* 36 (3): 535–53.

Lyson, Thomas A., and Judy Green. 1999. The Agricultural Marketscape: A Framework for Sustaining Agriculture and Communities in the Northeast. *Journal of Sustainable Agriculture* 15:133–50.

Machum, Susan. 2005. The Persistence of Family Farming in the Wake of Agribusiness: A New Brunswick, Canada Case Study. *Journal of Comparative Family Studies* 36 (3): 377–90.

Macías Barrés, A. A. 1998. An Assessment and Evaluation of the "Fruta del Sol" Ltda. Agricultural Credit System. Zamarano, Departamento de Economía Aplicada y Agronegocios, Honduras. Unpublished.

Magdoff, Fred, John Bellamy Foster, and Frederick H. Buttel. 2000. *Hungry for Profit: The Agribusiness Threat to Farmers, Food, and the Environment.* New York: Monthly Review Press.

Marsden, Terry, Jo Banks, and Gillian Bristow. 2000. Food Supply Chain Approaches: Exploring Their Role in Rural Development. *Sociologia Ruralis* 40 (4): 424–38.

Martin, Brett. 2012. Danny and the Electric Kung Pao Pastrami Test. *GQ Magazine*, December. http://www.gq.com/food-travel/restaurants-and-bars/201212/danny-bowien-interview-mission-chinese-profile.

Maye, Damien, Lewis Holloway, and Maya Kneafsey. 2007. *Alternative Food Geographies: Representation and Practice.* Oxford, UK: Elsevier.

McCarthy, James. 2006. Rural Geography: Alternative Rural Economies—the Search for Alterity in Forests, Fisheries, Food, and Fair Trade. *Progress in Human Geography* 30 (6): 803–11.

McCormick, Lynn, Rui Mao, and Yichen Tu. 2010. New York Chinatown's Food-Related Cluster. Department of Urban Affairs and Planning, Hunter College, City University of New York. Unpublished.

McMichael, Philip, ed. 1994. *The Global Restructuring of Agro-food Systems.* Ithaca: Cornell University Press.

——, ed. 1995. *Food and Agrarian World Orders in the World-Economy.* Westport, CT: Greenwood Press.

Méndez, V. E., R. Lok, and E. Somarriba. 2001. Interdisciplinary Analysis of Homegardens in Nicaragua: Micro-zonation, Plant Use, and Socioeconomic Importance. *Agroforestry Systems* 51:85–96.

Mingione, E., and E. Pugliese. 1994. Rural Subsistence, Migration, Urbanization, and the New Global Food Regime. In *From Columbus to Con-Agra: The Globalization of Agriculture and Food*, ed. Alessandro Bonnano, Lawrence Busch, William Friedland, Lourdes Gouvia, and Enzo Mingione, 52–68. Lawrence: University Press of Kansas.

Mintz, Sidney. 1985. *Sweetness and Power.* New York: Viking Press.

Morrison, Philip S., Warwick E. Murray, and Dimbab Ngidang. 2006. Promoting Indigenous Entrepreneurship through Small-Scale Contract Farming: The Poultry Sector in Sarawak, Malaysia. *Singapore Journal of Tropical Geography* 27:191–206.

Murdoch, Jonathan, Terry Marsden, and Jo Banks. 2000. Quality, Nature, and Embeddedness: Some Theoretical Considerations in the Context of the Food Sector. *Economic Geography* 76 (2): 107–25.

Murray, Douglas, and Laura Raynolds. 2000. Alternative Trade in Bananas: Obstacles and Opportunities for Progressive Social Change in the Global Economy. *Agriculture and Human Values* 17:65–74.

Nabhan, Gary Paul. 2002. *Coming Home to Eat: The Politics and Pleasures of Local Foods.* New York: W. W. Norton.

Newman, Jacqueline. 1999. Chinese Food Habits in the United States—Wok's Cooking. Unpublished manusript.

Newman, Jacqueline, and Ruth Linke. 1982. Chinese Immigrant Food Habits: A Study of the Nature and Direction of Change. *Royal Society of Health Journal* 102:268–71.

New York City Department of City Planning. 2000. Demographic Profile of New York, 1990–2000. http://www.nyc.gov/html/dcp/html/census/census.shtml.

——. 2010. Total Asian Alone Population. http://www.nyc.gov/html/dcp/pdf/census/census 2010/t_sf1_p9_nyc.pdf.

Ong Aihwa. 1997. "A Momentary Glow of Fraternity": Narratives of Chinese Nationalism and Capitalism. *Identities* 3:331–66.

Padoch, Christine, and Will de Jong. 1991. The House Gardens of Santa Rosa: Diversity and Variability in an Amazonian Agricultural System. *Economic Botany* 45 (2): 166–75.

Pareek, O. P., Suneel Sharma, and R. K. Arora. 1998. *Underutilized Edible Fruits and Nuts: An Inventory of their Genetic Resources and their Regions of Diversity.* New Delhi: India: IPGRI Office for South Asia.

Peng, Liying. 2005. Dietary Acculturation of Chinese Students in the United States. Master's thesis, University of Akron.

Peters, Christian, Nelson Bills, Arthur Lembo, Jennifer Wilkins, and Gary Fick. 2008. Mapping Potential Foodsheds in New York State: A Spatial Model for Evaluating the Capacity to Localize Food Production. *Renewable Agriculture and Food Systems* 24 (1): 72–84.

Perfecto, Ivette, John Vandermeer, and Angus Wright. 2009. *Nature's Matrix: Linking Agriculture, Conservation, and Food Security.* Washington, DC: Earthscan.

Ploeg, Jan Douwe van der, and V. Saccomandi. 1995. On the Impact of Endogenous Development in Agriculture. In *Beyond Modernization: The Impact of Endogenous Rural Development*, ed. Jan Douwe van der Ploeg and Gert van Dijk, 10–27. Assen, The Netherlands: Van Gorcum.

Ploeg, Jan Douwe van der, and Gert van Dijk. eds.1995. *Beyond Modernization: The Impact of Endogenous Rural Development.* Assen, The Netherlands: Van Gorcum.

Porter, Gina, and Kevin Phillips-Howard. 1997. Comparing Contracts: An Evaluation of Contract Farming Schemes in Africa. *World Development* 25:227–38.

Porter, Michael. 1998. Clusters and the New Economics of Competition. *Harvard Business Review*, November 1.

Porterfield, W. M. 1937. Chinese Vegetable Foods in New York. *Journal of the New York Botanical Garden* 38:254–57.

——. 1951. The Principle Chinese Vegetable Foods and Food Plants of Chinatown Markets. *Economic Botany* 1 (5): 3–37.

Portes, Alejandro, and Robert L. Bach. 1985. *Latin Journey: Cuban and Mexican Immigrants in the United States.* Berkeley: University of California Press.

Pretty, Jules. 1995. *Regenerating Agriculture: Policies and Practice for Sustainability and Self-Reliance.* London: Earthscan.

Rafie, A. Ray, and Carlos. F. Balerdi. 2002. International Marketing of Lychee and What Is the Future for Florida Growers. *Proceedings of the Florida State Horticultural Society* 115:88–90.

Ray, Krishnendu. 2010. A Taste for Ethnic Difference: American Gustatory Imagination in a Globalizing World. In *Globalization, Food, and Social Identities in the Asia Pacific Region*, ed. James Farrer. Tokyo: Sophia University Institute of Comparative Culture. http://icc.fla.sophia.ac.jp/global%20food%20papers/pdf/2_1_RAY.pdf.

——. 2011. Dreams of Pakistani Grill and Vada Pao in Manhattan: Reinscribing the Immigrant Body in Metropolitan Discussions of Taste. *Food, Culture and Society* 14 (2): 243–73.

Remizowski, Leigh. 2010. Wave of Hybrid Eateries, Fusing Two Asian Styles, Reflects Queen's Diversity. *New York Daily News.* November 21.

Rich, L. 2005. Shopper Alert: Grocery Stores Have a Future. *New York Times*. November 19.

Roy, Ewell Paul. 1972. *Contract Farming and Economic Integration*. Danville, IL: Interstate.

Santaniello, Neil. 2004. Seeing Gold in Rich Farmland. *Sun Sentinel*. March 22. http://articles.sun-sentinel.com/2004-03-22/news/0403220108_1_everglades-agricultural-area-hundley-farms-palm-beach-county.

Saxe, D. 1997. SoHo Produce Wholesaler Is Enjoined from Certain Interference on Street; SoHo Alliance v. World Farm Inc., Supreme Court, IA Part 18. *New York Law Journal*. http://www.newyorklawjournal.com/.

Secretaría de Agricultura y Ganadería, Departamento de Información Agrícola. 1999. Compendio Estadístico Agropecuario, Honduras, C.A.

Sidman, Amanda. 2011. Back in Business: Chinatown's Famed Nom Wah Tea Parlor Reopens, in Time for Chinese New Year. *New York Daily News*, January 30.

Smith, Michael. 2001. *Transnational Urbanism, Location Globalization*. Malden, MA: Blackwell.

Smith, Neil. 1996. *The New Urban Frontier: Gentrification and the Revanchist City*. New York: Routledge.

Sonnino, Roberta, and Terry Marsden. 2006. Beyond the Divide: Rethinking Relationships between Alternative and Conventional Food Networks in Europe. *Journal of Economic Geography* 6:181–99.

Spiller, Harley. 2008. Chow Fun City: Three Centuries of Chinese Cuisine in New York City. In *Gastropolis: Food and New York City*, ed. Annie Hauck-Lawson and Jonathan Deutsch, 132–52. New York: Columbia University Press.

Spindler, Audrey and Janice Schultz. 1996. Comparison of Dietary Variation and Ethnic Food Consumption among Chinese, Chinese-American, and White American Women. *Agriculture and Human Values* 13 (3): 64–73.

Stoller, Paul. 2002. *Money Has No Smell: The Africanization of New York City*. Chicago: University of Chicago Press.

Stonich, Susan. 1993. *I Am Destroying the Land! The Political Ecology of Poverty and Environmental Destruction in Honduras*. San Francisco: Westview Press.

Thorpe, Andy. 2002. *Agrarian Modernisation in Honduras*. Lewiston, NY: Edwin Mellon Press.

Thrupp, Lori Ann. 1995. *Bittersweet Harvests for Global Supermarkets: Challenges in Latin America's Agricultural Export Boom*. Washington, DC: World Resources Institute.

Tickell, Adam, and Jamie Peck. 1995. Social Regulation *after* Fordism: Regulation Theory, Neo-liberalism and the Global-Local Nexus. *Economy and Society* 24 (3): 357–86.

Torres-Rivas, E. 1993. América Latina: Gobernabilidad y democracia en sociedades en crisis. *Nueva Sociedad* 128:88–101.

Torquebiau, Emmanuel. 1992. Are Tropical Agroforestry Home Gardens Sustainable? *Agriculture, Ecosystems and Environment* 41:189–207.

Toy, Vivian. 2003. East End's Lost Link to Agriculture. *New York Times*, August 31, Long Island Weekly Desk.

Trinh, L. N., J. W. Watson, N. N. Hue, N. N. De, N. V. Minh, P. Chu, B. R. Sthapit, and P. B. Eyzaguirre. 2003. Agrobiodiversity Conservation and Development in Vietnamese Home Gardens. *Agriculture, Ecosystems and Environment* 97:317–44.

Troianovski, Anton. 2010. Groups Push Competing Plans for Chinatown. *Wall Street Journal*, June 14, New York Real Estate Residential. http://www.wsj.com/articles/SB10001424052748703389004575304960079231580.

Tsing, Anna. 2000. The Global Situation. *Cultural Anthropology* 15:327–60.

US Department of Agriculture. 1987, 1992, 1997, 2002, 2007. *Census of Agriculture*. http://agcensus.mannlib.cornell.edu; http://www.agcensus.usda.gov.

US Department of Agriculture, Agricultural Marketing Service. 2011. Farmers Markets and Local Food Marketing. http://www.ams.usda.gov/AMSv1.0/FARMERSMARKETS.

US Department of Agriculture, Agricultural Marketing Service, Fruit and Vegetable Division. 1981. *Fresh Fruit and Vegetable Unloads in Eastern Cities.* Washington, DC: USDA.

US Department of Agriculture, Agricultural Marketing Service, Fruit and Vegetable Programs. 1998. *Fresh Fruit and Vegetable Arrivals in Eastern Cities.* Washington, DC: USDA.

US Department of Agriculture, Agricultural Marketing Service, Market News Service. 2006. *Fruits and Vegetables, Custom Reports by Commodity.* https://www.marketnews.usda.gov/mnp/fv-home.

Vallad, Gary E., Joshua H. Freeman and Peter J. Dittmar, eds. 2014–15. *Vegetable and Small Fruit Production Handbook of Florida.* Florida Cooperative Extension Service, Institute of Food and Agricultural Sciences, University of Florida: http://edis.ifas.ufl.edu/features/handbooks/vegetableguide.html.

Vandermeer, John H. 2011. *The Ecology of Agroecosystems.* Sudbury, MA: Jones and Bartlett.

Ver Ploeg, Michelle, Vince Breneman, Tracey Farrigan, Karen Hamrick, David Hopkins, Philip Kaufman, Biing-Hwan Lin, et al. 2009. *Access to Affordable and Nutritious Food—Measuring and Understanding Food Deserts and Their Consequences: Report to Congress.* USDA Economic Research Service. http://www.ers.usda.gov/publications/ap-administrative-publication/ap-036.aspx.

Vietmeyer, Noel. 1985. Exotic Edibles Are Altering America's Diet and Agriculture. *Smithsonian Magazine* 16 (9): 34–43.

Watts, D. C. H., B. Ilbery, and D. Maye. 2005. Making Reconnections in Agro-food Geography: Alternative Systems of Food Provision. *Progress in Human Geography* 29:22–40.

Weis, Tony. 2007. *The Global Food Economy: The Battle for the Future of Farming.* New York: Zed Books.

Weedman, Mary Jane. 2012. The Year of Asian Hipster Cuisine. *New York Magazine,* July 8.

Wells, Pete. 2012. Why Downtown Needs Diners Now. *New York Times,* November 7.

Werbner, Pnina. 2001. Metaphors of Spatiality and Networks in the Plural City: A Critique of the Ethnic Enclave Economy Debate. *Sociology* 35:671–93.

Williams, M. 2001. Produce Company Loses Latest Round of a Pitched Battle. In *New York Times,* January 28. http://www.nytimes.com/2001/01/28/nyregion/neighborhood-report-soho-produce-company-loses-latest-round-of-a-pitched-battle.html.

Wong, Bernard. 1988. *Patronage, Brokerage, Entrepreneurship, and the Chinese Community of New York.* New York: AMS Press.

Yeung, Henry Wai-chung. 2000. Economic Globalization, Crisis, and the Emergence of Chinese Business Communities in Southeast Asia. *International Sociology* 15:266–87.

Yu, Renqui. 1987. Chop Suey: From Chinese Food to Chinese American Food. *Chinese America: History and Perspectives* 1:87–100.

Zarin, Daniel, Guo Huijin, and Lewis Enu-Kwesi. 1999. Methods for the Assessment of Plant Species Diversity in Complex Agricultural Landscapes: Guidelines for Data Collection and Analysis from the PLEC Biodiversity Advisory Group. *PLEC News and Views* 13: 3–16.

Zhou, Min. 1992. *Chinatown: The Socioeconomic Potential of an Urban Enclave.* Philadelphia: Temple University Press.

INDEX

Page numbers in italics refer to figures and tables.

Hong Kong, 123
Hong Kong Supermarket, 29
horizontal integration, 10
Howard, Phil, 185n4
Hunan cuisine, 136
Hunter College, 131; Department of Urban Affairs and Planning, 18; Urban Planning studio, 148
Hunts Point Food Distribution Center, 145–46; fruits and vegetables sold at, 7–8; Fulton Fish Market, 145; New York City Terminal Market, 67, 145–46, 185n3; volume of commodities, 9; wholesale food distribution, 4, 17; Wholesale Greenmarket, 145
Hunts Point neighborhood (South Bronx), 145
Hunts Point Terminal Produce Market, 146
Hurricane Andrew, 79–80

Ilbery, Brian, 75
immigration trends, 79. *See also* Asian immigrants; Chinese immigrants
Indian vegetables, 92
industrialization, agricultural, 13–14
irrigation, 70–72, 88, 113
Italians, 125, 127, 189n2 (chap. 6); in Arthur Avenue, Bronx, 148–49

Jacobs, Jane, 153
Just Food, 185n5

Kaffir lime, 80, 86
Kee, Wah, 129
Kissimmee River, 51
Koch, Ed, 32
kohlrabi, 60
Kwong, Peter, 30, 131

labor exploitation, 39, 69, 139
labor organization, 119, 139–40
La Guardia, Fiorello, 32, 149
Lake Okeechobee, 51–52, 69, 187n2 (chap. 3)
Lake Worth, Florida, 63
Lamberts, Mary, 187n2 (chap. 4)
land ownership, 66; in Honduras, 110; and South Florida homegardens, 83–84
Laotians: cuisine, 73; farmers, 81; tourists, 93
Latin America, 7, 49; contract farming, 97–99; diversification of agriculture, 97, 118; export-led growth strategies, 7, 97–98, 100; nontraditional agricultural export (NTAEs), 185n1 (intro.); produce, 92. *See also* Hispanic immigrants

Lauden, Rachel, 189n2 (chap. 6)
leasing land, 84, 110
Lee, Fred, 42, 47–48
Lee, George, 22
Lee, Karen, 22
Lee, Richard, 42
lettuce, 33, 65, 120
Levenstein, Harvey, 127
Lewis, Bob, 185n3
Li, Yuncong, 187n2 (chap. 4)
Li Hung Chang, 130
Lin, Jan, 31
Linke, Ruth, 125
litchis, 2, 35, 79–80, 90
local and global, tensions between, 14–15, 159–60
local food movements, xii, 4–5, 151–52; markets, xi; production, 144; relocalization of agriculture, 12, 15
longans, 31, 34–35, 79–80, 90–91
Long Island: agriculture on, 47; Chinese vegetable farms, 42, 47–48
Lower East Side, 18, 137, 150
Lower Manhattan Development Corporation, 147
Loxahatchee, Florida, 42, 63
Lu, Nan, 126
Lunar New Year, 34

makeshift stores, 30–31. *See also* micromarkets in Chinatown
Malaysian produce, 73
Malaysian restaurants, 137
mango, 79, 92
marketing infrastructure, 76
market liberalization, 13
Marsden, Terry, 76
McCormick, Lynn, 133, 149
medicine, Chinese, use of food in, 123–24
Medlicott, Andy, 189n7 (chap. 5)
Mexican farms: competition from, 48, 63, 65–66, 68, 90; seasonal produce, 34
Miami-Dade County, 77–78; Asian-operated farms, 81, 187n2 (chap. 4); Department of Planning and Zoning, 187n4 (chap. 4); development pressure, 78; diversity in agriculture, 95; farms, 42; land values, 78; leasing land, 84; Southeast Asian farmers, xvi; tropical climate, xiii, 77, 80
microfarms, xvi
micromarkets in Chinatown, 26–32
Mon Lay Won Company, 130
monocrops (monocultures), 2, 74–75, 82, 95, 158